# THE
# WATER
# HERE
## IS
# NEVER
# BLUE

# THE WATER HERE IS NEVER BLUE

*Intrigue and Lies
from an Uncommon Childhood*

## SHELAGH PLUNKETT

VIKING

VIKING
an imprint of Penguin Canada

Published by the Penguin Group
Penguin Group (Canada)
90 Eglinton Avenue East, Suite 700, Toronto, Ontario, Canada M4P 2Y3

Penguin Group (USA) Inc., 375 Hudson Street, New York, New York 10014, U.S.A.
Penguin Books Ltd, 80 Strand, London WC2R 0RL, England
Penguin Ireland, 25 St Stephen's Green, Dublin 2, Ireland (a division of Penguin Books Ltd)
Penguin Group (Australia), 707 Collins Street, Melbourne, Victoria 3008, Australia
(a division of Pearson Australia Group Pty Ltd)
Penguin Books India Pvt Ltd, 11 Community Centre, Panchsheel Park,
New Delhi – 110 017, India
Penguin Group (NZ), 67 Apollo Drive, Rosedale, Auckland 0632, New Zealand
(a division of Pearson New Zealand Ltd)
Penguin Books (South Africa) (Pty) Ltd, 24 Sturdee Avenue, Rosebank,
Johannesburg 2196, South Africa

Penguin Books Ltd, Registered Offices: 80 Strand, London WC2R 0RL, England

First published 2013

1 2 3 4 5 6 7 8 9 10 (RRD)

**Canada Council** **Conseil des Arts**
**for the Arts** **du Canada**

*Penguin is committed to publishing works of quality and integrity. In that spirit, we are proud to offer this book to
our readers; however, the story, the experiences, and the words are the author's alone.*

Manufactured in the U.S.A.

Library and Archives Canada cataloguing in publication data
available upon request to the publisher.

ISBN: 978-0-670-06699-5

Visit the Penguin Canada website at **www.penguin.ca**

Special and corporate bulk purchase rates available; please see
**www.penguin.ca/corporatesales** or call 1-800-810-3104, ext. 2477.

FOR MY PARENTS,
WHOSE COURAGE AND IMAGINATION
REMAINED UNDAUNTED
EVEN BY THIS DAUGHTER'S OCCASIONAL TRUCULENCE

# Contents

PROLOGUE: IT GOES WITHOUT SAYING    I

PART ONE
*Guyana*

1   ARRIVING   19

2   FLAMBOYANT   27

3   HOLLYWOOD   39

4   ALMOND STREET   51

5   *SERVIAM*   64

6   WU'DS   75

7   SU-SU   88

8   SHAKE-HAND   102

9   WHITE GIRL   120

10   WATER   132

11   LOVE: JUNE   151

PART TWO

*Indonesia*

12   ABLUTIONS   167

13   A SMALL, UNTHOUGHT-OF PLACE   189

14   KAMPUNG ORANG ASING   200

15   HELLO, BLUE-EYED WHITE GIRL   218

16 THE WIVES   234

17   THE LADY WITH A VIPER ON HER HEAD   246

18   MONKEY ISLAND   257

19   A BROKEN MONKEY   266

20   FLY AWAY HOME   271

EPILOGUE: HOTEL DREAMLAND   282

ACKNOWLEDGMENTS   296

# *Prologue*

## IT GOES WITHOUT SAYING

Patrick Plunkett, my father, died on June 21, 1993. He was fifty-eight years old. Five months before his death, he left home in North Vancouver for a job in India. While he was away he phoned me once and mailed me a postcard from Shimla, the town where he was living.

Shimla is high in the Himalayan foothills, and although my father took his last breath in Lions Gate Hospital, just down the mountain from my parents' home in North Vancouver, Shimla is where I always think of him dying. It is a faraway place, strange and exotic. The air is thin, the hills are steep and unterraced and thick with rhododendrons. It is a place that still evokes Kipling's India and the days of the Raj, a place of mists and shadows. Hidden in the forests above Shimla is a temple to the Hindu god Hanuman, white monkey, son of the wind, mischief-maker, and everywhere in Shimla, on its stone walls and its zigzagged roads, its tiled roofs, and steep stairways, there are grey-brown macaques hunched and watching. They are bearded and shaggy in the winter, bold, and sacred to the memory of the monkey warrior.

In his postcard to me, Dad wrote about those monkeys. They were, he said, just like the ones that roamed the forests of Bali and were related to those we swam with off the beaches of Timor.

Timor, Bali, Malaysia, Singapore, and Thailand. Guyana and Surinam, French Guiana, Barbados, Trinidad and Tobago. These are some of the places my father, through his work, took us, his family, but he went to many more places than we did. His work took him around the world. Work and water. My father was a civil engineer, and his area of expertise was water. Hydroelectricity. The designing and building of dams. The creation of power. And also, in some cases, irrigation systems.

Water was the reason my father gave for all his overseas contracts, and it drew him to some odd places. Odd places and interesting times. Water took him to the Mekong Delta in 1972, when Vietnamese communists were invading the area, and to the dry mountains of Afghanistan in 1974, during the military coup that deposed that country's last king. He spent time in Uganda soon after Idi Amin was driven out and made many trips to Swaziland and to Geneva in the early eighties. He was tear-gassed when his airport limo passed through a student riot in South Korea. He moved his family to Guyana the year after that country held what are now known to have been its most corrupt elections and around the time the socialist Guyanese government was seizing and nationalizing foreign-owned companies.

We lived for two and a half years on the island of Timor while the Indonesian government was slaughtering East Timorese a few hundred miles away. On the day the Indonesians invaded, December 7, 1975, my father was taking pictures of a Central Java flood plain. Within days he was on Timor, photographing riverbanks and stream beds, some barely twenty miles from the East Timorese border, and overlooking the construction of the compound where we'd all soon be living. We—my mother, younger sister, and I—arrived seven months later. (My brother, Stephen, stayed in Canada to attend university.)

My father's travels, his work overseas, the places he went, and the years he went to those places were brought up at his funeral in some of the tributes. His life revolved around travel, and so it made sense to talk about the places he had been. It was a balmy late-June day in Vancouver, and the small chapel couldn't hold all of those who had come to the service. A crowd stood outside, listening to the eulogy and tributes through loudspeakers. Most of the people there and at the reception that followed were strangers to me. Many had worked with my father or travelled with him, some had been fellow students at the University of British Columbia. A great many hadn't seen my father in decades.

My mother asked a man named Russ Fraser to give the eulogy. He had been a student with Dad and at one time the attorney general of B.C. His speech was informal and chatty, and in it he raised the question of what my father might really have been doing in the places he went to and in the years he went to them. What, Russ asked, was Pat doing in the Mekong Delta in 1972? What company, what country could have been interested in investing in hydroelectric dams or irrigation systems in that place at that time? Why was he wandering around the mountains outside Kabul just before that country's last king was deposed?

Russ Fraser made a joke. He said that wherever my father went, coups seemed to follow, that if Dad went to a country you could bet there'd be an uprising of some sort soon afterward. Maybe Pat was a spy?

It wasn't a new idea. There had been rumours and wonderings even before we moved to Guyana in 1974. By the time we were living on Timor, from mid-1976 to near the end of 1978, my sister, Chris, and I were old enough and aware enough to ask the same questions. What were we really doing there? Why were we fingerprinted? Why was our mail censored? Why were we told to keep a suitcase packed and ready by our bedroom door at all times? Why did my father's team, which did all its research in the interior of that small island, suddenly get a brand new fibreglass speedboat? We had a lot of fun with that boat, motoring out to atolls, fishing for barracuda, and diving off its deck over nearby coral reefs, but what real use could it have been to a group of engineers conducting an irrigation feasibility study?

Years after my father's death, my sister met two people who worked for the Canadian Security Intelligence

Service, Canada's version of the CIA. During dinner Chris told some stories about our life overseas, stories about Indonesian soldiers coming to tea and how they politely left their machine guns on the front porch, about the race riots in Guyana that left whole villages in ashes, about sitting cross-legged on the chocolate-brown carpet of our suburban Vancouver home in the mid-1970s watching film footage that my father brought back from Afghanistan, of *buzkashi*—a brutal Afghani version of polo in which a sand-filled goat skin is fought over and dragged from one end of a field to the other by harsh men on harsh ponies. She told them how my father's Land Rover had been squeezed up against a cliff when they'd encountered a Russian tank in the narrow mountain passes outside Kabul. As she talked, the eyebrows of my sister's dinner companions rose higher and they leaned toward her a little more with each story.

"What," they asked, "did your father do for a living?"

"He was a civil engineer," she said and then added, as we always did when that question came up, "but we joke that he was a spy."

"He probably was," her CSIS dinner companions said.

There was no doubt that the countries we lived in and those my father visited and spent time in were all suffering political and social upheaval. In 1974, the year we moved to Guyana, *The New Yorker* devoted twenty-four pages of its September issue to an essay about the country. Guyana was young, only eight years into independence, and the world was curious about it. Curious and worried. Forbes Burnham had taken power with the help of rigged elections, a bit of murder, and a lot of intimidation. He'd also had the help of the CIA. The reasoning seemed to be that Burnham was less of a communist threat than his opponent, Cheddi Jagan. But by the time we lived in Guyana, Burnham was actively courting China and the Soviet Union, had established compulsory national military service and launched a 160-mile march—the Great March—in homage to China's Long March, and was urging members of parliament to refer to each other as Comrade. The country was in turmoil, divided along racial lines, poor, and violent.

Guyana had been a British colony, and despite the chaos it was undergoing while we lived there, vestiges of its past coloured our lives. It was my father's first overseas posting, and my mother had to learn how to be the wife of an up-and-coming engineer who, though he wasn't yet the project leader, would be on his next posting. She had to adjust to managing household servants, setting menus, approving lists of supplies, and inspecting the daily cleaning of the house. She also had to learn how to be diplomatic with other expat wives who spent most of their days at the local club, by the pool, or on the golf course. She learned to mediate between our two maids who were always squabbling and to deal with the gardener—he was also our security guard—who slept in a hammock under our stilted house and who said he wasn't afraid of anything but thieves. We acquired two guard dogs, one of which, an Alsatian bred by a sugar plantation manager, wasn't afraid of anything except men.

I went to an exclusive all-girls school run by Ursuline nuns. Most of the nuns were Guyanese, but there were a few, all very old, who'd come over from Ireland when they were novices. Most of the foreign-born nuns no longer taught, but a few still did and all, both retired and teacher-nuns, lived behind the walls of the school. The school operated on the British system, and inspired hard work through a combination of threats of violence (girls were regularly caned), public humiliation, and appeals to our youthful devotion to the group. At St. Rose's High School, students were divided into houses, and we called each other chums. There was a tuck shop where sweeties were bought. Along with a rigorous slate of academic courses, we were taught penmanship, Greek and Roman classics, and how to paint a vase of flowers in watercolour. Some of this seemed familiar to me because I'd read lots of Enid Blyton and the entire Swallows and Amazons series when I was ten, but, of course, I was not really prepared. This wasn't England, and my fellow-students did not have peaches-and-cream complexions. I was the only white student in the school.

My awareness of the political and social upheaval in Guyana at the time was that of a thirteen-year-old who until then had led a boring middle-class life. Burnham's socialist revolution and his pledge to "house, feed, and clothe" the Guyanese meant even locally produced food was scarce. There were long lineups at Georgetown's few grocery stores, where shelves were sparsely stocked with dented, rusty tins. When visitors from North America wondered what we'd like them to bring from home, we asked for potatoes.

Before Guyana my life had been free of race issues. I was naively unaware of the colour of my own skin or the fact that skin tone held great significance. That changed in Guyana. The country was split along racial lines, a divide that widened further while we lived there. Burnham was Afro-Guyanese, but the majority population was Indo-Guyanese. I knew my friends at St. Rose's were concerned about the future, that their parents, particularly the parents of my Indo-Guyanese friends, were considering sending their daughters out of the country to avoid the compulsory national service that Burnham had recently introduced. I heard rumours that Burnham's military camps in the interior were places where girls, especially the Indo-Guyanese, were systematically raped. The theory, spread in whispers, was that Burnham's plan was to "sully the purity" of the majority Indo-Guyanese population. At school we all seemed to get along, but I became aware that none of my Afro-Guyanese friends socialized with my Indo-Guyanese friends beyond the walls of St. Rose's.

At home our phone was tapped and our movements carefully watched. When it came time to return to Canada, Dad instructed us not to let anyone know we were leaving permanently or to say anything at the airport. While the Guyanese customs official stamped our passports, we listened to Dad telling him that we were taking a short holiday in Surinam and French Guiana. Yes, yes, we would be returning. No, we were not taking any money or valuables out of the country. My mother had sewn a small packet of flaky, red, unprocessed gold and some uncut diamonds into the hem of her jacket. She later said she did this partly for the thrill of it, but also because we were not exempt from Guyanese law prohibiting the removal of these portable bits of wealth from the country.

We did not return to Guyana. After nine months in Canada, we flew to Indonesia. My father was now project head on a job based out of Kupang in West Timor. Dad had gone on seven months ahead of us, ostensibly to set up housing and ensure all would be ready for the team's arrival.

Despite the Indonesian invasion of East Timor a few hundred miles away and the fact that Kupang was overrun by young, machine-gun-wielding Javanese soldiers, my parents felt it was a safe place, much safer than Georgetown, Guyana, for two young girls to wander on their own. Perhaps they were right. My sister and I were the only blond females on the island. We were leggy teenagers, often mistaken for twins, who attracted a lot of attention. We were allowed to walk around town and shop by ourselves. We rode the *bemos*, ornately decorated minivans privately owned and run as buses. Whenever Chris or I were on board, the ticket taker, hanging off the open-ended rear of the van, would shout out in Bahasa Indonesia that he had the white girls on board. Dad told us the price for a seat beside my sister or me was double the regular fare. We usually drew a crowd that more than once seemed threatening.

On Timor there was no pretence made of the surveillance put on us. All our mail was opened and read. Private letters arrived with sentences blacked out and the pages of magazines, *Maclean's* and *Time*, stuck together because so much text had been marked by the censor's thick ink. Our fingerprints were taken and our movements controlled by the Indonesian military. We were required to leave the island at least once every six months, but before returning, had to gain permission from the army stationed in Kupang.

Unlike Guyana there was little on Timor that directly echoed its colonial past. Despite that, the Canadians, who mostly lived in a small compound with our house at the front, managed to recreate a tattered shadow of what might have been. The flags of Canada and Indonesia were always flown at the entrance to the compound, and we all had servants and gardeners. I remember there was considerable debate about how much to pay the servants. The concern was that overpaying them would somehow upset the delicate balance of the island economy. There was also talk as to which islands provided the best cooks and maids. We had one maid from Savu and another from Sumba. The old man who showed up at our door one day and became our gardener was from Roti. He wore a traditional Roti high hat, woven of palm and shaped to mimic a seventeenth-century Portuguese gentleman's hat. The brim was wide and the front rose up in what was supposed to look like an ostrich plume.

On Timor my mother was the wife of the project

head and so held a social position quite different from the one she'd had in Guyana. She took on the job of buffering my father, who had a short temper and wasn't particularly patient, from the complaints of the other expats, the members of the team and their wives. She gave English lessons to some of the island's prominent women, including the raja's wife and daughter, and arranged formal dinners when military or government officials came to the island. I remember standing in receiving lines at those events, shaking hand after limp damp hand, while smiling demurely. One of the things that gave my mother particular pleasure on Timor was the garden created around our house. When we arrived it was a barren plot of crushed coral, but when we left it was thick with bougainvillea, orchids, bamboo, and soaring trees. When I recently found our Kupang home, via Google Maps's satellite feature, the news that it appeared from above as a dense green blob made my mother very happy.

I celebrated my sixteenth and seventeenth birthdays on Timor. Along with my sister, who is three years younger, I began wondering what we were really doing on that island. We wondered why Dad went to the border of East Timor though the area was strictly off limits to foreigners, why we had a Coast Guard boat at our disposal, why we met and stayed with the Canadian ambassador while on Java. Who were the "Fretilin," what were they fighting for, and, if they weren't anything to be worried about (the answer my mother gave me), why were there so many soldiers in Kupang?

My father's final report filled nineteen volumes, and in its executive summary he notes that field operations for the project spanned three years, took up more than 250 expatriate man-months, and included experts from twelve different disciplines. Over the course of the project, twenty-nine foreigners were involved, seventy-five Indonesian professionals, and one hundred technical and administrative support staff. They were, ostensibly, all there to study the water resources of that small island. The project's recommendations, if implemented, would have benefited what was then a population of less than 750,000 of which 375,000 made up the workforce. In 1978 it seemed to my sister and me that a lot of work was being done for a relatively small group of people living on a very remote and seemingly unimportant island.

My sister and I still joke about our father the spy, but now we also acknowledge that the idea might not be just a joke. Was there a connection between my father's timing and the political upheavals in the countries he visited? What was he doing there? No one can answer that question. Not even my mother or any of my father's friends.

My father was a very secretive man. He rarely spoke of his work in detail. Though they were married for thirty-seven years, he never told my mother how much money he made or saved. She was given an allowance that grew as the cost of living did and as the family's needs increased. Dad had his own bank accounts, and Mom never saw any of the statements associated with them. When my father died, suddenly and unexpectedly, my mother had no idea if she was left destitute or comfortably well off. When we went through his papers, we found that he had an extensive stock portfolio, substantial savings, and numerous life insurance policies.

When he died, my father was working on contract for BC Hydro. I don't know exactly what he was doing in India, but I think he was conducting a feasibility study for a potential hydroelectric dam. He had been living in Shimla for five months when, ten days before he was expected home in Vancouver, he failed to meet his co-workers for breakfast. They went to his room and found him lying on the floor. He had been there for more than three hours. He was paralyzed from the chest down.

Two months later, after my mother and brother flew to India to have my father transferred to a private hospital, and once his condition had stabilized enough for him to be flown home, a doctor showed me an X-ray that he said would help me understand what was happening to my father. I saw the sharp outline of vertebrae, the silhouette of a skull, and a place about four inches below the skull where there was nothing at all. This empty space was where cancer had consumed the bone. This black hole in the landscape of my father was what had caused him to miss breakfast with his co-workers that day. He died a few weeks later.

He died without discussing his death with any of his three children or his wife. My mother brought it up during one of her visits to the palliative care ward, and Dad told

her there was no point talking about it, no point in getting
angry about it. He never explained to her why it was that
before he left for India he'd instructed her to leave him
there if he died and not to make heroic efforts to bring
him home if he became gravely ill while overseas. Despite
the dozens of overseas contracts he'd taken and the many
countries he'd travelled to during their life together, my
father had never before said anything like that to my
mother.

When I think of my father, I usually see him against a
tropical or exotic backdrop. I see him, almost six feet tall,
red-haired and splashed with freckles, over-tall and over-
white, provoking murmurs and drawing crowds whenever
he wrote notes or signed cheques with his left hand. In
most of the places we lived or he travelled, he was a clumsy
giant walking through markets, bending over woven
baskets holding ten-foot pythons, grinning while crowds
milled about him. We teased him, called him Bwana and
Tuan Besar, Mr. Big in Bahasa Indonesia. Bette, our maid
on Timor, baked him a cake every day and so then we
called him Tuan Kue. Mr. Cake.

Mr. Cake, Bwana Plunkett. I have a photograph of
him standing on the roof of a blue-grey and white Land
Rover. The kind with narrow vent windows that push
out near the bottom of the front windscreen and seats
in the back that flip down from the sides. The kind of
Land Rover that makes you think of adventure, of African
safaris, pale women in pith helmets with swaths of netting
wound around their faces, men who smoke pipes and wear

boots laced tight up to their knees, all polished hard and shiny like a red-brown cockroach carapace. In that photo my father, standing on the Land Rover roof, is looking out through a camera with a telephoto lens, looking out over thick jungly bush. The road curves off to the right but not sharply, and there is no one and nothing else alive within the photo's frame. He is wearing a safari shirt, one of many that his tailor in Hong Kong would custom make and mail out to him wherever in the world he was. He is standing there, in profile, looking out and away, far away, through a long lens.

In the last two days of my father's life, he began to feel pain and nurses gave him morphine regularly. He became delirious and argumentative. The last time I saw him, he told me to get him his cigarettes. When I reminded him he couldn't smoke in the hospital, he got angry. He didn't believe he was in the hospital. To calm him down, I finally said I would go out and buy him a pack of smokes. He looked at me and said with complete lucidity, "You're lying to me." He made me empty my coat pockets before I left the room.

My mother found me crying and laughing in the corridor. I had kept my cigarettes hidden. When we went back into his room, she told my father not to tease me like that. He shrugged and said, "It's my life." The next day he died.

The Hindu epic *Ramayana* tells of how Hanuman helped save Prince Rama's wife Sita. In return, the prince gave Hanuman a gift. He had written on a scroll, "As long as men shall speak of you, you will live on Earth. No one can equal you. Your heart is true; your arms are strong; you have the energy to do anything. You have served me faithfully and done things for me that couldn't be done."

Hanuman, the mischief-maker, snatched the scroll and answered, "It's nothing," while he tore to pieces the gift Prince Rama had given him.

# PART ONE

## Guyana

# 1

## ARRIVING

In Guyana the night is dark, true dark. In Guyana the night piles thick and velvet, Prussian blue from the ground beneath your feet to high above your head. It is all around you, not confined just to the sky, but lying too along the ground, at the side of the road, in the air above the canal water, and lurking among the grasses and the trees. Thick, so thick is the night that it comes in close and nudges you. It has a pelt that brushes cheeks, a weight that curls in the nape of your neck, and it fills your mouth with black and wet solidity. It is alive. Alive with sounds and smells, something you can almost hold in your palm. Night there is not like anything I had ever felt before.

Guyana, Guyana. True dark, true night was the first Guyana thing I learned. We left Canada in daylight and landed there, outside of Georgetown, in the night. Our plane touched down at Timehri airport. Out there, I saw "Welcome" and "International" written on a little whitewashed building beside the runway near the bottom of the rolling metal stairs. I stepped off the plane and out onto those stairs that shook and clanged metallic underneath my feet. Welcome to Guyana. There I stood, slapped to stillness by that water-thickened air. That's when I saw, for the first time, what true true dark could be, what night dark had within itself when left alone to spread and stretch and fill all nooks and crannies. How could it be so hot and yet so densely solid dark? You gulp air just from the shock of it. Taste greenness on your tongue. Jungly ancient vegetation sweetened by a hundred years of rattling sugar cane. Tasting too of other things, things hidden there among the canes, things my tongue could not detect, not yet. Trade winds stirred that sultry air, swirled it sluggishly round me in the velvet dark. The airplane's open door was there behind me. Back inside that plane was Canada, but I was standing on the edge and facing out, out to Guyana.

My father was already striding through the steamy dark and was almost at the whitewashed airport building. Behind me my impatient brother and my sleepy little sister waited for my feet to move. They leaned forward, my mother at the end, and all were pushing air. I felt it piling up behind my back. Hesitation time was past, and I must move, make my feet ting-tang-ting down metal stairs to first contact with Guyana soil. With each step my clothes were shaken, and all the little bits and shreds of northern air that clung, sunken into pockets and wedged in creases all the way from Canada, were driven out. Replaced, right then right there, by stronger, wetter, Caribbean stuff.

I was changing, without knowing it, before my foot had even reached the ground.

Changing as I walked, changing how I walked. Already feet were moving, a little bit, not much but some, already moving to rhythms never heard before. That's soca. It's a left-right sway. It was the Mighty Sparrow singing his calypso hits, pumping out of speakers in the terminal. Strange music clattered up the night, soca beat so strong it can change the tempo of your feet, can make your blood wash rhythmic in your veins. Welcome to Guyana with a steelpan trill, a rolling, high-pitched sound. The Mighty Sparrow sang, he sang, "Drunk and disorderly, always in custody, me friends and me family, all men fed up with me, 'cause I drunk and disorderly." Hear the jump in that, words that even spoken cannot sit still. That's a sound to make a white girl start to wind, and in Guyana wind is dance. *She winin though she just touch down, fresh fresh, she new and never been to Mashramani, never been to Carnival, but there she go, she swayin to that soca beat without knowing that she is.* Welcome to Guyana.

It was July 31, 1974. I was thirteen years old, and Guyana too was young. Guyana, a newly minted country, was just eight years and sixty-three days into independence. The country and I both young and restless, full of optimism, full of hope. Wide-eyed and credulous. We—my mother, little sister, brother, father, me—were fresh flown in from where I'd lived my life up to that day, a suburb of Vancouver. There the lawns were flat and weedless, kept trimmed and bound by pebbled borders.

Gardens were filled with annuals. My father liked Razzle Dazzle Petunias, their flopping heads all striped like candy canes in red and white. Dad planted tulip bulbs in lines so straight he must have used a ruler; spring blooms broke soil in even beats, uniform across the garden beds.

I came from a place where everyone looked just like me, and all my friends had names like Carpenter and Collinge. Where fathers, just like mine, drove off in mornings and returned at night to wives in aprons who served them Scotch and, later, dinner, chickens roasted, sometimes steak. It was a place where girls had long blond hair, blue eyes, pale skin, and some, like me, rode horses, English saddle, double reined. Black, velvet-covered helmets. Shiny leather boots. In that place the air was thin both night and day. Darkness there was cold and light, black linen faded out to grey. Where I came from nobody ever heard the word *Guyana*, not until they heard that I was moving to that place.

What was Guyana? Mr. Larson, my grade seven teacher, pulled down our classroom's world map and stuck his pointer on a spot in South America. A spot so small the pointer covered it entirely. This, he said, is Guyana. This is Guyana, and it is where the Plunkett family (necks turned and everybody stared at me) will be living in a few weeks. He tapped the map where a peanut shape was painted cotton-candy pink. The label read "British Guiana," and the colour matched Rhodesia, Uganda, Swaziland, and other places all in Africa. That map was out of date. I knew that even then, but no one seemed to notice. Mr. Larson smiled at me. Guyana, he said, is where you will find sugar cane and bauxite mines. And water, lots and lots of water.

You can't see that water on the map in Annieville, the elementary school where I was sitting listening to Mr. Larson, but it's there. Oh it is there, and plenty plenty of it. Water flowing as in rivers, water falling over mountaintops, water surging, water flooding, water in the air, and water on the land. Water bringing life and bringing death as in mosquitoes, cholera, filaria, and yellow fever too. Those things were also things no one where I grew up had thought of, but I knew of them. I knew because I'd had to have the shots for some, and each was now recorded in my yellow cardboard booklet listing all inoculations.

That yellow cardboard book was in my father's hand, stuffed inside my passport, the first passport I ever had. My photograph was inside too, in black and white, a grinning me, bucktoothed and shy, my freckles strong enough to show in light grey dots across my nose, my hair pulled back, my long blond hair that now was gone. Gone. The first and only time that it was cut, sold to a barber who said it would make a man's toupée. Fine and pale. "We are moving to the tropics," my mother said when we drove to the city on that day. "In the tropics it is very hot. We are moving to a place that's near the equator. You will be very hot with all that hair." My father didn't like that, but he agreed with her. He didn't like that I was going to lose my long blond hair. It reached way past my waist, and once when I was standing with my mother in a lineup at the grocery store I felt a man, an old man, stroking it, his shaky hand passing feather-lightly down my hair. My mother saw him doing that. I know she did. I saw her eyes flick overhead. I saw her smile. She smiled but it was small, and nudged me up so I was standing then in front of her. The tropics aren't the place for hair that's thick and long, that's heavy on your back. She said all that again while I watched in the mirror, sitting in the barber's chair and watching him with scissors in his hand. I saw him wrap a tail-like switch of wheat-blond hair, wrap it carefully in tissue paper, thin fuchsia paper rustled in his hands.

Sugar cane and bauxite mines. Hot tropic air. My mother and my teacher were both right. Guyana had all that, and plenty of it, but water was what brought us there. That's what my father told the customs men while we all stood, behind him, me, my sister, and my brother, good and quiet. Standing silent in the late-night tropic air. I was looking at my shoes. Standing in my yellow polyester travel suit, a skirt and matching jacket, poking with my tongue a stitched-up hole inside my mouth. That hole was where a tooth had been. It had wandered there, growing in the wrong place, and our family dentist had tried to fix it the day the barber cut my hair. When we got home that day and I was all excited about my new suit, special clothes to travel to a special place, my dad hesitated then reached out his hand and softly touched my hair as if to stroke it, but ruffled it instead. I was thinking about all of that and staring at my shoes and poking with my tongue at the stitched-up hole so new the wiry dentist threads still scratched. Meanwhile my father answered questions that the customs men, dark as night and shiny too, asked him, "Who are you?"

"You are Canadians?"

My father answered, "Yes."

"Five of you and why you here?"

How did my father answer? His back was there, just there in front of me and broad enough to cast a shadow, blocking out the light above the customs desk. I could see his freckled hands and even see the red-gold hairs that grew down his arms and even across the backs of his hands and out onto his fingers, faintly there, but there. But, I didn't hear him tell the customs man why we were there. Why, why were we there? Why had we moved? Why did we have to sell my horse, cut my hair, leave my dog with someone else, though I'd been told when we returned he would as well. I'd get my dog back someday, one day when we left this place. Why are we here? My mother says we're here to learn and for adventure, to see new things, to see the world.

My father might have said to Guyana's customs man, "I am a civil engineer. I'm here to map your rivers, assess them for their power and their strength," and that would all be true. That much I knew. Direct and true, straightforward, simple easy. He might have said, "We're here to serve the new Guyana. Comrade Burnham's vision brought us here," and that, as well, would also have been true, at least in part. It's true there was a Comrade Burnham, and it was his plan to power up the country using all Guyana's rivers as the source. It's true that hydro power, damming rivers, was my father's specialty. He might have said, "I'm here to watch," and that's a part of learning, and that would also have been true.

True, true enough. Stamp, stamp. The customs man banged down his inky stamp five times. He reached out to hand those booklets back to Dad who took them, red-gold hairs and freckles on his hands. I never realized how white white hands could be. Welcome. We walked through to where Guyana truly starts. Sugar cane and bauxite mines and water, soca music, blackest night, a place where water hangs in air.

## 2

## FLAMBOYANT

*I*f Guyana night was darkest dark, then day was just as unequivocally bright. White blaring sun. Its rays come down direct to earth when you stand there, that close to where the centre of the earth wraps round. Not slanted or oblique. Sun so bright and unambiguous it roasts a white girl's skin in minutes, crisps her up in seconds. She won't have time to see it happen, won't even know she's burnt till it's all done.

But, I sat in the shade, riding in a Land Rover that had a little fan bolted to the middle of its dash, turning back and forth to stir the soupy air. Air that's thick with smells of growth, of mud, of water stagnant in canals, and rotting reeds and things I'd never smelled before. Inside the car, the heat was woolly-blanket smothering. Air from open windows didn't cool; oh no, it was a furnace blast. Guyana heat came through the windows, open so that I could put my head outside and turn it back and forth, watch Georgetown scenes flash past despite my grumpy thoughts of never showing interest. I was resolved to hate the place.

We were being toured, our first day out in Georgetown, driving out to see the sights. My father wasn't there because, already, he'd set off. First thing, right after breakfast, he'd set off to work, to start the job that brought us to this place. My mother and my sister and my brother were with me, and we were seeing things that all were new.

Tree. Tree. Trees flashed past, white banded, bright rings around their trunks. They rose straight from the ground along the edges of the road, leaned out and over where we drove, fanned wide and flat at top and then exploded there in scarlet brilliant red. A canopy of flame. Flamboyant trees, our driver told us then. My mother laughed, she craned her neck to look up out the window, then turned to where I sat in back and said, "Flamboyant means exuberant." Yes, those trees, they were flamboyant, waving arms and shouting, "look at me." No discreet firs or cedars on that road. No monkey puzzle trees like those we'd seen on drives through downtown Vancouver. One Monkey Puzzle, two Monkey Puzzle, three Monkey Puzzle—that's what Dad told us to chant on the way back home after he'd been dropped off at his office. No monkey puzzle trees to chant at in Georgetown, not there where monkeys lived. I thought that I'd remember to tell my father that later, over dinner in the hotel restaurant.

No, there were no monkey puzzles and no walls of neat-trimmed cedar hedges there to block the views of passersby, creating privacy for those with money for that sort of thing. Instead, the trees were loud, flamboyant,

singing colours to the bright blue sky. One Flamboyant.
Two Flamboyant. Three.

Tree. Tree. Tree. Between the banded trees and down
the middle of the street, a boulevard that was wide wide
wide. Women walked, arms linked, some with umbrellas
open, arcing out and up above their heads, for shade
because the nearest rain was three months out to sea.
They swayed, sashayed, hips rolled, wrapped round in
cloth, bright purple, blue, and orange. Colours stamped
in flowers and in words. They slowly sauntered down the
middle of the boulevard, their flip-flops slapping up the
dust. Schoolgirls too, they're there. I saw them in their
pleated skirts and tunics, white and navy blue and checker-
patterned. They were there in groups of two or three, arms
round each other's waists. Friends. I saw them, but I knew
I didn't see myself dressed up like that. No, no. School,
that was a thing from the past, and how could the past, my
past, my everyday, fit into that strange place? It couldn't. I
was certain, sitting in that Land Rover with trees that set
the sky aflame above and flatbed trailers drawn by horses,
dun-coloured, just like the dust that rose as they passed us
at crossings, I was sure that none of what I knew and what
I was could fit inside that world.

That night, the first I slept in that new place, I had
dreamt of houses up on stilts. The kind of houses that we'd
seen when driving from the airport down to Georgetown
by the sea. The road was like a tunnel through the
rustling wall of cane fields, hidden green, invisible in
darkness. Land of Canaan. Hopetown. Providence and

Good Intent. McDoom. Those were villages we passed through on our way. But all we saw of them were lights off to the side, places where the darkness was made ragged, holes burnt in the night by amber lights. Those were lanterns hung below the houses, glowing there, out there in that Guyana night. Marks to show that people really did live in the village that we passed, the one they called McDoom.

"Look," my mother said. "Look at the houses. They're built up off the ground, on legs, on stilts." Stilts that kept what they called "bottom houses" cool, a place to hang a hammock in the heat, to sleep in the middle of the day. Not so, I thought. Stilts like legs, long leggy homes all ready, so it looked to me, to flee that place, ready set to run away, stride out of there, just go and head back home without a second look. Get out. Run now. Run from this place as fast as legs can run. And later, while I slept, dream houses crept through long long grass on legs thin as insects' and as bent. They watched with yellow eyes, then sprouted wings that clattered like a dragonfly's when they took off, buzzing, disappearing into blue-black velvet dark. Leaving me behind to watch them vanish into all that night.

Leaving me to wake up under sheets damp and limp as lettuce leaves, leaving me to hear the buzz-buzz-buzzing still. But that was an air conditioner, not wings, and it pumped air around me, smelling mildewed, thick as black. I lay silent in that bed inside a tower in a hotel called the Pegasus, just lay there while the white of day came pouring in and shattered everything that I could see inside that room. Shattered sight at least. Blinded just as much by light as earlier I was by dark.

But even sulking girls, all grumpy mad and stubborn, can't lay long in places new as that. New new day and new new world. I had to get up off that bed. I did, I got up and felt hard tile cool on my feet, saw where brightest light lured me out to a balcony. Below my feet, I saw what looked like Hollywood: a turquoise pool, not square and straight-edged but curving, sinuous, and all around it, lounges waited. Waiters, white sleeves contrasting with dark hands, swayed from a thatch-roofed hut, holding trays of drinks. I heard steelpan music, ruffled metal trills. Beside the pool, a band was always playing. That soca sound again and that's why waiters swayed. Palm trees ringed all of it and over top of everything the sky was stripped of blue, washed out by that bright sun. This was new. All that was something very new.

That sound, that music, it played everywhere we went that day. It seemed to set the pace of clouds, the rhythm of the leaves that shimmied there in trade wind breezes always blowing, the dance of grasses stirred by slow-motion cyclists wheeling past. The way feet took steps, unconscious and unbidden. That Mighty Sparrow or Lord Kitchener singing everywhere we went. Singing inside everything you saw.

We went down to Stabroek Market. Our driver said, it's most famous, a building made of iron, cast iron, and old, and everything there was for sale, everything to buy and to be seen. But first, across the street from Stabroek's pointed four-faced tower clock, we saw a sign painted red and white. It read "Trafalga Square," and even I knew that wasn't right. At least, not right in any other place, but maybe here where English jumps and jerks in unexpected ways. Perhaps in that new place that sign might be right. Trafalga Square was not a square at all. It was a plywood stall that smelled of chilies frying hot in oil and curry-goat, but I didn't know what I smelled until our driver told me. Trafalga Square, he said, is where to buy the best goat roti. The stall was red and white and striped and hung with other signs that told us, "Drink Red Spot Soda!" and boys and men were lounging all around it, ringing round and leaning backward, elbows on the counter, eyeing everything that passed by, sniffing curry-air. We passed by and we were eyed.

Our driver said, "Stabroek, it is Georgetown, history and hucksters, all together. All of Georgetown here tight packed in this one place." He pointed at the tower. It was squat and topped with rust-red tin that looked like a pointy witch's hat. It had a tiny bell, and every one of its four clocks told a different time. Stabroek was built along the riverbank, in Georgetown harbour, where sweet water from the Demerara River mixed with the salty south Atlantic sea. It was built out hanging over water where boats bunted up against its piers. The piers were stellings. "That's what we call them here."

The stellings stretched out long and low and over water muddy brown and sluggish thick. The river flowed beneath the stellings, slow slow, a slow backdrop to all.

The Demerara River: They call it sweet, but it looked bitter bad to me; it seemed to barely move, so wide, so thick with silt, so dirty looking, greyish brown. It flowed silently, didn't splash or even gurgle there beneath the stelling boards. But on the stellings, that was a different scene. Everything above the river was a jagged jumble, a juddering shoving crowd. And what didn't move was frantic too, with scent, or feverish with sound. Bales of goods—I didn't know what they were because they were bound in rope and cloth—were piled to tottering heights beside the water's edge, just then removed from boats it seemed. People squatted on the ground beside pyramids of fruit all spiky bright and strange. Things called breadfruit, soursop, and sapodilla. I saw bananas, those I recognized, but they were were short and fat and black.

A woman with her head wrapped in a flowered piece of cloth shouted, "Mauby," and waved an empty glass. "Best mauby. Fifty cent." It's a drink, the driver said, and offered us a taste. Mauby, made from bark, was sweet and bitter, brown and yellow-gold, light and dark together. I took a sip and thought of Coca-Cola mixed with liquorice. The driver took the glass back to the mauby woman, then winked at me and said, "Look, look, dem boys. Georgetown boys got champagne taste on mauby pocket." I saw those boys. Boys with Afros brushed out wide and perfect round and other ones with long straight hair. They wore pants high-waisted tight and flaring wide on platform shoes and shirts with buttons deep undone in front, tucked in to show their narrow hips. Flash. They strode past, and I

saw one that had a rooster tucked up underneath his arm.
Its yellow legs were scaled and barbed and crooked out
the back. Fighting cock, the driver told us. Tail feathers,
iridescent purple, colours like a gas leak in a street-side
puddle, waved at us as the boy walked past. Tail feathers
bounced as if the Mighty Sparrow's song was tugging on its
tip. I saw that fighting cock's sharp eye on mine. I stared
hard at it as it stared equal hard at me. The bird craned
its coloured neck to catch a long last glimpse of that new
thing, that freshly pink just-off-the-plane white girl.

*My, my, it is hot out here. Gyal, you far from cool and pink is
turnin quick to red. Get out da sun. Ya burnin up.*

I shivered when we hit the cool inside of Stabroek
Market. Murky dark was banded randomly by shafts of
light, fiercely speared into the dark through punctures
in the high tin roof. They'd blind you if you looked too
hard. In there the air was old. As old as Stabroek was itself,
at least a hundred years. Old air, so old that you might
think the air you breathed was stuff the workmen puffed
when they were building it so long ago. The smell of all
Georgetown, history to hucksters, it was sunk into the
floor, the walls, the ceiling. Everything all mixed, confused,
and fused into a smell that was new and only in that place.

But the smell would shift and alter as we wandered
up and down the aisles. "Aisles" makes it sound just like a
store. Stabroek aisles were more like narrow streets, high
walled and canyon-like, bound in by stacks of what's for
sale. The narrow aisles trapped smells and concentrated
them. A breeze from off the river stirred up the smells,

wafting some from far far back, beyond what you could see, and spread them thick or thin, but mostly thick, on you and on the ground.

The first thing we smelled was dye and cloth. Bolts and bolts of fabric towered over us, rolled and stacked and tidy-tall above as we craned necks. We stopped and stared too long. A man brought out a ladder, quick, to scramble up. He sent the cotton down like ribbons or like waterfalls, cascades of printed fabric. Red and white and purple, pink flowers stamped on bright lime-green-and-paisley swirls with dots of shiny gold along the edge. As colour fell toward us through the air it carried smells. A smell of thread and bobbins, zippers, buttons, safety pins, and patterns tacked to cloth. I smelled my mother's sewing room and that was unexpected.

We moved on. Down the aisle and around a corner was where all Guyana's past, its history, was hung up near the roof. It was a history in furniture, the furniture of those who'd come and gone. Things left behind, first by the Dutch and then the English, there, up there above our heads. We saw straight-backed chairs for formal teas, credenzas, and card tables, their felted tops stained, bug eaten. Dutch tiles inlaid, bright blue-and-white and showing scenes with windmills over water. There was a desk of purple wood, shiny dark and heavy, roll-topped and with every drawer and flap secured by shiny brass locks. There was a chair slung low with cane and curved just right to hold a rich man's back in lolling pose. That, the driver said, was what they called a Berbice chair, and

you will never see a one like it in any other place. He
showed us how its arms could pivot, arms that swung out
wide to hook a lounging leg, feet up and over. The driver
said this was a chair where plantation bosses lounged when
heat set in, spread-legged and smoking pipes or sipping
rum while others worked the sugar. Up there, up near the
ceiling, all those legs of chairs and tables bristled down
at us. Sharpened teeth that showed with knowing grins.
They might be saying, sure, the sitters and the drinkers of
the tea, they all are gone, but we are here, we still are here.
We see it all pass by, and you, they grinned down hard at
me, *you gyal, watch out for what is commin next.*

What next? Next was something new again. Next
we came to where the concrete floor of Stabroek Market
was sticky, sticky on our shoes. Our steps were sounded
out with crinkly notes and sucking sounds, of something
grubby grabbing at the rubber soles of shoes not made
for this. Oh no, those sandals, they were made to show
off toes all clean and delicate and not to cross on ground
like that. That was where the beef and fish and chicken,
pork and all the meat that any Guyanese might eat, and
that included some we didn't know, was hung up, laid out,
stacked and piled and oozing out onto the floor. Oh my.
The flies were thick and made a sound as loud as any air
conditioner, same buzz-buzz-buzzing there. Sharp and,
yes, flamboyant.

Fish, some with gills still flapping, caught right there,
right off that Stabroek stelling in that dutty water, that
dutty greasy Demerara River there. They curled and

gasped and glistened on the slimy scales of others that had just been gutted, entrails dumped onto the concrete floor. Chickens being killed, heads off in one loud chop, and feathers plucked and singed right where others waited, inside slatted wooden crates all steepled up along the aisle. They watched and squawked and screamed. They flapped their wings as if to rise and fly from there, fly fly away. Fly, crate and all. My daydream broke. I knew those birds, I knew that they weren't flying anywhere. They were curry bound, and no amount of flaps and squawks would save their lives.

Nor would chicken cackles or fish gasps keep our eyes from rising, slowly slowly, up and up to what was much more new than all of that, more new than any of the things we'd seen so far. Up high, above the heads of everyone, up on the posts of stalls, that's where the cows and goats were hung, mostly stripped but some with hooves and horns, eyes and even tongues in skulls. White bone, red meat. Those, the horned and eyeballed skulls, were hung on lintels, thick strong wood posts dyed dark from many years of being what they were. Skulls of cows and goats hooked over rusty spikes high up so all could see from any aisle that this was where the meat was sold. Fresh meat. Sold here. Don't let imagination run away with you. It might have looked like something more, but really it was just a message. Just a sign so anyone could see from almost any aisle in that dim dusty place of criss-crossed aisles, so all could see that if they wanted meat, well, it was over here. We stepped carefully away, slipped and slid, while big round eyes stared black and blankly down and watched us try to learn how to keep feet dry when walking there in thin-soled sandals made for other sorts of ground.

# 3

## HOLLYWOOD

The first place that we lived was called the Pegasus Hotel. The Pegasus stood on the shore, in Georgetown, in a corner where the river met the sea. The Pegasus was a round tower looking down to where the Demerara River opened up its mouth and spat the silt of all Guyana's flat-topped mountains out into the ocean. Silt blurred the water all along that shore, fogged and muddied it for miles and miles out into the sea. We are in the tropics, but the water here is never blue. Not blue, that is, unless contained inside a hotel swimming pool. No, no, the beachside water there was dirty grey or brown and sometimes frothed like chocolate milk. Frothed along the wall that stretched out along the beach, vanishing from tower views into the distance. That was the seawall. My father said that Georgetown land was below the level of the sea, three feet below, and so there was a wall to hold the sea, to keep it off the land. Canals were everywhere throughout Georgetown, along its roads and down its streets, there to channel water back, water coming in the form of rain that floods that place. My mother said that's why all the houses there are built on stilts. Water water.

Look down, look out from tower-heights and you could see the dirt mixed up with river water, mixed up with sea, dirt dragged from the land and carried to the country's very rim. Some people said that water, that very water flowing out into the sea, carried more than just rich soil. Some said it tumbled diamonds too, mixed with the dirt, and some said gold. Grinning wide, its mouth agape, the Demerara River smiled a big wide smile, a smile inviting people to come, come in, come up this water all the way to deep inside Guyana. Come one, come all. The river invited everybody in.

Not so the Pegasus. It was different. It was uninviting. Strangely so for a hotel, a place where people came to stay awhile. The Pegasus, its tower, was the tallest building in Georgetown. Tall as Stabroek's belfry with its clocks. And, just like Stabroek's belfry, the Pegasus was seen from everywhere, and that meant it could see most everything. It stood tall and looking down on everyone and everything in Georgetown. It looked and didn't touch because it was ringed and held in tight by walls. Those walls were very high. You couldn't see over them, you could not see in if you were on the other side, the outside. But, from inside and up the tower, from the bedroom balconies, it was easy to see past those walls, despite their height. And that was where we lived, there inside those walls.

Our room, the one I shared with Chris, looked out over the swimming pool, so any time of day or night we could stand out on the balcony and see its turquoise water shimmering below. We could hear calypso steelpan music rising up from poolside. It drew us out each morning. Every day we'd wake up, step out, and look down at that walled-in turquoise pool and steelpan band with band-boys playing through the daylight hours and at the waiters holding high their discs, their trays above their heads, ready all the time to serve.

My father went to work right after breakfast every day, breakfast that we ate together, all five of us together in the hotel restaurant just off the lobby. There the tiles felt cool as we kicked off our sandals underneath the bentwood bamboo table. I would order kippers, smoked fish my father had taught me how to love, crisp skin and thin thin bones that bent beneath my tongue. It was fine to order kippers there. They didn't fill the room with stink the way they did at home. There in Georgetown, they understood those sorts of things. They understood that kippers are for breakfast and that toast is served not hot but cold. These were things my father learned when he spent time in England at my Uncle Michael's wedding. Dad came home and after that had toast brought to the table in a silver rack, slices standing separate not stacked, and he would wait for them to cool before he spread them, thick, with marmalade and butter. At breakfast my father smiled and told us stories, talked about that place we'd come to live. He talked about Georgetown and its colonial past. He liked that we, his children, sat straight and tall, held our knives and forks the way he'd taught us to, chewed quietly, and took small bites. He liked that we ate everything we ordered and were served, but waited to start until he himself began to eat. My father liked that we were mostly quiet, that we listened, thanked the waiter when he brought our plates of food, smiled up into the waiter's face, looked everybody in the eye when speaking, and said thank you. He liked that I ate kippers as he did.

After breakfast my father, wearing khaki pants and safari shirts in beiges and pale-blues, patch-pocketed and left untucked—because that was the way men dressed in jungly places—met his driver in the blue-grey Land Rover out front and went to work. Then our worlds diverged, his and mine, and didn't cross again until he returned, sometimes later on that day, sometimes later in the week; it depended on how far he went away, across Georgetown perhaps or off into the wild blue sky, the yonder he might say, to fly above a river somewhere in Guyana. I didn't know, really know, just what he did, and then, right then, I didn't care because there were other things to think about, to learn, to see, to smell and hear.

Learning started right after Dad had left. That was when we put on bathing suits and learned to lounge and how to wave a hand so waiters skimmed with trays right to our sides and gave us dewy bottles of Lime Rickey or Red Spot. They all knew our room and knew our names. We didn't have to even sign a chit. At first they thought my brother was a girl. He was sixteen years old, his hair was wavy blond and long, silky and luxuriant, while my sister's and my own was cut off, short and straight. I was only ever called a "Miss" but people sometimes mistook Chris for a boy, and around the pool Stephen might have been mistaken for a girl, except when he lounged there he wore a Speedo bathing suit. Soon enough my sister and I were wearing bright bikinis bought in the hotel lobby shop and shining up our skin with baby oil, trying hard to brown, but that was never going to happen, no, not ever. We got blonder though, our hair bleached out in sun; in the pool that was mostly what we saw, blond heads and light brown ones. Our skin burnt red in double time, quick quick, then peeled and then returned to white, perhaps more freckled than before, but otherwise fish-belly white, my father said.

I began to let my feet do soca rhythm sways when walking to the pool. I set them free with knowledge that those feet were setting hips to roll and sway. I knew they were. And next I learned just how to look and see without my eyes full staring, how to check on others' eyes without them seeing mine were looking just as much. I saw things. I saw teeth that shone far whiter bright beside the darkness of the skin. I saw sweat that gathered in a band-boy's hair to make it sparkle. I saw it too along his arms. I saw these things as I walked past, and I didn't even look. I saw, and then I took my lounge and closed my eyes and lay in sun and listened.

Soon, very soon I liked that life inside that wall, beside that pool, and soon I thought that that was how it would always be. Life there would be a string of days spent lying by a pool and sipping cold Lime Rickeys, cool tangy soda in a bottle brought right to me by a boy who calls me Miss.

Just like Hollywood, I thought. Flick flick my hand and lie under that Guyana sun while my white skin was dotted reddish brown and eyes filled up with blue.

Oh, but we weren't lounging by the pool and playing starlets on our own. Oh no. My mother was always there watching, swimming, mostly reading, underneath her floppy flowered hat and big dark glasses. Underneath all that I knew she watched. I wondered what she saw. That was what the wives of expat working husbands seemed to do. They watched. They watched and talked and congregated at poolside almost every day to lap the pool in lazy pace, to lounge and tip the waiters for the drinks they sipped. Tips were big and bigger, bigger best. Some had husbands like my dad who worked as engineers, some in banks and some were diplomats, and some were there to help the new Guyana grow. The husbands were, not wives. Oh no. Wives of expat husbands didn't work. They ran households, managed gardeners and maids. That was a sort of work. At least, it did take skill, skills that must be learned, and poolside lounging's where my mother started learning how to run a household in the way an expat wife should know.

Talk talk. That's how things beyond the wall that bound the Pegasus Hotel crept in to crack the perfect picture. Talk and talk and storytelling time.

One said, "It was a terrible time. It happened right outside my husband's bank. Broad daylight. In broad daylight."

That was the woman who swam the pool in laps each

day, but always kept her hair hard dry. She swam back and forth and back and forth in constant, never slowing never speeding steady crawl. Her arms seemed weighted as they limpy arced up and then flopped down into the water, her head above it all to keep the moisture off her tight-curled hair. She had a breast just like a pigeon, jutting out, and I wondered sometimes if that shape was there because of all her swimming. She lived in Bel Air Park. Her husband worked at Barclays Bank.

Lying there beside my mother, all dripping bathing suit and curled grey hair, head laid back, eyes behind her glasses closed against the sun, she talked. She said, "Middle of the day. People all out shopping. Everybody saw it. Everybody saw the plates. It was a government car."

She's telling stories of two years before. Two years before and still it's news.

"Everybody saw it. At least a hundred people did. Broad daylight and a car pulls up, a Burnham car with Burnham plates and Burnham thugs. They shot the man right there."

Talk talk. Oh yes, this is the place your husband brought you to. This is the place where men get shot for agitating for the poor, politicking on behalf of people down in Tiger Bay. Now there's a place you do not want to go.

My mother asked what happened next.

Curled head turned and looked through darkened glasses at my mother sitting innocently there. "Nothing. Nothing happened next."

No newspaper report. No arrests. No investigation. No talking out there on the street, at least no talking loud enough to hear. Oh no, no talk like that.

"You know about the election count? About the ballot boxes too? You do?"

No, no, my mother didn't know about the ballot boxes either, but she learned. She learned that Burnham called the army out to commandeer those boxes on election day the year before. She learned about the votes all cast, cast and far outnumbering the people who could vote. She learned about the ballots stuffed inside the boxes, and yet neatly bound in rubber bands, already counted, locked inside the boxes when they were handed over by the commandeering army who had taken them, sealed and still unopened, from the polling booths. Hmm. Hmm. She's told, as well, about intimidation: men drowned in Georgetown's deep canals, and newspapers and magazines that Burnham sued if editors gave hints or even whispered of the goings-on.

"Poor Cheddi Jagan didn't have a chance. He couldn't possibly have won that election."

It's the CIA, the women said. The MI5. The Americans and Brits. Hmm hmm, they nodded heads in unison, flapped hands. Another round of drinks came gliding up. The spies are all around you. They are everywhere. Oh yes, just look, you'll see. They said to Mom, "They've all got spies down here. You know, you could be one too. At least, that's what the Guyanese might think." Could we be spying too? Laugh. Laugh. Oh my, that made everybody laugh, shaking off the water droplets left behind by cooling dips and laps swum back and forth to keep the shape that's right for bathing suits.

I listened and I learned as well, but those women's su-su-suing whispers mixed all up with the calypso music wafting over water from the other side of that blue pool. Sun heated skin and trade wind breezes cooled. Their buzz-buzz-buzzings, stories of the goings-on beyond the wall, confused. Burnham. Cheddi Jagan. Politics and shootings, voters bribed and shot? The CIA and MI5—what's that? Tiger Bay and poverty. Who would spy and why? But then another woman joined the lounging group and shifted the talk to subjects like maids and cooks, how much to pay and where to find the best. I grew restless, and wanted to wander where I could inside those walls. Wanted to wander off where talking wasn't heard and mothers were not seen. There was a garden, there behind the poolside deck. Tile edged gravel, gravel edged grass, thickened water-storing succulents of green, not like the grass at home but grass-like all the same, and that led in the distance off to something yet unseen beyond where broad banana leaves fanned out, dipped low, and vines of hot-pink bougainvillea sprayed their thorny branches wide. That was enticing. What was beyond that wall of untamed vegetation?

I wanted to see, but I wasn't brave enough to go alone. I called my sister, Chris, to come along. We slipped away. We slipped beyond the bougainvillea and banana leaves, and poolside talk faded out and even steelpan music barely

penetrated that green place. Lizards flashed in curving
paths up rough papaya trunks. They ran a scalloped route
with stops and starts and rolling black-ball eyes. Birds.
Something called a Kiskadee, yellow with a banded black-
and-white-striped head. Nests of others, later known as
Crested Oropendola (my father learned these things and
passed on the information morning, noon, and night), their
nests hung overhead, long droops of woven grass. They
looked like tennis balls inside old ladies' nylon stockings
suspended from the trees. We recognized parrots, green
with yellow heads and looking just like ones we'd seen in
shops in malls at home. Birds. The air was shivering with
screeches, chirps, and shrieks. Some squeaked like toys
and others sang, high-pitched, drunk and laughing. Some
were water bubbling over stones. Here was another world
that's new.

A chop-chopping sound came through the trees and
over there there was a man, a gardener we thought. He
was bending over chopping at the ground. No, he was
smacking his machete at the base of vines that thickly
wrapped around the trees, choking trunks and strangling
the fruit we saw hanging near the top. Chop chop. We
stood and silently we watched through green air that
shimmied with the sounds of birds. His back was to us.
He was bent down over ground and wore a cricket cap,
a cap that was dirty white and brimmed and rimmed
with sweat. But there was another man, standing in deep
shadow, looking at us through the same green air that we
were looking through. Ragged shorts and a shirt with

sleeves torn off. Darkest skin I'd ever seen, darker far than any out there by the pool, than any playing music, than any serving sandwiches and drinks. Skin so dark it fell into the shadows; it was hard for me to see where skin began and shadow ended.

Tiger Bay. Is this a man who lives in Tiger Bay? I couldn't hear the women talking then, yet I heard them in my head. They shot him in broad daylight. Not that daylight's broad where I was standing then. Oh no, it was narrow bands and speckles there in that lush garden. Dappled at my feet.

The chopping stopped. Both men were looking at us, at my sister standing there with me. We were still. *Shrreeee-sha-sha-sha-sha-shreeeee.* A crazy creaking sound of rapid rising notes, then heavy silence. All the birds were waiting for an answer. All the lizards watched. What would we do? I felt something shift inside, and later, in an hour or two, I realized that must have been, right then and there, when my first period began. In Guyana they say that when that happens to a girl, her mother should give the girl an egg, a hard-boiled egg, to eat. My mother didn't do that though.

Right then, right there, two men were watching us as we watched them, and changes happened, silent shifts. Birds screamed again. That time they laughed.

Listen hard and you might even hear calypso coming through the jungle trees into the garden where you stand. It's there, you just can't hear it yet. Birds laugh and so do men. The man with darkest skin backhands his brow, flings sweat into the air and says, "Gyal, don vex me now wid starin at us at we work." This garden here, it's not for you, not now, not for you today. Come back another time. Go back to sit in sunlight by the pool. Go back to Hollywood.

## 4

## ALMOND STREET

A clean white house. That's what we moved to when we left the Pegasus Hotel. We left the Pegasus and moved into a house, a proper home, on Almond Street. That name, Almond Street, made me think of Vancouver and of pink blossoms filling up the gutters in the spring. But Almond Street was not like that, because Guyana trees don't put out pale-pink fluffy blooms. And yet the house on Almond Street was a little bit like that.

The Guyanese would call that house a "proppah" house. Proppah Georgetown house. That house on Almond Street was old and standing long in Queenstown borough. It was stilty tall and made of wood. Flounced all around by Demerara shutters, scroll-cut and delicate, top-hinged and pushed out at the bottom to look just like a crinoline of stiffened lace. Standing there, set back from Almond Street, a band of grass and wide canal between the dusty road and where the house walls rose, it looked poised, skirts all gathered up, long legs exposed as though about to step most daintily across a mucky landscape. It looked like a debutante in spring.

And it was white and that was proppah Guyanese as well. Bright white. Think of sugar. Think of sugar cane that has been chopped and crushed and stripped of green and bleached of all its brown. Sugar white. Refined. Purified and processed. Made ready for a cup of English tea. White white, bright white. It shone. The outside boards were whitewashed every year to shine and turn away the high Guyana heat. Reflect it back onto the street so as to keep the inside cool and dark, all shadowy and secret.

From the poolside wives, my mother learned the house was up for rent. Short term, just while the family who lived there took a sabbatical in Amsterdam. They left behind, for us to use, their beds and chairs and tables, sheets and plates and glasses, brooms and dustpans, even books (all those in Dutch, but some had photographs in black and white of naked women). They left behind, as well, their maid, and she became our first. Mary Santiago. A Puttagee, that's what the Guyanese would say instead of Portuguese, with short black hair, thick legs, an apron always tied around her waist, and a daughter just about my sister's age, nine or ten years old. That girl, her name was Anne, she was surely dougla. That's what the Guyanese would say because her father surely wasn't Puttagee. I don't know what he was. We never met her father, but Anne looked as though her father might be black or Coolie. Coolie. That confused me because I'd heard that word before we moved, but only in Vancouver's Chinatown. Coolie in Guyana didn't mean Chinese. In Georgetown, Coolies were West Indian. But we didn't use that word. We understood it was an ugly word.

All proppah Georgetown houses like our house on Almond Street had maids. They didn't live on Almond Street or even in Queenstown, not nearby, but came each day on bus or foot or bicycle or maybe even donkey cart from somewhere else. They carried string bags stretched and bulging, weighed down with what they'd bought that morning at the market on their way to work. Sometimes papaya, sometimes breadfruit or bananas. Sometimes chickens. Sometimes ducks. Live chickens and live ducks, legs bound together, feet thrust out, and beaks pushed through the netting of the bag, feathers all forlorn. Once our maid, not Mary but a later maid, brought us a cat to be a pet and not to eat. That cat was mottled yellow, brown, and black. Milky-eyed and bandy-legged. Thin in body and in hair. My father named him Scrofulous.

Mary brought balanjay in her string bag. That's eggplant in Guyana. Fat purple fruit, white pulp inside and outside skin all tight and shining like a bruise. She called it choka when she baked it with pepper, garlic, and tomatoes. The smell was through the house and out the Demerara shutters, out as far as Almond Street, and everybody who passed by then knew what we were having for lunch. It was my mother's favourite lunch, and even I could eat an eggplant cooked as choka if Mary Santiago was the one to cook it up.

Mary stopped at Bourda on her way to Almond Street. That's where she stopped to fill her string bags. She shopped there early every day. Bourda Market, where the stalls were all outdoors in rows, not covered, not like Stabroek, though as old. You could buy a lot of things at Bourda but not everything, like you could buy at Stabroek. Bourda Market was for food. Some stalls were really only baskets on the ground or piles of fruit and vegetables all laid out neat in rows or balanced one atop the next on burlap sacks spread out on hardened ground. But other stalls were raised above the ground, made from planks, some painted bright in bands of red and blue and yellow, some left to weather in the sun. Inside the painted boards or pyramided on the ground, you'd find okra, cucumber, plantain, and more, all the green Guyana grew, everything you'd need to cook Guyana food, laid out in rows or mounded high in stacks and pyramids.

"Now Sally," said the women by the pool, "if you shop at Bourda or at Stabroek, don't ever take your money. Or don't shop. That's best. Just give the maid a list."

"Not just for market shopping," said another. "Never carry money. Ever."

"Shopkeepers keep a tab for you. Then send your maid to pay or have them come right to the house."

But, my mother liked to shop. The markets, Bourda and Stabroek, could be fun. Walking there was an adventure.

"Just order what you want and take it then or leave it for the maid to fetch. Send your maid, send your maid with cash. They carry money. We do not."

Those women added, almost all in unison, "It isn't safe. White women are not safe to carry money in their bags."

But my mother liked the markets. She liked to see fresh coconuts piled high inside a red-planked stall. She liked to talk with women selling what they'd grown. Those women were what Guyanese would call the hawkers and the hucksters, and my mother liked to talk with them. She listened to the poolside wives (and to my father too, who said as well she shouldn't carry cash) and never paid for things herself, but she would stop and talk. She would talk with Mrs. Boyo. Mrs. Boyo might have been the richest of the hawkers selling things in Bourda Market. Certainly she had what seemed a proppah stall, not just a piece of burlap spread out front or even just a box raised up on legs to hold her papayas and plantain. Mrs. Boyo's stall was like a little shop with sides and even with a roof. But Mrs. Boyo never sat inside her little shop; perhaps it was too hot in there. Instead she'd squat outside. Out there she'd hung an oil-can parrot cage. An old round can with sides stripped off, replaced with mesh, and painted, long ago, bright blue. Mrs. Boyo's yellow parrot dangled upside down, twisted its head side to side to keep a shiny eye on everything at once.

Mrs. Boyo squatted out front beneath a rusty black umbrella, and she always wore a hat that drooped. She oiled her long black hair with coconut, and all her teeth were solid gold. She smiled a lot and flashed her golden teeth at us when we stopped by to talk. She said those teeth were savings, all the money that she had. She said she'd sent her son to travel in Toronto. It was a city she considered moving to, that one day she might use her savings—her golden teeth—to start a new life in. So, for now, she'd sent her son to see what sort of city it, Toronto, was. She smiled. She had a lot of golden teeth, even I could see there were a lot. I tried to see if any had been pulled. Had she spent a golden tooth to send her son to Toronto?

Mrs. Boyo liked sweet things. Her favourite breakfast, she told us, was a glass of sweetened condensed milk mixed half-and-half with Bedessee's West Indian Queen Cream Soda. Frothy, cloudy, sweet sweet sweet. You must try it, she said to me, and grinned a golden grin just thinking of her breakfast. Do they have that? she would ask. Do they have Bedessee's Cream Soda in Toronto, in your land?

No, I never tried that drink. I would try to smile and swallowed jerkily whenever Mrs. Boyo said that I should try her favourite drink. I was afraid she'd mix some up right then and there, and I, to be polite, would have to gulp it down. It never happened, but there were other sweet things to drink, and special too, in Bourda Market. Cane juice sold from a cart an old man wheeled from place to place. He'd grind a stalk of sugar cane, crush it in between two metal plates, and fill a plastic glass with cloudy juice, pure cane juice that stickied up your fingers as it dried.

That was proppah Guyanese as well. Like maids and Demerara shutters, like people wanting out and sending sons to places like Toronto, sugar cane was proppah Guyanese.

Sugar. Sugar at the root of all that is Guyana. Sugar cane once covered all that is now Georgetown. Cane fields grew wherever land was rich enough, and it was rich enough along the coast where all those rivers dragging all that silt and dirt made perfect sugar-growing land. Almond Street and even Bourda Market had once been sugar fields waving sweet sweet stalks. Cane fields still rim Georgetown, rustling all around its edge. You don't have to wander far, just down this road or that, past where the pavement ends and further out a bit, and then you'll be surrounded by it, high walls of wide green blades like giant grass.

Sugar built the country, made Guyana what it is. Stocked that country well with people. Dutch and then British. Growing sugar made them rich, so they brought slaves from Africa, then others, indentured workers all the way from Portugal and China, and later, last of all, from India. Indians, the "coolies," were still the ones who worked the sugar fields, who ran the big estates. The Africans, they left the fields as soon as slavery was stopped, but the workers from Calcutta and Madras stayed on. And didn't that cause trouble.

That was what my father said, he said Guyana was the land of six nations. That's what the Guyanese all said as well. Land of Six Nations. We heard it on the radio when the politicians spoke. We saw it on the billboards and on banners. Six Nations: Europeans (Brits and Dutch), Afro-Guyanese and Portuguese, West Indians and some Chinese. But that's just five. The other is the group that I forgot most often. The sixth is rarely seen, but it is there and always has been there, somewhere, its members living in Guyana's flat-topped hills and hidden down its jungly river gorges. The Amerindians. We did see them sometimes, but only when we left the coastal sugar-growing lands to go upcountry or inland. Guyana's Indians were not found downtown, and I don't think they ever were a part of sugar history.

Six nations of Guyana, and all but one were strangers there. We'd hear the Guyanese on celebration days say, "All a we is one family." All six in harmony. But that's not true. Not then, not now. Those six got proppah vex, each one mad at all the others, and everybody bubble up and fight. Then the song was more a chant of hatred than of love, and what they sang were things like, "all a we best do sumting 'fore sumting do to we." That's right, get what you can and get it now. It is not safe and things are getting worse, so Mrs. Boyo saved her money as gold teeth and sent her son to see what life was like elsewhere.

At first I didn't understand all that. I didn't understand exactly why that trouble brewed. I didn't understand that Mrs. Boyo's teeth were all that she might have to take beyond Guyana's borders. I didn't even understand why she would want to leave this place. Behind our Demerara shutters, in the hush-hush dark where fans stirred tropic air in constant lazy fwumph-fwumph-fwumph, I could sit and watch and not be seen. I could spy. Out there, past the Demerara shutters, out on Almond Street, nobody bubbled up. It all looked calm, people walking

Georgetown-slow, not even voices raised. Maybe the air was just too hot to aggravate at each or anybody. No no. No aggravating there, not there on Almond Street.

But. Just like my mother said, one reason that we moved to there was to have adventures and to learn about the world and how the people in it lived. I learned.

One day our maid Mary's daughter Anne was playing with my little sister, Chris, out back. They played together at our house almost every day. Two kids, one dark, one light. Blond hair and black. They played outside, and that day in the garden, two ducks were tethered to the fence. Mary bought those ducks at Bourda, brought them all the way to Almond Street caught and wriggling, a weight inside her bag. Each had a coloured string around its leg that bound it to the fence, and there they stayed, hand-fed on bread and fruit. I fed them every day and talked to them and gave them names, and Chris and Anne were feeding them that day.

Squatting there in our backyard and feeding tethered ducks, Anne asked Chris to come and play at her house. Chris could go with Anne and Mary when they went home that afternoon; she could stay the night, and they'd return together in the morning. Chris could see Anne's house. She could see her toys and bedroom, see her garden and her neighbourhood. My mother thought this was a good idea. Chris could see another part of Georgetown.

Mary Santiago didn't live in Queenstown borough, oh no. She lived someplace else where houses were not painted any colour, certainly not whitewashed every

year. Her house and every other house nearby was made
of silvered planks and unpainted sheets of tin that
overlapped and metal roofs that rusted orange and red.
The houses in that neighbourhood were jumbled up, with
thin-railed stairs out front that shivered with each step. It
was a neighbourhood where crossings of canals from road
to house would all be done in single file because the planks
weren't wide enough for two by two. That neighbourhood
was where the grass grew long and rough, but only in
the rainy season, and where horses and donkeys, that in
daytime pulled the flatbeds piled with bags of rice or tires
or concrete blocks, at night were hobbled at the canal's
edge. In Anne Santiago's neighbourhood, the roads were
made of dry dry dust, not paved like Almond Street.
But, underneath Anne's house, it was sandy and cool.
Hammocks hung between the stilts that held the house
above the ground, above the floods, and that, said Anne,
was where the family slept sometimes when things were
too hot inside. Chris said that was nice. The cool and
sandy bottom house was nice. That's where they played
most of the afternoon in musty air.

Most of the afternoon, but not all. They grew bored,
and Anne led Chris back out into the sun so she could
show her banana trees that grew along the road. Bananas
are a type of grass, my father had told us, and those by
Anne's house had fruit, huge long clusters of bright-green
bananas curved inward on themselves. At the bottom was
a giant purple blob. It was the flower, and was coloured
and was shaped just like a heart, a human heart, a real one,

not a drawing on a card. They poked it with a stick. It was dense and hard. Now that they were out from underneath the house, why not look for guppies or for other things that can be found in Georgetown's canal waters? So, they wandered down the lane, hunting guppies, scuffing dust up in the sun. Walking, arms around each other's waist, long skinny legs together. New friends. Out and off and down the road, and Chris had some coins, not much but just enough to buy a little candy, and Anne said, there was a shop just close, just down the road, and it sold sweets.

That shop was on a corner, open-sided, wide wide wide, with doors that folded back flat to make a mouth that yawned full-walled and wide enough to drive a truck in there where it was too dark to see. Smoke and sound curled out the open sides and brushed past where Chris and Anne were walking down the lane. Rum shop. Inside were men, and they were getting sweet on rum and playing dominoes. Standing in the blinding sun, you cannot see them there inside where murkiness hides lots of things. But you can hear them. You can hear them playing dominoes the Georgetown way. The Georgetown rum-shop way means slamming down the dominoes to make a gunshot sound, bang bang, on the table. Music wandered out as well and danced round the bang bang bang of dominoes. It's that song, that Mighty Sparrow song again. Hear him sing, he's singing, "Drunk and disorderly, always in custody."

A man is sitting outside in the sun. He's smoking and he's drinking blackest rum held inside a murky glass. His chair is tilted back, front feet off the ground and tipped against the turquoise paint that's flaking off the frame around the door. Anne says the man is liming. That's what he's doing, liming in the sun. He opens up an eye, sees Chris and Anne as they walk up to go inside to buy their sweets. They have to pass him where he sits. Calm calm. He looks at them. He looks at Chris and spits. He arcs a line of smoky rum-dark spit that flies through air and hits my sister, Chris, on her pale and skinny arm.

"White bitch. White Limey bitch." Chris told me that he grit his teeth and stared, and that his words were whispered, barely heard but loud enough, though they were mixed up with the Mighty Sparrow's song. She was scared. She and Anne turned back then without their sweets to play beneath the Santiago house where it was cool and dark. No, no, they didn't talk about it; no. They didn't say a word about what "Limey" meant or why that man said "bitch." Why was he so angry, why was he so mad?

Next day when Mary Santiago came to work on Almond Street, she brought my sister back but didn't bring her daughter Anne. That afternoon she served us curry for our lunch. Curried chicken, so I thought, but found that it was duck when I went out into the garden later. I was standing there, staring at the duck-foot-flattened grass where there were no ducks, and Chris came out and stood there too. That was when she told me all about Anne and Mary's house, about the cool cool place to play, about banana trees and that their flowers look like hearts, how to spot them on the road and in the gardens up and down our street, and also what to look for if you wander out to where a rum shop fills the street with music and with gunshot sounds of dominoes. Don't go there. Just don't go there. Stay away from rum-shop sounds and rum-shop dark and liming rum-shop men. There are scary things that we don't understand. Together we just stood there staring at the place where ducks had trampled all the grass. Staring at that space and feeling sick, because we felt like we'd just eaten something that we'd loved.

# 5

## SERVIAM

*Serviam*. That was the motto of my school. My Guyana school. *Serviam*, that means "I will serve." It is the motto, also, of all schools created by the Ursuline nuns, and they've made schools around the world. They say, as well, that *serviam* is what Saint Michael said when Lucifer told God, *"non serviam."* That's what the nuns explained, and they said we must all say *"serviam"* as well.

I learned that once the nuns accepted and enrolled me at St. Rose's High School.

My mother said enrolment was ensured, because my father's contract stipulated that his children would be schooled at what the Guyanese considered their best schools. But, it seemed enrolment wasn't really guaranteed, not for any of us. Not for Stephen, who, they said, was too old and too far down the schooling road to go to Bishops' High School, the best for boys. They said if they allowed him in, he'd drag the average down, down, down, he'd drag the whole school average down to where it would affect them all, all the Bishops' boys. I thought that was very strange. Who thinks of things that way? Who thinks about school averages? Who cares about those things? And school wasn't guaranteed for me; at least, that's what Sister Hazel said. She was headmistress at St. Rose's School. She said, St. Rose's was not run by government officials. It was a convent school, started and continued by the nuns, and they, the nuns, decided who could and could not wear the St. Rose's uniform.

She told my mother we must come to see her in her office. It was summer and we'd not been long in Georgetown. No students filled the corridors or passageways of that old school, but there were lots of nuns, because behind the walls around the school, there was a convent too. Back, in behind the buildings where the classrooms were, behind the gym, and past the playground courts where girls in navy-blue uniforms—our gym gear to distinguish it from pastel-coloured academic wear— would run relays and play netball, were the convent buildings and the convent gardens. Most of those nuns were very old and didn't teach. They were the ones who'd come to Guyana as young girls themselves, come from places far away, from villages in England or in Ireland.

I had never seen a nun. But that day I saw one up close, right across a wooden desk, the nunnest nun of all St. Rose's nuns. Sister Hazel. Headmistress Sister Hazel. She was Afro-Guyanese and neither old nor young. St. Rose's was her home and her domain. That day she pinned us with her nun eyes, we were caught; and I could tell my mother felt about as pinned as I was feeling then.

Sit up straight. Put your two feet on the floor, flat flat and
ladylike. Look forward, don't look sheepish, don't look
down. Sister Hazel wore a blue-grey headdress, wimple I
was later told, that covered up her hair and swept down
long and out the sides. It was very smooth, its edges and
creases perfectly sharp. She wore glasses that swept up too.
Pointy cornered. Pointy eyes and pointy stare. No smiling
on that face. No "Welcome to St. Rose's" from that nun.
Oh no. Her hands were folded in a disappointing way on
top of papers that my mom had brought. Those papers
told the story of my education up to then. Those papers
made Sister Hazel frown.

I think we knew that it would come to that. I think we
knew that it would end with Sister Hazel's frown.

Why? The whole place led to that conclusion, giving
plenty of warning that it would not be a hello-hello-all-
are-welcome-here experience.

First of all, St. Rose's told you clearly that the inside
and the out were separate. The world was divided in
two parts: St. Rose's and the rest. The rest included
Georgetown, and Guyana, and the whole wide world.
Two parts, and they don't mix. St. Rose's started at
Church Street, ran down along that road, a long high
wooden building painted white. Three high flights up and
windowed, rigidly in even beats along the side, the first
row far above the heads of anybody walking down that
road. Nobody was going to catch a peek inside. Topped
above all that there was a fourth floor, narrower and not
as windowed, high up; snugged underneath the eaves it

made me think the entire place looked like a giant chicken coop. Solid, solid like a fortress down Church Street. But there was a way inside, a portico, a porte cochère, that was gated equally solid, gapless as a wall, and guarded by a man who sat outside all day. Nobody ever wandered aimlessly through there.

Through the portico, St. Rose's opened up. The school was not a single building (as it seemed from Church Street's verge), but many joined together in a great big square by walkways and footbridges, steps leading up and down, windows looking out on other windows, closed passages, and corkscrew stairs. Some buildings, looking newer than the rest, were up on concrete pillars, and underneath were tables and chairs. That's where, I later learned, we had our lunch. In the centre of this square of buildings was a garden with a great big statue of a nun, all shiny white in plaster. She was bent over just a little bit, her hands spread wide. She looked down at white begonias dotted round her feet. Brown earth was reddened where a living nun, I guessed, had watered each, sparingly, before the day grew hot.

I saw that just flashing past as my mother and I were rushed along. We were met by a nun who had waited for us in the portico and took us through the buildings, up the tightly corkscrewed wooden stairs, along the covered enclosed walkway stuffed with heat, past all those wooden doors, all locked, and then to Sister Hazel's office door where we were left sitting on a bench to wait. She walked away, still silent, grey skirt sweeping, a big cross bumping on her chest. The only noise was the squawking of her squeaky crepe-soled shoes that faded as she vanished down the hall.

We waited. We waited long enough to start to fidget, then Sister Hazel called us in. She looked at us from across her desk. Her glasses reflected light, sparked light at me when she looked up. She was unblinking and unsmiling. We were waiting. She began.

"Your daughter's academic standing is quite poor."

I was frozen, staring straight and blankly like a fish. Out of the corner of my eye, I saw my mother gather up her words. She sat a little higher in her chair, about to speak, speak probably about that guarantee, but Sister Hazel wasn't waiting for an answer or a comment.

"Though her grades are not all bad, the quality of her education is substandard. The overall result is poor."

Oh Canada.

I saw my mother straighten up her spine a little more and saw her words collecting in her throat.

"She will have to sit a test before I can consider her for possible enrolment in St. Rose's."

Puff. Puff of air, no words came out. No talk of promises from governments. We both were quiet on the long walk back to the exit, out into the other place, out into the world where flamboyant trees and parrots line the streets.

I took the test. I failed the test. St. Rose's High School standards were quite high.

When we returned to get the test results, it was

explained, again, that Canada was lacking in its standards, and as such, my knowledge was so poor that it would drag the whole and entire school down down to some low level that St. Rose's would not tolerate. As such, my entry to that school would cause a lot of suffering for all the girls who studied there.

That sounded bad. It sounded worse to me than when I'd heard my mother telling Dad the same result had come when she had gone to Bishops' with my brother. But, then Sister Hazel told us there was a chance. My admittance to St. Rose's might be managed if I were tutored by the nuns every morning all that summer. Then I could sit the test again and maybe pass.

I did that. I spent mornings every day in July and August inside a high-walled room, one of those along the covered walkway where the silent nun had led us on that day, and in that room, one nun and I went over what my school in Canada had failed to teach.

Penmanship. Not just the way to hold a fountain pen so ink won't smudge, but also how to shape the letters perfectly the way they like them shaped in schools where British nuns still teach. How to paint a watercolour of a vase of flowers. How to sing the special anthem written for St. Rose's. At Annieville, we'd sung "God Save the Queen" and "O Canada," standing stiff-necked beside our desks, hands behind our backs, chins up, and mouths all open wide. But in Guyana, the new Guyana, nobody sang "God Save the Queen." I learned, instead, to sing the special St. Rose's song.

But, the most important thing I lacked was knowledge of Guyana. Did I know how to draw Guyana? Did I know its borders, even those disputed by its neighbours, Venezuela and Surinam? Where are the inland plains and where the flat-topped mountains? Could I name the rivers, all the large ones? No. You must learn them and the mountains and the towns. Even children know those names. They are: Essequibo, Demerara, Cayuni, Corentyne. They are: Kanuku, Acarai, and Pakaraima. They are: Good Hope—that was easy—Bartika, Parika, Mabaruma. That twisted up my tongue so tight it took a while to learn to chant those names. I learned that Fort Zeelandia was built in 1744 and that Greenheart trees grow taller than the Crabwood do. That Mora trees have buttress roots and that Wallaba don't. I learned the months when it was wet and those when it was dry. I learned the word *alluvial* and learned it was the reason why the Europeans came. Alluvial and sugar go together. Taste sugar on your tongue when *alluvial* rolls off.

I also learned some maths, and learned to call it that, some Roman classics, and some poetry that rhymed. I learned a summer's worth of facts, enough to pass the test, enough to join the other special girls allowed inside those gates so they could serve.

In September I was back again, early in the morning at the gates, this time in uniform. Then I was a true St. Rose's girl. First day of school and girls flooded through the gate and past the portico and up the stairs to gather in a great big room called the assembly hall. It had wooden floors and wooden walls, a ceiling soared somewhere far above our heads. Windows, tall and arched and multi-paned, showed treetops and blue sky.

We swirled together, seven hundred of us, in our uniforms; we were like petals stripped from flowers on a windy day. Our uniforms were pastel-blue or yellow, green or pale rose-pink. Box-pleated skirts hemmed to the middle of the knee. Tunic of same with white collar, this to have a tab sewn on the left-side breast where one can wear the school pin (optional). White knee socks. Black Oxford shoes.

That room was in the original part of St. Rose's, built when nuns first came from Ireland. Up front there was a stage and in the back a door that I had followed everybody through. Two nuns stood like sentries and said hello if some girl greeted them, but otherwise were silent, watching us flow past. Inside that room, all movement seemed to stop, and everybody stood, face forward, in long straight lines, row on row on row. All of us sweating in the closeness and the heat. This was assembly; and, I learned, it happened daily, at 7:15 A.M. exactly, each and every day of school. The doors at the back stayed open until the nuns who flanked them heard Sister Hazel's shoes squeaking along the waxy floor. When they heard that, the doors were closed, and any girl arriving after that was held and later questioned, all reasons for her lateness jotted down, recorded in a great big book that daily went to Sister Hazel's office where her secretary tabulated and cross-referenced names and dates, times and reasons why.

But on that morning, my first, I'd yet to learn those rules. I stood, face-fronting like the rest, and while they fussed and fidgeted, and said hello in low soft voices, I stared down at my new shoes, my new and shining shoes, and felt the temperature around me rising from the press of bodies in that room. It was already hot, but all the girl-sweat and exhalings thickened up the air. Tropic hot and stuffy. Two rows over a girl gulped air, she hung her head and slowly swayed. I saw her wilt and crumple. I watched her slip down to the floor where cooler air puddled at our feet. She had fainted. Two others hooked her by the arms and pulled her out of line and out of sight. My stomach washed like a tide, and I gulped too. Mary's early morning breadfruit pudding breakfast, something I had grown to like, felt grey and lumpish. My uniform, all special starched-up for the day, poked and prodded me in the neck. I gulped some more.

The fainting girl's two friends had just got back in line when everybody in the room took a breath. They'd heard a sound I hadn't heard, but I heard the sound that followed. Whoosha-whoosh of closing doors. And in the quiet then I heard her steps. Sister Hazel's steps. She rose up the stage in front, stared out across our heads, and all the other teacher-nuns gathered on the stage, they stood too. Everybody was standing then, staring back at us as we all stared in silence back at them. Sister Hazel nodded to her left. A nun, in profile and the only one who sat, banged down on ivory keys, and then around me everybody sucked in air and seven hundred voices sang.

They sang, "*Serviam* shall be our watchword. Marching on we'll sing. Battling against the pride of Satan. Serving Christ our King."

A room tight full of brittle voices. Everybody seemed to know the words. I could see and hear that the girl in front of me liked to sing. She lifted up her chin, tilted back her head, her long black braid swept past her skirt's waistband and wagged.

She sang, "Storm or cloud will not dismay us. We will do and dare. When it's dark we'll just remember that the stars are there. If we fail we'll rise unconquered, set our armour right. Hope and love will heal our bruises. Faith will win the fight."

The last line wavered off into the ceiling and was followed by another silent moment as the girls around me caught their breath and teacher-nuns sat down. The only sounds were scrapes of chairs and swishing long grey habits. They all sat, but Sister Hazel stood. Her glasses flashed. We held our breath.

She said, "Girls. Welcome back to St. Rose's. I hope you were productive during holidays and that you are ready to direct your energies toward achieving the realization of better and higher standards on a total level."

My thoughts of pride at having known the words of that school song were pushed right from my mind.

"Welcome, too, to the new Form Ones. Look to your older sisters for guidance and example.

"And, another welcome, this to a girl who has come all the way from Canada. Shelagh Plunkett has joined Merici House, Form Two. Welcome, Miss Plunkett."

Her glasses flashed directly at me. I was caught, head up and staring.

"It is my hope that the special school spirit of St. Rose's will move and inspire you to direct your energies toward the perfection that human nature is made for."

A rustling sound rose up, and I heard whisper whisper, sensed the nudge nudge nudge as some poked others and all stretched necks to see that girl, that girl from Canada. Oh, there she is. She there, she standin there and lookin lost. She lookin scared.

I was. I was scared and staring at the ground. My blond head bowed. I knew it was a yellow stain inside that room filled up from side to side with heads all glistening black. I wore the selfsame box-pleated skirt that everybody wore, my tunic tucked in tight just like the rest. My shoes were shiny black like theirs, my socks pristine and cuffed just right. But I stuck out. I couldn't hide. I was the only white girl at St. Rose's school.

# 6

## WU'DS

At St. Rose's the teacher-nuns spoke words that anyone could look up in the dictionary, the Oxford English dictionary. And they were strict about the way we talked at school. We could not be heard to say a girl's a "liard" for her tall tales or mention that Elizabeth was "lickerish" at lunch when "she pass a scraven eye" on all that curry-chicken left on plates. No, no, the nuns were sharp about these things, and there, inside St. Rose's walls, we all were told to use the words the British brought, to say those words in ways the British colonists would understand. We said "sweeties" for the candies that we bought inside the "tuck shop" on our break. If it was cold, we put on "jumpers," and we wrote in "copybooks" and used our "leads" for drafts.

Sure sure, the nuns were usin proppah English wu'ds, and some, the pale-pink ones who had arrived from Ireland long ago as girls themselves, were stringing their plain words together in a plain and proper way. But that was not the way the Guyanese strung words. So all those

teacher-nuns, the ones both born and raised in Guyana—
and they made up most of the teacher-nuns—they sang
their words. Oh sure they did. Even teacher-nuns singsong
their sentences the way that Guyanese singsong. The
English language there was full of skip and jump, with
sentences that writhed along the ground, slunk low until
they leapt, exploding up in places where, at home, they
would have stayed docile. Some words were squeezed tight,
shrill and high, and others were spun long, acquiring twists
and torques I'd never heard. In Guyana a simple sentence
full of simple English words caffuffled with my head.

On that day when I first wore my uniform and joined
the others as a full-fledged St. Rose's girl, I listened closely
to their talk. We left assembly in an ordered column, led
out of the assembly hall by the top girl in the front. We
followed, ducklings in a row, across a footbridge overtop
the baby-school where Chris was having her first day, to
a room with walls of concrete breeze-blocks and desks set
out in tidy rows. All around me I heard voices singing,
except they weren't. They weren't singing. It was talk,
Guyana talk that rippled like a song. I heard, "Gyal, yu see
she fallin fallin now?"

"First she wobble, shakin in her legs, then sudden,
braps, she down. She full out four-and-a-half."

"Dis hot so high it mek all a we see ning-ning too, we
standin all jes so so long so long."

"Eh-ehh! Stop ya gyaf na, teacher cyum."

Me, I was feeling faintish faintish too, but not because
of heat. I was stretching ears to try to understand this

talk. It was English. Yes, it was. That's what they speak in Georgetown, in Guyana, but that English, it was full up with words I'd never heard before; and though I was sure the messages conveyed were simple things that even I should clearly understand, I couldn't. I could not understand. It was weeks before my ears were tuned and I could hear where words began and ended.

Away from school my friends let tongues go free and plunged deep deep into Guyana's well of phrases, terminology, and special words. I was quickly lost again. I might have understood the rhythm, but that didn't help when, with my mouth on fire, Farida's brother shouted at me, "don't take swank" to douse the wiri-wiri I'd just eaten in the curry at her house. Swank. That's lemonade and, I learned, you shouldn't drink it when you've chewed a tiny pepper hot enough to stream tears down your cheeks. Farida's father handed me a glass of buttermilk, warm and thick with cream on top. Pale-yellow and the temperature of blood. It soothed my mouth but left my stomach "squinged."

"Hardpants," I learned, were jeans, and if I'm "jooked" that meant that I'd been poked. The little fish that I called guppies swimming in canals along the road were there named "millions." To "lime" was just to lounge, but why was "Limey" then a nasty word? My best friend, June, said, "If I don't study hard, the game come." She'd be in trouble then. "Don't worry" meant don't try, don't do; and if she said, "I ky'an do dat," she meant she could not do it. "Nuff" was lots so you could say I was confused nuff nuff.

Confusion came in other ways as well. Things weren't always what they seemed.

My mother became bored with sitting at the Pegasus poolside each afternoon. That Hollywood lifestyle was not for her, not every day. She was used to working, had always had a job, at least most of the time before we moved. She'd been a teacher, then a counsellor who worked with unemployed people, helping them find jobs. She'd liked that work. But, in Georgetown she found that household management was mostly done by maids. We'd moved again. Our new house was on Kaieteur Road. It was bigger and more modern. The floors were wide-plank purpleheart that glowed deep amethyst when waxed. They were waxed most days by Victoreen, who was even shorter than I was. Almost as short as Chris, who wasn't yet eleven. Victoreen was our new housemaid and Daphne ruled the kitchen.

Daphne ruled the house. She heard my mother talking on the phone one day, making plans to help at someone's wedding. Two expats were getting married. They were older than my parents and had both been married in the past. Daphne thought their plans to marry were ridiculous. She heard my mother talking on the phone and laughed so hard she had to slap a hand across her mouth to muffle snorts and coughs. We could hear her even when she'd retreated to the kitchen, her domain, to clutch the kitchen counter because she shook so hard with mirth. That was disrespectful, but Daphne didn't care because she ruled the house.

She'd been married. Once. That's all, she said, a woman needed. One marriage was enough to call oneself a Mrs., then she'd never be a Miss. Why would any woman bother getting married, again, after that? Daphne's marriage, her Mrs. marriage, had been a long time back, and since that first she'd had a lot of children with other men. I didn't know how many, but there seemed to be a lot because Daphne would talk about them, say their names, and there were a lot of names.

Daphne's men were always coming to our gate and our back door to sit on our back steps, the ones that led up to the kitchen, where they'd cool themselves with mauby made by Daphne. The drinks man who rode a bicycle that had a rack on front to hold his crates of bottles, tink-tink, tink-a-da-tink. He came every week. The gardener and the butcher boy; the delivery man from JP Santos bringing tins of butter, jars of jam; and the men from Bookers where my mother bought books and cloth. Other men came by with burlap sacks of rice or bags of fruit and even furniture. They brought things they knew we wouldn't want to buy, but came so they could chat with Daphne on the kitchen steps. There was a man who came to Kaieteur Road with antique bottles for my dad to buy. Dark-green, almost black, thick glass with bubbles caught inside that only could be seen when those bottles were held up to the brightest sun. Some were wider at the top with four flat sides and others squat and round. My father said that they'd held rum two hundred years ago and since that time had been sitting deep in Demerara silt. Daphne liked the antique-bottle man. She liked them all.

Daphne bossed Victoreen and nobody bossed Daphne. That meant my mother didn't really have a job. Daphne, like most maids, knew what must be done, and then she just went ahead and did it. Most of the time she told my mother, but that was as far as that went. The only time Mom told her what to do was when she'd found Victoreen wiping the purpleheart floors, not polishing them the way she should. Mom got down on her hands and knees to give a demonstration on the proper way to put the beeswax on the wood. Daphne saw her do that. So did Victoreen. The point was to show Victoreen how to polish the floor the way Mom wanted it polished, but the effect was something else. It's true, after that the floors were polished well, but Daphne, when she watched my mother, the lady of the house, on her hands and knees, she shook her head and tut-tutted while she crossed her arms across her chest. That was a lesson.

The expat wives at poolside started to sound like parrots. Stories were being retold, and my mother was hearing once again about the men in Tiger Bay. We'd been in Georgetown long enough that she wasn't scared by that story anymore. Besides, she liked to wander through the markets and talk to hucksters there. She didn't like to lie out in the sun so much, not like the other expat wives, not like those who flapped a hand so often for another drink and what they drank was not Lime Rickey. She began to not fit in; at least, not every day.

She was bored. She got a job. She took a volunteer position with the library. Oh boy, that raised voices by the pool. Sally, you know, Sally Plunkett. Well, her husband's often in the field, and now she's working. She's doing volunteer work for the library. They've got her taking books to the men's ward at the hospital. What, what? A job?

Yes, she took a job. She took a volunteer position along with another expat wife from Canada, one who also didn't fit in so well with those who lived poolside every day. The women at the library sent Mom off with a pushcart full of books to take around the wards. They gave her two instructions: Tell the patients, the ones who are not crippled or dying, to get out of bed to pick their own books from the cart; and don't walk down the path that runs alongside the building. Why? That path is not safe. The patients and the staff dump bedpans out the windows, out and down onto the footpath there and down onto the head of anybody foolish enough to walk along that path.

She followed her instructions, and she liked that job. The men, sometimes two or even three on top a single bed, were mostly friendly, and they liked to talk with her, sometimes about the far-off place that she'd come from. Canada. Snow. Toronto. Everybody seemed to have a friend, a brother, uncle, cousin, nephew, niece who'd moved to Canada, or wanted to. Most of the men were strong enough to stand and walk, to get up off their beds and come to her and her cart to pick their books. There weren't too many cripples, not too many missing legs.

One man had a bed just to himself. He looked big and strong, he looked fine and well enough to get up and walk, to choose the book he wanted, but he just lay there when my mother stopped her book cart at the foot of his bed. He stared at her, lounging with his arm crooked back above his head, and said, "Crime stories. I like mysteries. Stories about cops." My mother remembered her instructions. She said, "You look strong. Come pick a book yourself."

"Well," Mom later said, when she told us stories of her day, when we were eating dinner that Daphne cooked and served. "He wasn't crippled. I could see he wasn't crippled."

No, he wasn't crippled, but he glared at her. He glared and snorted, sort of rolled his eyes and smiled, but not a friendly smile. He didn't say a word. He said nothing, then he lifted up his arm from where he'd had it tucked beneath his head. Lifted it and shook it. Clank clink clang. Handcuffs tinged against the iron bedpost there. Later, on another day, the buzz-buzz talk around the hospital is that one of the men, one who should have been chained to his bed—maybe he was handcuffed, maybe not—the talk is that this man escaped. Squeezed through the little window in the bathroom, there behind the curtain in the ward, squeezed out and dropped down two floors, and then was gone.

Next my mother gets a car. There was no driver sitting there behind that wheel except for her. She drove that car herself. It was a Vauxhall Viva. Boxy, white, and British-made; the seats were leather, navy-blue and piped in white.

It was jaunty, and that's a word that any nun might like. Old perfume smells were caught inside the leather seams, lipstick, cigarettes, and salty water air, warm leather. The Viva had a flat-nosed grille with headlights bugging out and round. Its rear-view mirrors mounted on the hood were angled, pointing outwards like a shunna-foot old man. That's a word the Guyanese would use: shunna-foot. It means toes out, duck-footed, that's what we would say. If that Vauxhall Viva could have walked, it surely would have shuffle-shuffled, comfortable and slow.

My mother drove her Vauxhall Viva everywhere, all over town and out of town as well. She drove herself and quickly learned that in Guyana driving means you travel on the left while sitting on the right. The opposite of all the driving she had done up to that time. It felt unsafe at first, as if at any moment any other car or truck could meet her Vauxhall Viva face face on and then that flat-nosed grille would flatten further. At first it felt unsafe, but she learned quick.

My father was driven in a special car and taken by a driver to wherever he would go. His driver came to pick him up on mornings when he wasn't in the field. In the field, I learned, meant that he was off away and mapping rivers in the jungle. In the field meant in the jungle there because, except for in the distant Rupununi lands, Guyana had no fields except for sugar fields along the coast. So on days when Dad was in Georgetown with us, his driver picked him up and dropped him off again at night. His driver always waited in the car and double-parked in any spot my father had to be. He'd double-park right there downtown when Dad was in the bank or at a meeting with a government official. Right there, out front and blocking traffic. That was okay in Georgetown. It was okay if you were in a chauffeur-driven car. Nobody seemed to mind. Other cars or donkey carts or long-necked horses hanging heads and pulling flatbed trailers piled with lumber or with bags of rice or tires, they just flowed around, passed by that driver sitting waiting in his big car. They ky'an fuss wid him.

But not my mom. She never doubled-parked. She was not official, not enough for double-parking right downtown. She would have got a ticket had she done that, left her car and walked away to shop. Oh no, there were some rules, and she was mindful of them.

So there she was one bright and breezy day, driving out to Timehri airport to meet a visiting Canadian. She was alone and wearing on her face her best don't-careish attitude, because it's just too fine a day to feel a care right then. She was driving down the long green tunnel, out and out and out from Georgetown. Down a narrow strip of road, two lanes, clean-sliced and straight between the cane. Tall green walls of sugar bordering the road. Her car was little and white and shining in the sunlight, driving straight through those tall swaying walls of rattling green. Nothing else but green for miles and miles.

Nobody was on that road but her. It's nowhere and no place. It's just the road to Timehri, and right there it's sugar cane for fields and fields, waving all green leafiness in sunlight and in breeze. No villages. No houses. No cars upon the road, not even long-necked horses pulling trailers. Nothing to be seen but green.

But suddenly there was, there was a thing to see that wasn't waving green or sunny blue. There was a man. A policeman suddenly just there just there ahead, beside the road. Out he stepped from somewhere past the sugar wall, from somewhere out of sight. He was there beside the road and fully uniformed, with a hat and shiny badge and all. He put up his hand, palm facing at her car, and braced his legs out wide. He had stepped out from the sugar cane and then, policeman-like, was saying silently to her to stop.

She slowed her little car. She pulled up by the side where sugar cane came close to tarmacked road, and there, before she passed him, she stopped.

"Where you going?" That policeman leaned in her window and said this to her. Maybe he said ma'am first, I don't know.

"I'm on my way to Timehri. To the airport." That's all she said.

He asked, "Will you give me a drop?"

She hesitated. She was thinking. She was thinking he's police, but she was also thinking, "I'm not carrying money," and, "It should be fine." He was polite. He smiled. He wasn't young or old or large or small or anything particular, except that he was black. But, that was nothing odd, because all Georgetown policemen were black.

"Yes," she said. "I'll drive you up to Timehri."

He hopped in, and she pulled out and back onto the road, and down the road passed nothing anywhere along that strip but fields of sugar cane.

They talked. She said she was from Canada and newly living there in Georgetown. He said he had cousins in Toronto. He had heard from them what life was like in Canada, where things are what they seem. He's heard that streets there are clean clean clean, people all polite; and everybody there, in Canada, is nice, and there are no snatch-tiefs, no criminals who grab your jewellery and run, or who might stick you with a knife, no slash-robbers there in Canada.

And all that time he sat beside her with his clean and shiny uniform, his hat and all, his Georgetown police badge glinting in the sun.

When they were closing in on Timehri, he said she could drop him in the village just before the airport gates. Here, here, he said, right here, right here. Waving his hand off to the side, showing her to stop where there was nothing to stop for, just sugar cane. She slowed the car and pulled up on the roadside where no houses could be seen. He sat a moment, and then he turned to look at her, his hand was on the handle of the door.

He said, "You didn't want to pick me up, did you? I could tell you didn't. You didn't."

"No." She was honest, so she told him no. She remembered that she'd hesitated when he asked her for a ride. It was true, she hadn't wanted to pick him up, just for a moment, even though he was a Georgetown policeman.

"You were right to think that way," he said, "to think you didn't want to pick me up." He said, "You were lucky. This time. This time you were lucky. But don't do that again. Don't you pick up people asking you for rides. No, not ever. Policeman uniform means nothing here. Not here," he said. "Don't you ever stop for anyone again." In Guyana, tiefman don't-care-damn for Canada. The rules are not the same.

# 7

## SU-SU

Oh my, this land is full of things outsized and over big. Creatures grow much larger than they do in other lands, much larger than they should.

Guyana's marabuntas—those are wasps—grow big as hummingbirds, deep-black with yellow wings and three-inch legs that hang below their bodies, barbed and swaying side to side as they fly past. They fly past and shake up all the air around. They vibrate the air, and it thrums deep, low low, as they pass by. You hope they do. You hope that they pass by, because the story is a marabunta sting can kill, and sometimes you don't hear those marabunta wings until the marabunta is about to land beside your head. Who knows if that story's true. I never met a Guyanese who ever got a marabunta sting. But, just in case it is, in case it's true, run run away when marabunta wings set air vibrating. Spiders too, the ones they call Goliath, spin their webs across streams and creeks. They catch leaping fish and flying birds. Like something from an Aesop's fable, that Goliath spider grows as large as a dinner plate. My father told us he'd seen such spiders in the jungle, and there were pictures of them in our schoolbooks at St. Rose's.

Rodents. The largest rodent in the world lives there, but it is not rat-like at all. The capybara comes in sizes like a Labrador, a dog, and wanders through the swampy forest on its two-toed feet. They call it water pig. Its nose is blunt, its ears are small, and it looks innocent. The labba, that's a rodent too, with spots all down its sides just like a deer. The labba comes out only in the night, and the Guyanese will tell you that this creature is a special treat. If you eat the labba and you drink black water from the creeks, the Guyanese su-su that you will come back to their country. You will return.

"Su-su"—that means gossip, talk and whisper, spread rumours and tell tales. Spread rumours of one sort or another, tell tales about your neighbours. All sorts of things su-su in that strange place. Marabuntas. They su-su, su-su a warning of their coming. Buzzing just to let you know they're on their way. Crickets too. Crickets racket up the air at night, competing with the Who-you birds that sing, but only in the dark. Frogs too. Frogs in all canals make deep drum calls from one to all the others. Dogs bark, bark out in pitch-black night from places you can't see, but you can hear them barking in those hidden spots. Screen door slams somewhere and sets the dogs to barking, each one setting off the next down darkened streets and through the neighbourhoods. They wake you with their canine shouts. "Soft-foot, soft-foot! I hear you. I smell you in the dark. I know you're there."

Other things su-sued as well.

Our telephone su-sued. Click, click, the call ended, but the noises did not stop. Be quiet now, and wait a moment more before replacing that heavy black receiver. I could hear it, a soft, sleepy-sounding breathy air that echoed carefully all down the line. A hollow waiting sound. Somebody's out there. Someone's listening.

My mother told me with a little shrug the phone was fine. It was just somebody listening in on all our calls. She shrugged and said, "We're being tapped."

Tapped? I knew what that meant. Oh yes I did. I had watched Watergate. I watched the Senate hearings back at home in Canada before we left. My father told us history was being made (it is always being made), and he made us sit, day in day out, the curtains drawn to make a gloom so we could catch the details on our black-and-white TV. It's true. We learned it's true that people lie and others spy, and sometimes both get caught. And now we were being tapped. There was someone out there, somewhere in Guyana, who was breathing in our phone. I heard him breathing quietly. He was listening. He was spying.

What secrets did we have to hear? What secrets did he listen for? Listening to my mother make a bridge date or to my brother plan a tennis game? I thought, again, of Tiger Bay and women by the pool and other stories that I'd heard since then. Maybe that listening man was hoping we would talk about potatoes. We had asked the next expatriate who was coming down to Georgetown to smuggle in potatoes, just a few, because we missed them.

We missed potatoes. Potatoes weren't allowed in Guyana, because they wouldn't grow in that hot place. Burnham and his government had ruled Guyana was a self-sufficient country. No imports, like potatoes, were allowed. Could that be why the someone out there listened to our phone?

I picked the phone up almost every time I passed it in the hall. I hoped to hear him listening as I listened back. Now I was spying on the spy. He'd been listening to me talk with my friend June, two teenage girls complaining up and down about our homework, complaining all about the nuns who never seemed to take a break from watching us. Listening while we made plans to meet up at the Astor to see *The Towering Inferno*? I wanted to say into the empty phone, after June had hung up at her end, I wanted to ask the listening man if he had seen the movie, if he liked it. I wanted to ask him what his name was, what he looked like, if he was bored.

Listening to listen just because you never know what you might hear?

It seemed that everybody listened in that town and everybody also su-su-sued. The man at JP Santos, where "one good tin deserves another" but all were dented and rusty, that man listened to my mother talk while we were waiting in the sugar line. That line was long despite the fact that sugar was grown right there in coastal fields. But sugar grown in coastal fields was not for Guyanese, oh no it wasn't. Sugar grown in coastal fields was sold to sweeten foreign cups of tea. All was sold except a little bit that was rationed to the people who had grown the stuff.

So we stood in lines to buy our sugar ration. Some people grumbled and complained, but all were careful to keep their voices low low low.

While we waited, that man listened to my mother talk, and then he sidled up, sideways shuffling, to stand beside my mother. He bent low and, after swirling round his eyes, asked her in a su-su voice if she would sponsor him to Canada. Oh Canada. He even knew the words. Oh, Canada was where he wanted to be, not there in Georgetown, no no no, not there in that fresh country so recently released from its colonial ties, not there. Not in that place that then, just four years after independence, was already having new words like *Co-operative* tacked onto its name. Co-operative, where everybody worked together to make everything the best. Where everything was shared. He didn't like the sound of that. Things were changing up too fast, he said, and he wanted out. Here, he said, it's all a mess, a mess and chaos too.

We'd heard that before. He was not the first. Everybody knew we were Canadian, and everybody wanted to ask—and some did ask—if we could help them leave their home. They wanted to leave that place, that place where parrots decorated trees and bananas grew on boulevards. They wanted to leave that place that had just become their own, and that was a thing I did not understand. I liked it there, even if sometimes some things were said at me with voices laced in anger. I did. I liked Guyana.

We'd heard that before, that "will you help me leave" su-sued at us by men we'd never met, and so my mother had her answer ready. No. No, we cannot help you move to Canada. Well then, he said, could he buy money from us? Cash? Canadian, American, or Brit, he didn't care so long as it wasn't Guyanese. Anything would do. He'd buy it all. Now that was something else we'd heard before, as well, and everybody knew it was illegal. It was illegal to own money that wasn't Guyanese. Even I knew that, and my blue eyes were watching as that stranger man in JP Santos shook out his sweating whispered words, his hope for foreign cash, which everybody knew you were not allowed to sell or even carry in your purse or in your bag, can't put it in a drawer at home or in a safe or in a box or anywhere. Can't have it anywhere. We all knew that, and so I wondered why he asked. Why did he ask for something that he knew he could not have? What su-su stories would he tell if she said yes? Who would he tell? What would he say? Now I start to wonder.

Everybody su-su-sued. At school my friends and I su-sued. We talked at school while we ate lunch, oily Chinese noodles tasting faintly curryish. We sat outside, beneath the science wing, long tables in between the concrete pillars holding up St. Rose's newest classrooms. We sat at tables spread with white paper-cloth, on benches lined by girls in pastel uniforms. Everybody there su-sued. Breeze blew and paper lifted and fell, our plastic plates were lightened as we ate our food, and in that breeze we had to hold things down or plates would fly and make a mess. We did that automatically while bending heads together, theirs all black and mine bright blond, but then I'd been there long enough that I didn't think of that. These were my friends. I was one of them, and I'd forgotten how much my head and skin stuck out.

We talked, our voices low as any JP Santos lineup man's. Things were changing. Change was what we talked about. St. Rose's, some had heard, was being taken over by the government. What? That can't be true! Oh yes, it is. The nuns, the Ursulines whose school it had been right from the start, from back as far as 1847, had given our St. Rose's school to Burnham and his government. They had to hand St. Rose's over. Farida said that they were told they must. No, no, said June. They gave it freely to the state. That's what we all must do. The state, the people, that's what that means, doesn't it? The state, the people now, are taking everything: sugar fields, big big plantations, bauxite mines. I'd heard my parents talking about the companies that once were owned by Canada but then were owned by Guyanese. That's what nationalization meant. Guyana was a Co-operative Republic, and all must work together hard to make Guyana's future shine.

That was something we St. Rose's girls could understand. We wore our pins. Those pins said "*Serviam.*" We were St. Rose's girls and we all worked together, everyone for all. Farida, June, and me, we were in Merici House, green coloured to mean vigour, and our motto was, "Where there's a will, there's a way." We understood. We knew how to work together, because we did that every day at school. That year Merici House beat all St. Rose's others for points. We bested all, and that meant beating

Breschia and Lima and Loreto and Cologne. We took a
first in sports and also in the drama competition. We'd
staged *Odale's Choice*, and even though the curtain dropped
and left the body, played by Kim, on view for all to see and
all did see her wriggle-wriggle back beneath the curtain
like no dead body ever has, despite that, we won the cup
because the teacher-nuns all said we showed a spirit strong
in teamwork. We understood co-operation, sure we did.

June poked her finger on our leader's face. It was
there, glowing in a halo, on our notebooks. Comrade
Prime Minister Linden Forbes Burnham on every book
that each and every student in Guyana used. Smiling all
the time. June tapped her finger on his face and said he'd
lead us all to greatness, but only if we worked together.
Co-operative, she said, meant that everyone must share
and share alike, and all things Guyanese (and things that
once belonged to others like the British and the Dutch
and even Canada), they would be spread and shared
amongst the entire population. That's what June said. It
was our duty as St. Rose's girls to work hard hard to help
Guyana be the wonder it could be.

It's not just St. Rose's that is going to change. The
government is taking over everything. Farida said that
in her su-su voice. She said it right at June. But, why so
hushed and secret sounding? That's no secret. *Socialist* and
*socialism*—those were words we read each day. Headlines
big and black shouted: GO OUT AND SPREAD SOCIALISM,
SAYS PM. Things will change, and Burnham said that
change must happen fast. So every day we read that mines

and corporations, banks and stores and farms, plantations growing sugar and rice, and smelters where Guyana's bauxite was made into something else more valuable, all these and even things like schools could not be owned by anyone except by all. Share and share alike.

No need to su-su-su. The headlines told us: EDUCATION MUST BE TOOL FOR SOCIALISM, and we'd been told this face to face, right inside St. Rose's walls. Comrade Reid told us. Deputy Prime Minister Ptolemy Reid—but just called Comrade since parliament had voted "yes" on that—came to our school and explained it all to us. We were the people's students. He named us that. We were the people's hope. That sounded like a title: The People's Hope. His words wafted out from where he stood up front onstage, wafted out across our turned-up faces. We sat in straight-backed chairs neatly lined in rows across the floor in front of him, all seven hundred of us listening to him tell us we were Guyana's biggest hope, or one of them at least. We had a job to do. We had a job to do in this new revolution. Revolution? We opened up our eyes. Oh yes, that's what he said. He said "revolution" and said we all had a job to do. He said that we, St. Rose's girls, The People's Hope, would have to be courageous and determined. We, he said, would have to sacrifice some things. What? What would we have to sacrifice?

He said the way that things had been must be destroyed, smashed totally and replaced quick-quick with something new, with something different. He called it "the old order" and said it had to go. It had to be replaced

with socialism, with everybody sharing everything. He
said there was a struggle coming, a struggle up ahead, but
we, The People's Hope, we would lead the fight. We sat
silent. Some were wondering what all that meant, and
others knew just what.

I didn't understand, at least not very well, and when
I asked my father, he just snorted. He was sitting in a
Berbice chair out on the balcony with breezes blowing
smells from passion flowers growing on the fence below.
Soon we would eat the fruit. Yellow globes with soft-
pink interiors. My father dipped his paper down and
looked at me. I had interrupted him. He paused, maybe
wondering if this question was a worthwhile one. His blue
eyes were creased and crinkled up a bit, so I thought that
he was going to tease me. I told him about the minister,
about what Comrade Reid told all the St. Rose's girls
when he came to the school and said we were the people's
hope. My father put his paper down beside his chair, sat
forward, looked at me, and said that legislating attitudes,
passing rules to force people how to behave never works.
Wind shifted the paper at his feet. I saw a headline there,
something about China and a loan. Twenty-two million
dollars to the Guyanese. Who do you think will spend
that money on their own big houses and big cars? Who do
you think will get to make the rules? he asked. I wondered
about that. It was true, at school we worked together, we
all co-operated, but we did not make the rules. Would
people have to sneak and su-su-su if they all liked each
other, liked the rules, if they all got along? Maybe that's

the sacrifice. He said, that sort of thing, that talk of all for everyone, was just a ruse. A ruse, I knew, meant a trick.

My father told me that the government, "the Burnham crowd," he said, was playing tricks on the Guyanese. That socialism talk masked dictatorship and that would make some rich and leave the others poor. It would not make them better off. He said that communism-socialism legislating attitudes wouldn't change a thing for most. Guyana and the Guyanese would suffer for this change; this was dictatorship, it was the rule of fear. Don't you see that? He crossed his legs, one sandal dangled at me from the end of his pale freckled toes. He settled into talk about corruption, about greed, about scare tactics, pitting little people against each other. He leaned forward, stared his clear blue eyes at me. I knew that look. I'd seen it on his face before. I remembered when he used to tease me, long before we left Canada, he'd tease me with that look. He'd ask questions that confused me. He'd ask me things like, "If no one sees the tree fall in the forest, no one's there to hear it fall, does it make a sound?" I would answer back, "Of course it does." But, that was not the end—of course it wasn't—because you never really know the answer to that question. It's assumption. That's what he explained and then went on to where he always meant to go. He'd say, "When you're in bed at night and in the dark, and nobody is there to see you, nobody at all, how do you know that you exist?" Long before we moved to that strange place, my father's clear blue look and what always seemed to come with it would often make me cry.

Not anymore. Oh no, I wasn't five years old. I knew that
look and didn't cry anymore when I became confused.
Sometimes, by then, I even liked my father's tricky-
teasey questions. Don't be fooled. Don't assume. And
don't take anything for granted. Think clearly, think the
problem through, line up your facts in tidy rows, make
sure the beats are even and don't jump and jive. Use logic
in the answer that you give. His crinkles smiled at me.
Encouraging. You know you can. I said, "People want to
leave Guyana. Some are scared. Not everyone believes the
speeches." That's right. My father picked his paper up,
leaned back, and flicked that paper open wide. Let him
read in peace. There were headlines staring at me then:
PRICE CONTROL COPS SWOOP DOWN ON CITY SHOP-
OWNERS. A crime was solved through OPERATION SILENT
WITNESS.

Sacrifice. In speeches and in papers I saw "sacrifice"
most often when I saw "co-operation." June said that it
was not a sacrifice if everybody worked together for the
new Guyana. She said that was why St. Rose's nuns had
given Burnham's government their school. June told us
that meant there would be boys among the girls next year.
What? Oh yes, oh yes, there would be boys. Why else, she
said, was Mr. Sankat with his black beard and thick black
hair teaching maths that year? No other men had ever
taught St. Rose's girls. That year he had joined the teacher-
nuns and taught maths to girls about to graduate, the
older girls, the ones who soon would head off to university
where men, we knew, were common. They weren't inside

St. Rose's walls, but June said that was a change, a sacrifice, that was coming soon.

In midday heat cicadas sang, droned high and loud. In Georgetown they were big as mice, big and grey and scaled but hardly ever seen. Their song started small and almost tentative but quickly grew to deafen and to shatter all your thoughts. They sang, it seemed, from right inside your head. It's heat that sets them off. They sang loudest on the hottest days. It was hot right then. Farida and I sat in shade on steep stairs that led to open doors, wide and high and very bright out there, outside St. Rose's walls. We were in the shade, inside the walls and looking out and waiting, surrounded by cicada sounds, waiting for our parents' cars to pick us up.

She said in su-su voice that mixed in my head with insect song, "Nah all who go ah church house go fuh pray." Not everything was as it seemed. I knew. Some people lie. She said, "I'm scared." Her parents talked. She heard them say Guyana was a mess. The country was in crisis, and it was quickly getting worse. And now, and now she said, there is the National Service. Guns and mud and uniforms. No girl, no boy or girl, could go to university, not there, not in Guyana, unless they first marched in mud and wore an army uniform and shot a gun. Unless they spent a year or more in camps, camps far from home, far in the middle of Guyana where nobody lived. Far far away where nobody was watching. You've seen the photos in the papers. Yes, I have. A girl, fourteen years old, was marching with forty other girls who marched among two hundred and eighty others. They were marching then. The Great March, that was what the papers called it. Great Marching all the way from Kimbia to Georgetown, one hundred and sixty miles through swamps and creeks and forests that the papers said were "virgin." That fourteen-year-old girl posed with a gun, a machine gun in her hands held up across her chest, her fingers spread and one was on the trigger. She didn't smile, but that was okay because the march was serious and hard. The job's important. Sacrificing for the greater good. She was helping Burnham lead us, lead Guyana, to our future. Far away. That day, the paper said, they would march from something called the Burnham Ideological Institute to someplace called Garden of Eden. Ideology and Eden. I thought that sounded nice. I liked the name. It seemed, to me, just right.

But, Farida whispered, "far away." Those camps were far away. She heard her father su-su words like "rape" and "race extermination." Those roots of discord run deep, but Burnham found a way, her father said, to shift the balance. Shift Guyana's racial balance in his favour. Shift through sacrifice, through rape. Farida's father said this in a quiet voice, but Farida heard. She heard and said to me she would not be The People's Hope, she was not going to be a people's student. Oh no. She is getting out. Her parents, they were looking for someplace for her to go. She was leaving for some other place. It might be Canada. Far far away. Oh, Canada, where Burnham's revolution cannot reach.

# 8

## SHAKE-HAND

*L*and of Six Nations, that was what they called Guyana, and it was. That and more. Six nations, five races when you counted Portuguese and early colonists (the Dutch and then the Brits) as one, as white. They never did though. They never counted those as one. Nations are not races, I supposed, yet no one ever said why Africa, a continent, was counted as one nation, just one of Guyana's six.

They said "nation" when they talked about Guyana's six, but everybody was really talking black and white and brown. Skin colour. Eye tone and the texture of your hair. Those were all important. And historic roots were too. The roots of where you were before you landed in Guyana. Where did you come from? How did you get here? Were you a bringer or a brought?

Even at St. Rose's that was there, lurking underneath, quiet and unspoken, behind those uniforms that we all wore, beneath our *Serviam* and our Merici House. It was hiding even when we sang the St. Rose's song each day. It was hidden so well I didn't see it. I couldn't spot it with my blue eyes, the only blue eyes in the school. All I saw was what officially was there to see, and that was six, including me, six nations holding hands, together, altogether making what was then the newest, latest version of Guyana. The Co-operative Republic of Guyana. Six nations made the country strong. That's what Comrade Burnham said. Each nation had its strengths, and each one was just as equal as the rest. That's what June said, officially. Farida said it too, sometimes, but more and more she also said Guyana's future wasn't one she'd share. Quietly, she said that Burnham didn't want her nation, her history, her past, her India, her skin. Unofficially.

Six nations. Five races. Four different shades of brownish-blackish amber skin and one that's pinkish white. If I fit into any part of Guyana's six nations, then I'd have to find a place among the pinky-whitish one. That's what I was thinking while I hid behind the counter at Booker Brothers store. I was thinking that while seeing all around me that the nation I could count myself among was there in force, at Booker Brothers store. Above me, choirboys, white as any rosy cherub ever was, were staring down at me with open mouths. It was Christmastime, and on the shelf so high above the shoppers' heads, the porcelain English choirboys were out. Golden hair and flowing robes and hands in prayer. Their eyes were blue as mine. Their mouths were open. Silently, they sang.

The Booker Brothers choirboys were proppah Guyanese, and Bookers store, where I was hiding from a nun, was most official. It had history. Bookers store had roots. They were definitely one among Guyana's six. In fact, the Booker brothers had once owned so much of what is called Guyana that the entire country was considered theirs. Unofficially. That was when Guyana was called "Booker's Guiana," because that's how much the brothers owned. All that land. They covered most of it in sugar cane and owned the factories that processed cane to sugar, the trains and tanker ships to carry it across the sea, and everything between and more besides. All of it was owned by Booker Brothers. Sugar, sugar, sugar. They owned almost all that grew in rich Guyana soil. And rice as well. And stores. Stores for selling everything from tractors down to shoes and shirts and socks.

Shoes and socks was what I watched while ducked down behind a counter full of men's dress shirts, starched and pressed and flawless white. Thick-soled shoes and thick white socks that wrapped around a nun's dark ankle. Those were what I watched as china choirboys stared down at me and gasped. There was a nun coming down the aisle toward where I was hiding. I held my breath and hoped she'd take a turn, pass down a different aisle. What was she shopping for in Bookers store? What sort of things would nuns want in this store?

One thing I knew for certain was she wouldn't like the sight of me in my pastel-yellow uniform. Not there. Not in Bookers store. Not shopping and, especially, not hiding. The nuns were clear on that. St. Rose's girls should not be seen wearing their uniforms downtown.

St. Rose's girls must never wander Georgetown's stores
or saunter down its streets among the rum-shop sippers
lurking cornerwise. Should not be seen in uniform
because St. Rose's girls should always be busy studying or
volunteering at an orphanage. The nuns told us that we
were never to be seen, in uniform especially, engaged in
frivolous endeavours. But, there I was, in uniform and
frivolously hiding. Shopping with my mother who ignored
me as I ducked and hid, who never took it seriously when
she picked me up at school then drove down Church
Street toward the shops instead of home. She thought it
was funny when Chris and I froze up in fear whenever
we saw a nun approaching. But, if that nun saw me, she'd
make a point of telling Sister Hazel. Then the ledger book
would have a mark against my name, and I would have to
answer Sister Hazel when she called my name and asked
me at assembly why was I in Georgetown in my St. Rose's
uniform. I'd have to answer her while everybody stood and
listened silently. She'd tell me it wasn't dignified to stroll
downtown in uniform. I knew she'd also say that hiding
in a store, in Bookers store, in my St. Rose's uniform, was
most undignified of all.

I crouched and held my breath and watched. All
around me Christmas carols filled the air. I heard "Away in
a Manger" while I watched for nuns. Bookers piped music
in when it was time to put out the porcelain choirboys.
Songs about the cold and snow and chestnuts roasting.
Santa Claus is coming. Bells are jingling. You better watch
out, I'm tellin' you why.

I was going to have to explain why I was hiding to my grandmother. She was there with us, shopping too and looking puzzled about my behaviour. We called her Gradgy, and she was visiting us for Christmas. It was the first time she'd ever been to a tropical country. Maybe it was the first time she'd ever travelled outside of Canada. A lot of things puzzled Gradgy, things that had stopped surprising us, like when our maid Victoreen tried to talk her into joining the Baha'is. Most of the time we had to explain what people said, as if we were translating from another language. "She said 'dove,' you know, 'simmer down' the meat," when Gradgy asked our other maid her recipe for Guyana stew.

Gradgy was my father's mother, and every year, before we moved to Georgetown, she would come to our house for Christmas dinner. She and my uncle and my aunt, two cousins, also cousins twice removed, my mother's parents all the way from Virden, Manitoba, and my mother's oldest friend. Sometimes we had more than twenty people eating turkey dinner at our house. Turkey dinner, stuffing made with chestnuts, mashed potatoes, Brussels sprouts, and gravy. Turkey, like potatoes, was something you had to smuggle into Guyana if you wanted to eat it for Christmas dinner. Every year, except when she came to Georgetown, Gradgy made the trifle. Fruit and cake and whipping cream in a big cut-crystal bowl with a jagged toothy rim. Everything was soaked in brandy. She called it boozy cake.

All around in Bookers store it was Christmasy like we were someplace else, not Christmasy like anything you'd ever see in Georgetown. That was weird, but it didn't puzzle Gradgy. I sweated in my St. Rose's uniform, but the songs piped in were all about frost nipping at your nose, and the Bookers aisles were filled with cards and decorations glittering with fake snow. Real snow didn't shine like that, I told my friends at school. They asked me about snow. What was it like? How did it feel? Was it hard, like shavings from the icebox when it's all built up in there, or soft and fluffy on your face? If I said yes to that, to fluffy on your face, it made snow seem like something almost warm, but, no, it wasn't sharp like crystal ice. How could I tell a girl who'd never stepped on grass that crunches underfoot from frost or stomped to shatter thinnest ice on autumn puddles, how could I tell that girl what any of those things were like? They didn't know what snow was or even ice, but they gave me Christmas cards with pictures of rosy-cheeked girls and boys ice-skating on a pond.

We had a Christmas tree at home in our Guyana house. It was green and had skinny branches that drooped and long limp needles that the ornaments slid off if they weren't clipped on tight. There were few branches on it and lots of airy space, so my mother wrapped ropes of fuzzy glittery stuff around it to make it seem full. It was a sort of tinsel we would never have had on a Canadian Christmas tree. On those trees the tinsel we hung was made of thin strips of silver foil, and each piece had to be draped individually. Our hands would sweat from clutching it as we carefully chose the next spot to hang a piece of tinsel. In Georgetown we could have had a plastic tree as thick and bushy as a live one grown in Canada. There were no trees growing in Guyana that looked like that, but the Guyanese knew what Christmas trees were supposed to look like. Even there, in the steamy tropics where the seasons were "dry" and "wet" and temperatures between the two ranged only by five degrees, even there you could buy a fake Christmas tree at Bookers and in other shops. Some even came with sprayed-on snow. But, my mother didn't like plastic trees. My father didn't either, so we had a live one, thin and pale, its trunk stuck into a bucket of sand that my mother wrapped up in red paper. It smelled tropical. My father said it looked like Charlie Brown's Christmas tree, but when I told that to June she looked puzzled. There was no television in Guyana.

My father photographed us sitting by our Christmas tree. He put the camera on a tripod, set the timer, rushed to his chair while we all froze and stared. *Blink. Blink. Blink, whirrrrrrr-click.* There.

That's a picture of our Christmas in Guyana. I'm there, cross-legged on the floor, just behind my sister, Chris, who's also sitting on the floor, and Stephen's in the corner in a chair, and on the other side are Mom and Dad. Frozen, caught inside a plastic square. Our Christmas tree almost hits the ceiling, and we all sit in front of it in shorts and sleeveless tops. See my brother, Stephen, sitting by himself, off to the side? He spends his days playing tennis with his friend Dennis Ramsahoye. That boy's father is an engineer, and Stephen says that Dennis will be sent to

Canada to study. He is Stephen's only Guyanese friend. His other friends are expats. See my father's white white legs? He doesn't often wear short pants, and so his skin's the palest of us all.

The choirboys at Bookers store and the Christmas carols were traditional. My grandmother seemed to like the china choirboys and the music piped inside Bookers. She stopped to talk with people begging near the door outside, out front of Bookers. She never gave them money, but she bought them chocolate bars. Cadbury chocolate bars flown in from England. Those chocolate bars were as traditional as Bookers choirboys. My friends said that to them Christmas meant Cadbury bars with crinkly golden foil. Those chocolate bars, on edges and on corners, usually had a greyish-whitish colour overtop the chocolate brown. Sometimes tiny holes too. Chris and I learned to check for those little holes before eating any chocolate bars, because that was where the worms had burrowed in and were hiding.

When we left Bookers, passing through the crowd of beggars there around the door, Gradgy handed out Cadbury bars to children begging with their families. The children smiled and cheered, but their parents didn't. My mother shook her head at chocolate bars for children living on the street. It was not what they needed. It was not a good idea.

There was a man outside. His skin so dark with sun and dirt I couldn't tell which one of the six of Guyana he came from. He could have been white or black or something in between. His shaggy hair was knotted up with sticks and leaves from sleeping in the dirt out there where cars were parked, out there beside the watery canal. His clothes were torn and shredded, pants were turned to shorts because they'd ripped so much. He was always there across the street from Bookers, always holding a boulder in his arms. It was worn smooth, and even shiny in some spots, because he'd held that rock so long. He held it high above his head and over the heads of other people too sometimes. Sometimes he held it up above my head and shook it, saying, "bloody British." He didn't know I was Canadian. As we left Bookers, the "bloody British" man smiled at Gradgy when she handed him a Cadbury bar. He tucked his boulder in his stringy arm and took the chocolate and smiled. He didn't shake his rock at her or call her "bloody British." Gradgy smiled back at him while my mother shook her head.

I wasn't British or Dutch, but I was white, and that was good enough for me to count as one among Guyana's six. That nation, the white one, included colonists (the bringers, not the brought), and some of those were Brits and some were Dutch. They were the ones whose history included Booker brothers, Fort Zeelandia, and kokers, the sluice gates controlling water flowing through Georgetown's canals. I was the closest thing that they could find to china-choirboy pink, so I was asked, or told, to stand out in the sun on Company Path and represent my nation.

There were six of us, the six nations. The government officials found us all at St. Rose's. I was sitting at my desk, alone because my classmates all were off at weekly chapel. They were Catholic, but I was not. I was Anglican, officially, which meant I didn't have to pray. The government officials gathered us and took us off to Company Path, where we were photographed in what the paper called a "shake-hand ceremony." That's what the headline said, atop the photograph, on page two of the *Guyana Graphic*. SHAKE-HAND FOR SCHOOL KID. I showed my grandmother the photograph and told her what a shake-hand ceremony was and why there were six of us standing in a line. I told her about the history behind the Six Nations of Guyana. I showed her and everybody else. See. I'm there, right there and standing with five others, standing in as Guyanese. There I was, right there, mid-line and barely visible, but there, and you could see me if you looked hard enough. Look hard all day, and yet you'd never catch a glimpse of Gillian, Gillian Da Silva. She was Portuguese, and you couldn't see her where she stood at the end, the far end of the line, because her face was blocked by Farida's head. Farida stood beside me. We were both looking at the camera. I was smiling, full up with thoughts of being there, of being Guyanese and proud of that.

But first, before the photograph was shot, we were told to line up tidily on Company Path. Company Path, I explained to Gradgy, was not a path at all. It used to be a walk between two sugar fields, estates most likely owned by those Booker brothers, a path for owners strolling down among the high green sugar cane, hearing their riches rustling tall, down to the riverbank. But when the shake-hand photograph was taken, it was not a path at all. Then it was a little park that anyone, not just the wealthy sugar lords, could use. And there we were, even an Amerindian girl, standing in a row on Company Path, where someone had raked the gravel freshly that morning; it was sharp and shining in the bright bright sun and newly weeded clean. Stand straight. Stand tall.

We were in that place to shake the hand of Tanzania's President Nyerere. He'd come to lay a wreath at Company Path where there were statues of four men, the leaders of the non-aligned nations. Heads on pillars. Wreaths on gravel. You can see Nyerere in the photograph, just past where my blond head is leaning forward. Just then, just as I was leaning out to watch him greet the Chinese girl who bowed and looked so solemn, the damp imprint of his palm had still not faded from my hand. Shake hands with each nation of Guyana.

I felt that, then, I was a part of that. I was, officially, recorded in the newspaper for everyone to see, one of the Six Nations. My father said it was important to know the place that you called home. In Canada we went camping every summer. Driving over mountains and up river valleys. Stopping to see where towns were flooded out by hydro dams. Climbing on the boulders outside Hope, B.C., that a few years before had been a mountainside. See the scar, my father said, pointing at the messy, pale-grey slope. We stood beside the highway, and Dad told us about the Frank Slide. He said a baby was the only thing that lived.

The miners found it when they came up to daylight from the deep, and there it was, a baby in a bassinet balanced on a boulder as big as a house, as big as an elephant. Nothing else was left. No town, no homes, no schools. We saw the Fraser Canyon, we saw the old highway across that narrow Fraser Canyon, rock carved by the frothing, raging Fraser River far below. We saw all that and more on summer camping trips. We drove through mountains via tunnels that my father had helped build. We drove to places where the loggers lived and cut down trees, to other places where the fishermen canned salmon, metal-sided buildings built on wharves out over water where the fish guts could be dumped, where the smell was tangy—Dad said that was the iodine in kelp—and where the seagulls gathered thick as flies in Stabroek Market.

For Christmas we would do the same, except this time we'd see the things that made Guyana what it was. Because it was Christmas and because my grandmother was there, Dad took holidays and spent more time with us. He'd made a plan for us to travel inland on a boat. We'd see the coastal plains, the land that first drew bringers, colonists, to that land in search of gold, in search of land to grow their riches. We'd see rivers.

Muddy rivers. They slowly clarified as we went up the Demerara River, up the Pokeraro, up Kamuni Creek. Muddy water slowly clarified to the colour of strong tea, golden amber when the sun struck through. In Guyana they call that "black water." Dad said the water was that colour because of jungle vegetation rotting down and staining it. It was stained, but clear and sweet. Slowly slowly up down water, jungled banks moved closer in and creeks narrowed. The boat was almost silent, but the jungle, it was not. Howler monkeys roared warnings. They knew we were there. Birds shrieked, birds clicked, birds craw-craw-crackled out their calls from somewhere we couldn't see, beyond the impenetrable walls of jungle green. My mother said we were in a boat that looked just like the *African Queen*. I didn't know what that was, but I liked it. Africa sounded even more exotic and exciting than Guyana. We sat beneath a striped canvas awning, and the sun and shade were dappled where the cloth had rotted through. We all wore hats. My grandmother was in the stern, her red hair billowing out around her face, and she leaned back with her freckled arms along the gunwales and smiled.

We stopped at Santa Mission where a path of sand, white shining sand, led from the creek bank up to a church. An airplane had crashed on the other bank, across from where the church was. It was nose down, nose buried in the river reeds, tail up, and skeletal with age. Somebody had hung a bell inside the fuselage, among its struts and ribs. That was where they'd hung the bell that rang to call the Amerindians to church. We stopped at Santa Mission and walked up the sandy path to where the buildings were, just three, and one was really just a roof on poles, no walls. The other two were silver sided, made from corrugated tin, and all were thatched with shaggy palm, sun-bleached to silver too.

Amerindians watched us as we watched them. We wandered through their village. I'd seen an Amerindian just once before; she was there on Company Path, although I'd never seen her at St. Rose's where they came to gather the six of us. The Amerindians at Santa Mission were not at all like her. We saw mothers, topless, with their babies on their hips. We saw fathers who looked worried where they sat and watched us watching them. They all wore bright red strings bound tight around their arms and just below their knees. Bright-red cords wrapped wrists and made their calves bulge; a loop of coloured strings criss-crossed an infant's chest, around his arms vest-like. Red string and three red stripes of pigment, maybe blood, stroked down a cheek, another smeared along a nose. Their eyes were deep dark amber like the creek. We watched women pound cassava root and lay it out on flat tin discs. The discs were put on palm-roofed huts that were held up off the sand by stilts. White cassava circles drying on palm roofs above white sand.

It was hot. The sand reflected the heat, and the only shade was where the Amerindians in hammocks watched us silently, so we swam, diving in the black water of the creek below the church. Beneath the water, amber clear, I saw my arms and legs, no longer white. Darkened like mahogany. And then later, back inside the little boat, back to chugging up the stream, we saw that what we thought were logs were really crocodiles, lurking on the banks beneath the jungle's overhanging, drooping edge. No, not crocodiles, my father said, they're caimans. Smaller and, perhaps, less dangerous. Exotic, said my grandmother, who also said, "you're brave."

Exotic. Howler monkeys howled. Bright macaws flashed yellow, purple, blue, and red, more red: red heads, red wings. Green parrots, toucans, eagles, harpy eagles too. The Guyanese called them flying wolves. My father took a picture of a long-legged bird, all brown but richly so. It was a jacana, also called a Jesus bird because it seems to walk on water, walks on lily pads.

Our boat trip ended at Lama, where we spent that Christmas holiday. Lama was a conservancy, a place where water was pooled, dammed up, and saved in case there ever was a drought and coastal sugar fields dried out. The Lama guesthouse had a striped tin roof. Red-white-red-white-red-white. We slept beneath its widespread eaves in open air, swaddled in white gauze mosquito nets. Rain fell and beat on the tin roof to make a sound that swallowed up all others, even howler monkeys, and I was quickly lulled to sleep. In the morning Gradgy's arms and legs were dotted over with bright-red itchy spots. She asked Mom what those were, and Mom pretended not to know that they were bedbug bites. "I think you may have got too much sun. Stay in the shade today."

We swam at Lama too, and after swimming, our bathing suits still wet, we'd hook bacon, dangle it in the water where we'd swum, and catch piranha, little silver-sided fish that looked like flattened coins. My father caught the largest one. At Lama he was, again, the fishing dad I'd known. The fishing, hunting, napping dad I'd known, except that there, at Lama, he didn't wear his chocolate-brown suede coat that smelled of smoke from cigarettes and campfires. I missed my father in his suede coat. I missed the smell of campfire smoke he carried home sometimes along with mallard ducks he'd shot and which he'd hang above his workbench in our basement. Iridescent green and royal purple on their necks. I didn't miss the ducks, but missed my camping dad. At Lama he was back, holding up piranha for the camera to catch. We all caught piranha there, and they had jaws much bigger than you'd think and those were full of jagged teeth. The man at Lama said piranhas wouldn't fuss with us when we were swimming, so we swam and we were never bit, and bacon brought the fish to us, their beaten-silver colour turning pewter grey when they stopped flapping on the dock. When we went home to Georgetown later, we put those fish out in the sun. Ants came. Long lines of ants swarmed thick then left the bones and teeth. Fish jaws, saw-toothed, to show our friends.

That was what I showed Farida. When we were home, I showed Farida piranha teeth from fish I'd caught, and I told her about the caimans and the howler monkeys and the rain. Black water isn't black, I said. I showed her photographs of Lama and of Santa Mission too. Showed her pictures of the Amerindians I'd seen and palm-roofed huts, cassava discs, and Jesus birds. She'd never seen or been to either of those places. She said she hadn't travelled any of the creeks or rivers threading through Guyana. She'd never swum black water, never flown above the flat-topped mountains inland where Sir Arthur Conan Doyle once flew. Those mountains, I'd seen them, lost worlds cut off from coastal plains by jungles that filled valleys, vines and trees and flowers. Farida had never seen those hills or famous Kaieteur Falls, not walked inside the oldest fort, Zeelandia, built by the Dutch three hundred years ago, even though it wasn't far from Georgetown, just a short boat ride up the Essequibo River. She hadn't ridden horseback on the Rupununi plains or picked a lemon off a tree where lemons grew inland. Farida had never met a man who's goin in de bush to pan for gold, a pork knocker who, just like Walter Raleigh, still hunts for El Dorado. Farida said she'd never heard a howler monkey howl or watched macaws, bright smudges in the air, flushed out from the jungle canopy below a plane. I knew all those things. They were some of the things I knew of as Guyana, the place that stretched back beyond the sea, behind and down below Georgetown. But, Farida knew only Georgetown. She knew Stabroek Market, scroll-cut wooden shutters, kokers holding water back, and Bookers store. She knew Christmas brought the choirboys out and chocolate bars from Britain. So we talked about the things she knew, the things we both had shared.

We talked about six nations and our photograph, our picture in the newspaper.

"Look at you," I said. "Your great big head is hiding Gillian. You can barely see her there."

Farida laughed. "Look, gyal. Look you, standin there

and grinnin grinnin big. Your skin. You lookin like a ghost, nah. Your skin so white it hidin you."

I looked and I laughed too.

I looked again. I stared, and then I knew that she was right. My shape was more a blank of space outlined by all the others. My edges in that photograph were defined by what was around me. My skin so white, my hair and eyes so pale, the ink dots barely there to fill in where I was.

# 9

## WHITE GIRL

*I* was standing in bright sunlight waiting, once again, to shake a famous hand. Canada's Prime Minister Pierre Trudeau was coming to Guyana, going to land that day, and I was there to shake his hand, or hoping to at least. That shake-hand time I wasn't there to represent a nation or a race, not there to be photographed as one of Guyana's six. I was there because I was Canadian, and all Canadians in Georgetown had been invited out to smile and wave the flag at Timehri airport. That April day at Timehri we all were white, all one race, no shades of gold or brown, just pinkish white where we all stood behind a barrier. I was at the very front, the perfect spot to shake our Trudeau's hand.

Asphalt shimmered black and hot. It had rained earlier, and afterward the puddles steamed. Soon they would all be gone. It was that hot. It was very hot, but we didn't sweat because we'd been living in Guyana long enough. We'd acclimatized. They say in heat your blood thins, and you don't sweat the same as if your blood was thick, thick enough for winter and for snow.

In postcolonial Guyana, boys lounge at Trafalga Square across from Stabroek Market, gyaffing and passing sweet-eye on every girl. Georgetown, Guyana, 1975.

All-girls St. Rose's High School was like a fortress. Behind its walls nuns kept their sharp eyes on the students while, in the wet season, the students kept a lookout for glimpses of market boys bathing naked in the Church Street canals. Georgetown, Guyana, 1974. *(Photo by Sally Plunkett)*

Pierre Trudeau seemed as happy to greet us as we were to see him when he landed at Timehri International Airport. Every Canadian in Georgetown was on the tarmac to shake his hand. Georgetown, Guyana, 1975. *(Photo by Stephen Plunkett)*

Following Sir Walter Raleigh's lead, pork knockers sought riches in Guyana's murky rivers. Sometimes they found gold, sometimes diamonds. My father bought both from this man. Later, Mom sewed them into the hem of her skirt and smuggled them out of the country. Guyana, 1975. *(Photo by Patrick Plunkett)*

Knowing there were piranha in the river didn't stop us from swimming. At Lama Conservancy we used bacon as bait to catch this one and then waited an hour (on the caretaker's advice) before jumping into the water again. Guyana, 1974. *(Photo by Sally Plunkett)*

Santa Mission was a small clearing in the jungle accessible only by Kamuni Creek. The Amerindians living there showed us their bright whitewashed church and sold Mom the tools needed to extract poisonous juice from cassava. Guyana, 1974.

We were told that Guyana's interior, with its prairie-flat mountains and sheer-sided valleys, had inspired Sir Arthur Conan Doyle's *The Lost World*, and it did seem like a fictional landscape that we walked through. A jungle trail brought us to the lip of Kaieteur Falls, formed by the Potaro River. Stephen, Mom, Chris, and I stood at the top of a 900-foot drop and were cooled by the updraft of Guyana's most famous waterfall. *(Photo by Patrick Plunkett)*

At fourteen years old, I stood just five feet tall, yet Daphne, formidable ruler of our house, was shorter than that. She and I flanked Stephen beneath the passionfruit vine on Kaieteur Road. Georgetown, Guyana, 1975.

Saying goodbye to June and the other Guyanese friends I'd made at St. Rose's left me sadder than I remembered feeling when I'd left Canada. Georgetown, Guyana, 1975.

Kupang in 1976 was like a frontier town, dust and guns and half-built structures, where cheese was grey and came in tins, and blond-haired girls drew crowds. Kupang, Timor, 1976. *(Photo by Patrick Plunkett)*

Bette (l) and Lin (r) wore traditional sarongs that identified
where they came from, and Chris (l) and I (r) wore what we'd
identified as the hippest clothes that Kupang could offer. Kupang,
Timor, 1978. *(Photo by Sally Plunkett)*

Kerosene stoves exploded, all water had to be boiled, monkeys
made havoc, and every grain in the kitchen had to be sifted for
stones and bugs. Lin worked hard for her monthly $15. Kupang,
Timor, 1977.

Quibo would snatch sunglasses off the face of anyone who let him get close enough; he was intrigued by his own reflection and wanted a closer look at it. Perhaps that's why Dad was photographed without the aviators that seemed to be always shading his eyes. Kupang, Timor, 1977. *(Photo by Christine Plunkett)*

At Penang's Temple of the Azure Cloud, Dad and I were also draped with snakes, but with a pit viper on her head, Mom's delightfully intrepid spirit showed best. Penang, Malaysia, 1977. *(Photo by Patrick Plunkett)*

Quibo and I shared the rare treat of a little beer. After a few sips, he'd run around the garden on his hind legs, arms waving in the air above his head, then trundle back to my lap for a good sleep. Kupang, Timor, 1977. *(Photo by Christine Plunkett)*

Dad, Tuan Besar, or Tuan Kua, depending on our mood, as I most often remember him and as he was most often happy. Kupang, Timor, 1978.

An honour guard of Guyanese marched past, forming lineups on the shiny black tarmac. Bright jackets gleamed white, red berets, red sashes, and black pants striped down the side in red. A military show. There were hundreds of them out there on the tarmac where the rising steam made everything waver. Water being pulled into the air, maybe to make shady clouds. No, not likely. It was just burning off. Out there on the tarmac, it was one race too, just like it was where we all stood. One race, not six, to represent Guyana's past or future. It's the present, and that shake-hand ceremony was a different kind of show, not like the show we did on Company Path for Julius Nyerere. All the faces there, out there in uniform, were black. The military show, Burnham's power marching black on black.

My foot was cocked up on the lower rail of the metal barricade that separated the Canadians from the Guyanese. I leaned out and held my tiny flag ready-set to wave it when the plane landed. Red and white, red pants, white shirts, and cricket caps with Canadian flags sewn on; a cricket cap was not a thing to wear in Canada, but it was in Guyana. That's what everybody all around me wore. I looked back at them behind me and saw that all together we Canadians were less than sixty people dressed in red and white and waving flags. Not many, and yet many more of us than we knew even lived there. Who were all those people? Engineers who mapped the rivers like my dad? What kinds of projects could have brought this crowd to this small shifting place? Maybe some were bankers, watching out for money lent by Canada? What else, what else could all those people do in Georgetown, in that Co-operative, that newly minted state that then, already, was calling itself socialist?

My mother said, "Who knew so many Canadians were living here in Georgetown?" She said she wondered where they all had been when she and some others, Canadians we knew, were cooking doughnuts, drizzling maple syrup (smuggled in), frying bacon for the Canadian booth on International Day when all the embassies showed off what made their country special.

We all must have been Canadian though, to be there on the Timehri tarmac, because the High Commissioner had invited us to come. Later, in the evening, there'd be a reception for the adults to meet Trudeau. The Commissioner would host that cocktail party, and my mother and my father would be photographed, in black and white with Trudeau. Later, after that reception, Mom told us that she "fell in love" with Trudeau. She fell in love with him because, instead of coming through the big front doors at the High Commissioner's reception, Trudeau entered through the kitchen, and he stopped and greeted all the staff and thanked them for their work. Mom said that showed Trudeau was a gentleman.

Mom also said he was a "playboy." That was why everybody was excited, grinning, dressed in red and white, and waving flags out on the steamy tarmac. My father even liked Trudeau, but I'd heard him snorting when he read the newspaper just days before. He was reading about Trudeau's visit to Venezuela. Trudeau's wife had sung a song to Venezuela's leader. My father liked Trudeau, he said, the man but not the politics, but thought that his wife, Margaret, was embarrassing. But we had learned that Margaret would not be there at Timehri. She wouldn't sing a song for Comrade Burnham, not that day.

The Air Canada plane landed and rolled slowly down the asphalt runway. Heat waves made the maple leaf on its tail flutter like a flag. People all around me cheered, and then I heard my father say, "How soon we forget what they do to our luggage." But that maple leaf was all it took to make some people teary-eyed. We leaned further out to show our pride, and the honour guard fidgeted in the steam. Then a tiny flag held in a hand poked out the pilot's window. A tiny Canadian flag just like the ones we held. It was Trudeau, our Trudeau, waving at us as the plane approached. We screamed and yelled and cheered.

Photographers and cameramen and others with boom mikes rushed in and squatted on the tarmac facing us. They took photographs, and there I was in centre front. I wasn't dressed in red and white, and I didn't wear a cricket cap. Beige pants with wide bell-bottoms flared over my platform shoes, and I wore a madras cotton shirt with sweeping sleeves. My shirt was blue with multi-coloured embroidery around the neck. Beside me was another girl with long blond hair. She was my best friend, my new best friend, and we were dressed like twins, except her shirt was green. Her name was Annette, and I never called her Annie. She had picked out my clothes, had told me what to wear that day. Her green shirt was tucked into the top of her pants because she was thin, but mine was not.

Annette's hair was long and feathered blond and banged. Her arms and legs seemed longer than they were, and that was because she was thin. She showed me, once we were good friends, how to judge one's weight. She showed me, lying on her side, stretched out in panties and a bra one day when we were at her house and lounging on her bed. She said, "Lie on your side like this. See." She hooked her finger underneath the waistband of her underpants and showed me that the elastic there stretched straight from her hip bone to the bed, where her other hip bone disappeared into the coverlet. "See. See, it doesn't touch anything." Her stomach was concave. The elastic didn't touch it anywhere. If you can do that, she looked at me, then you are thin or close to thin enough, you are thin enough to wear your shirt tucked in. There had to be a hollow gap, a concave scoop, no belly there. I didn't bother testing that by lying down right then and there. I knew I wouldn't pass the panty-top test. I knew I wasn't thin enough. She could tuck her shirt into her pants, but I could not.

Annette was Canadian, but I didn't know that until we heard that Trudeau would be coming to Guyana. I thought that she was American. That's what she'd always said she was. But, there she was that day, right beside me at the front. She even had a flag to wave. Her parents and her sisters were there too.

Annette was always talking about New York, where they had lived for years before they moved to Georgetown.

When I asked her why she would be at Timehri, she said she had a Canadian passport. Her mother was Canadian, or Québécois, and so, she said, closer to a Trudeau-type Canadian than I was. I was from B.C. Annette told me she'd been born in Montreal. But, the U.S.A. and New York was what she always talked about, the place that she called home.

Her father was an engineer, just like my dad. Annette didn't know why he was there or what project he was working on. She said that sort of thing was irrelevant. She just didn't care. She didn't care why he had dragged them to Guyana, to the boondocks. She didn't ever want to talk about Georgetown. She liked to talk about New York. New York, she said, was where the entire world wanted to live. If they were smart they did. That's how good it was. It was the place to be, she said. It was the place to be, and Georgetown, in Guyana, sure was not. She said her sister Barbara, who my brother took to movies, stopped traffic even in New York. Even there, where people were accustomed to that sort of thing, to that sort of beauty. Annette said that Barbara might be walking down the street, just out for a walk, and cars would stop, just stop, and everybody stared. That was how beautiful her sister was. Barbara always wore flowered dresses, ones that frothed and floated in the breeze, stirred by even little puffs of air. Her legs were long and tanned and smooth and always ended in platform shoes that made her feet, because her legs were very thin, look thick like horse's hooves. That was something I never said out loud.

Annette showed me what her sister Barbara used to make her skin so smooth. Creams that melted hair. Annette said that sort of cream could not be bought in Georgetown, not in any shops. They had looked and couldn't find it in any of the Georgetown shops. Annette told me that her sister had her friends back home send packages of creams to melt her hair, eye shadows, lipstick, rouge. They regularly mailed those packages to her. But I had seen makeup in the stores, in Booker Brothers and in JP Santos too. At Fogarty's there even was a special place, a cosmetics counter full of bottles labelled Chantelle and Lisa Kay and even Avon too. When I said that, Annette looked at me. I'd seen that look. I'd seen the wives beside the pool look at my mother that way too. She looked at me and said, "That makeup's not for us. That makeup is for dark-skinned girls and not for us." All that I could say was, "oh."

She was my newest friend and my only friend with skin like mine.

It happened, just like that, one day. One morning at St. Rose's I was not the only white girl standing at assembly in the heat to hear Headmistress Sister Hazel speak. I hadn't even noticed that another head was blond, another one was standing out among the heads of shiny black. I hadn't noticed, not until her name was said aloud and Sister Hazel told us all to welcome Annette from the U.S.A.

That morning I was one with seven hundred others. I was with them all as we craned necks and nudge nudge nudged to see the new one standing looking strange and all alone among us there inside that high-walled room. I was one among the rest who started rustling whispers and who shuffled feet to get a better look. There she was, just two rows over, in her brand new uniform. Form 2, like me, but I was glad to see she wasn't standing in the line for Merici House. That day I didn't want another blonde to share Merici House with me. I didn't want this new girl from the U.S.A. to join my friends and me, to work with us while we all worked together.

She was standing in the line for Lima House, and even I could see she didn't look so scared as I knew I had looked on my first day. Not scared at all, and different, she looked different from the rest of us. Her eyes were pale and stared unblinking back at us. She didn't bow her head when Sister Hazel said her name, she didn't blush. She looked up and out and flicked her long blond hair. Her hair was not cut short for tropic heat, and she didn't tie it back or pull it tight into a bun. She stared at us with pale pale eyes and flicked her hair, and then she looked away and we looked down.

I know we all felt something shifting in assembly hall that day.

At lunch when I sat down with all my friends, we looked around, down all the tables to see where she was sitting. But she wasn't sitting anywhere that we could see, and we would certainly have seen her sticking out, the only other white, if she'd been there. June didn't bother looking. She watched us stretching back to see beyond the other heads down the table, and then she told us that she'd seen that uppish new girl—"biggative" is what June said—she'd seen da gyal sashaying out the gates when all a we had tumbled in our pink and blue and green down the stairs to jostle into lineup for our food. "She takin lunch at home. She daddy driver com fah she." Her driver? Oh, we thought, and bunched up closer on our bench, put heads together overtop our lunch, and didn't speak of her again. Oh, but we wanted to. Farida, she and I, had questions then that only June could answer. Questions like, what kind of car, what sort of driver was it, was there anybody else inside, and did she speak to anyone before she stepped inside that car? Did she look back at you? Did you see her smile?

Uppish. Sure, she was, and later we all thought that that was fine. At least, I did, and maybe others did as well. She was uppish at St. Rose's. She was uppish everywhere she went. She never ate with us. She never ate at school. She went home each day to eat. She later said, when we were friends, home was where she ate real food like peanut butter sandwiches. Curry, which we ate at school, she said it made you stink.

Curry. It was never cooked inside Annette's house. Not ever at her house in Bel Air Gardens. That house was unlike any house I'd ever seen. Not Guyanese at all and not like houses I remembered from before Georgetown. Curry smells would not have lasted there. I think they would have fled that foreign place. I wondered if Annette's mother cooked their food or had she taught the maid to make those peanut butter sandwiches, those dinners lacking curry, lacking spice?

That house was filled with everything brought from their home in New York State. They'd filled it up with furniture and carpets, lamps and filmy window covers they called "sheers," photographs of their blond heads all smiling in a studio, and beds with covers that were ruffled, tucked, and flounced. The colours were all wrong, at least that was what I thought at first, all wrong for there, for Georgetown. There was no purpleheart, no dark plank floors like ours. Their floors were covered up with pale-pink woolly carpets. There was nothing Guyanese about their house, except that it was standing there in Bel Air Gardens and that was near the seawall out along the east coast road.

Oh, but you couldn't keep Guyana out. Not there, not if your house was in Georgetown by the sea. Guyana came in through the windows and the doors even if you kept those closed and cooled the air inside with air conditioners you'd had shipped down to the country from the U.S.A. It seeped inside. Guyana found its way inside no matter what you did.

Guyana found a way into their house when seas were flooding high and sea walls weren't enough to keep the water out. Then a snake came up the pipes and right into the toilet in their strange and foreign house. It did. And that was Guyanese true-true and never would have happened in a house in New York State.

At school Annette wasn't in my class, but I saw her

every morning at assembly and in gym class once a week. She was athletic, she could run and jump and even climb up ropes, and that was something hardly any other girl could do. My friends and I watched silently and stood with necks bent back when she scrambled up a thick hemp rope the teacher-nuns had hung down from the ceiling. We had all tried to climb that rope and we had all failed, but Annette climbed it right away, right to the top. It was the thing, the one thing, that she was really good at, or, at least, the thing she seemed to work at and do better than the seven hundred other St. Rose's girls. Her marks, we learned, were not so good. She was often late and didn't put in the effort that Sister Hazel said she must. And that was different too. She didn't care. She didn't care when Sister Hazel made her stand while all the other seven hundred of us sat and listened to her marks read out, listened while the days that she was late were counted out. She didn't hang her head or shuffle her feet or blush. She didn't even stand up straight. She almost shrugged when Sister Hazel asked her why her grades were not as good as they should be, or why she hadn't managed yet to get to school on time each day. She almost shrugged before she sat back down. Oh my! We almost gasped when we saw that, and so did Sister Hazel.

It was sometime after that, after that assembly when the newest whitest girl had shown she didn't really care and we'd all seen her almost shrug to prove she didn't care to Headmistress Sister Hazel, sometime after that I started wishing she would stay at school for lunch sometimes.

And it was after that that I began to watch for her when we, all seven hundred of us in our uniforms, were swirled inside those walls, inside St. Rose's walls where all a we, they said, were working hard to be the people's students. All but one were working hard. And it was sometime after that, as well, that I began to think of us as two and all the other girls as seven hundred. We were two. Two white girls then.

Two blondes in matching shirts that day at Timehri International when Trudeau was about to land. Sure, some were Canadians just for a day, but that was fine, just fine for me. The plane had taxied to a stop, and all the soldiers in their fancy uniforms were perfectly lined up. Red stripes in perfect rows. The metal steps came rolling out, and soon enough Trudeau was waving at us. We screamed and waved our flags and stretched to try to grab his hand. He came right up to Annette, right to the barricade where she was standing next to me. People pushed behind and squished me up against the metal barrier, reached overtop my head to touch Trudeau. Cameramen and diplomats and Burnham were all looking sombre and solid, but Trudeau grinned. He grinned at us and reached across and shook my best friend's hand.

# 10

# WATER

Water took us to Guyana. It took us from our home and brought us to that place. Looking down and out the airplane window, I remembered that. We were flying inland, flying in a little plane that skimmed the jungle tops, the canopy, my father said. I guess he knew it well because he skimmed it in that same plane most every day. He knew the pilot and called him by his first name, George. George let my brother take the controls for a while. It was safe, that day the sky was unruffled and clear. But on another day when we flew home with George in monsoon season, a hurricane came up. The sky was thickly grey, and winds shoved the little plane up and down and side to side. I threw up into my hat. That was the only time I was sick from being in a plane. My sister was sick as well. The rain was like a solid wall. George couldn't see ahead to where the airport was. He dropped the plane as close to ground as it was safe to do, and there, just there below us, palm trees bent, branches waving crazily, along the ground beneath the wind. Then I was scared. Everywhere were cane fields; we were close to Georgetown though we couldn't see its buildings, but the fields were thick and cut apart punt-filled canals. No place to safely land. We skimmed the palm treetops until George found a landing strip that he could put the plane down on.

But, that day, when we were flying inland and when Stephen flew the plane, the sky was high and crystalline and all the way serene. I was looking out the window, looking down and wondering what I couldn't see through the canopy below. I saw the shadow of our plane, stretched, compressed, and bent; it flitted below us like a piece of silk dragged over humps of green. I looked closely, looked for faces, our faces at the windows of the plane, but, of course, I couldn't see them. Just silhouette, an even-coloured grey. The jungle canopy was green, every green there was or ever will be on earth. And there were silver flashes too. Silver, that was the water, flowing through the jungle. From there I could see that the land was shot with rivers. Water coursing over, coursing through. I could see why Guyana was called the Land of Many Waters. That is what the word *Guyana* means in the language of the Arawaks. A watery land named by the Amerindians—one nation of the six—when they first met the Europeans searching there for gold.

Mists rolled in and rains fell down. Rivers flowed long and wide, and falls fell there like nowhere else. Some cascaded from such great heights the air around them rumbled up to heaven and palm branches flew like little twigs. Other waters hugged the land and jangle-jittered

low for miles and miles, running over steps of rock.
Water there was sweet and salt, and black and amber too.
Sometimes clear and other times clouded.

Twice yearly monsoon seasons stormed the coast,
filling Georgetown's ditches to their brims, but all those
houses standing high on stilts were fine, and all who lived
in them were fine as well. Inside they were dry. Rain fell
too thick to see across the road, and all you could do was
laugh with the exuberance of water, turn your face up and
count the seconds till de rain mek yuh whole skin soak.
You might be tempted to join the children on Camp
Street, splashing in water that was suddenly knee-deep.

Water of life, water of death. All that wet made the
country leak and burst, and green grew faster there than
anywhere. Sticks that lay stacked on barren ground rose
from the dead if driven into soil; dry brown Lazarus come
to life, they sprouted leaves and flowers, and, in time,
brought forth fruit. Our gardener built a fence of sticks,
and not much later, we watched, amazed, to see the fence
was living, saw it come alive. Lush paradise was born
overnight from naked ground, and there was food for all.
It was magic.

But if the heaviest rains met the highest tides,
Georgetown's streets were stinking rivers, and then you
membah dat cat ketch a rat, and that's why you keep him
around. Cats are also thieves, and the proverb ends with
"he tief he massa's fish." Good and evil came together,
and then the muddy waters floated the bloated carcasses
of goats and cows. Wild dogs feasted. Crops rotted. The

man in his high-stilted house was stuck up there. He must catch a boat or wait for all that water to recede, and that, sometimes, took time and he waited long, and while he waited things bred. Cholera and yellow fever, filaria that made a market women's legs swell thick like bolsters, puffed up and rolled over the tops of her brown Bata sandals until I wondered why the skin stayed whole and why it didn't split. Dengue fever, also called break-bone, bone-crusher for the pain. And, of course, that water brought malaria too, and also leishmaniasis, a fly's bite that made flesh dissolve in spots, yawn inches wide, and ooze. Your spleen might grow so big it could outweigh your liver.

Water of life. Inland, that water jammed up the land with every kind of life. Even the Rupununi savannah had its watery moments when flat grasslands turned, for a while, to vast deceptive lakes. Jungles dripped dense, rain fell down and then steamed up, rivers flowed as wide as seas, and little golden frogs lived out their lives in puddles caught between the bromeliad's leaves. We walked a footpath through the jungle. We were on a flat-topped mountain, on the edge where Kaieteur Falls falls down down down. Around us air was filled with tiny water droplets, water shattered into little bits from falling so far down. Kaieteur is 741 feet straight down without a bump or stumble, then another 81 feet tumbling to total the heights of five Niagara Falls. It stuns you with its power. We were standing on the edge, the lip of Kaieteur Falls. My mother clapped her hand onto her head to keep her floppy hat from flying free. My brother inched up to the precipice, put his toes closer to that straight drop than the rest of us. I went as close as my heart dared and felt the wind push my body back. We saw ten-foot-long palm branches fly past us, fly up and overhead. My father said that that was air displacement. Branches blown by air pushed up by water falling down. I wondered if that air could fly a body, fly a person, fly me up and overtop the jungle all around. Spread arms and lean out over misty air.

Guyana's many waters are filled with many-toothed creatures. Silver-disc piranha flash and caiman crocodiles lurk in mud, even the dwarf one there is five feet long with scaly ridged eyes all liquid-brown and hidden. In Guyana's waters lives a fish called arapaima that grows bigger than any other in the world. That fish can measure fifteen feet from end to end and weigh four hundred pounds. That fish breathes air and catches birds to eat. It is an ancient monster fish from fairy tales, and yet it swims those waters.

These were things I'd learned from textbooks at St. Rose's and from stories that my father told on days when he was home.

Water brought us there, and I looked down and out the airplane window thinking of that fact and wondering. Our plane was following the silvery trail of rivers. That was how the pilot navigated. There were no flight paths or instruments on board that plane to show the pilot where to go. Just rivers, flashing through the jungle, showing us the way. My father said he was there to chart those waters, map the rivers, test them for their power. That was why he spent so much time inland, camping at the base of waterfalls and walking through the jungle, where the jungle is a solid wall and every step by step by step is cut with sharp machetes arcing overhead. He told us stories that he heard and things he saw. Watch out, he said, when walking through the jungle, for the two-step snake. A snake whose bite is filled with poison, strong enough to drop you to the ground before your foot can take its second step. Another snake is called the third-man snake. This one kills you if you're walking third in line along a jungle path. Why? Ah, he said, the snake is startled by the first, takes aim to strike the second, hits the third. "One time," my father told us, "when we were marching through the jungle all along a great wide river flowing there beside the path, we stopped to rest. One man sat on a log, or what he thought was a big thick fallen log." Thought it was until the log beneath him moved, lifted up its head, its forked tongue testing air to taste and smell what sort of creature sat upon it. Green Anaconda. A snake that big, so big that it might be a fallen log.

At first I thought those stories that my father told us over dinner when he was back from days away, at first I thought he'd made them up. Stories like the ones he told when we were camping in B.C. Those were full of creatures he'd made up—Ratchet Owls and Side-Hill Gougers— invented to explain the way the landscape looked. "Did you see the ridges in the dry dry hills we drove through earlier today?" he'd ask. Hills near Kamloops shallow terraced, rings around the sides. Those, he'd say, are made by Side-Hill Gougers, always born with legs on one side shorter than the other. They can only walk in circles, round and round, because their uneven legs make walking straight impossible. Some are born to only walk clockwise and others only counter-clockwise. They spend their lives gouging rings around the hillsides they are born on. Ratchet Owls are their natural prey, but the Gougers have a way to kill the owls. The Gougers kill the Ratchet Owls by running fast around and around the hill, again and again and again. If they run fast enough before the owl swoops, the Gougers cause the Owl's head to twist right off.

I thought, at first, my father's jungle creature stories were just like his camping tales; but no, the creatures in Guyana are mythic, but they are also very real. Guyana's Green Anacondas are so big that they might be mistaken for a log. They are sometimes thirty feet from tip to tip. Their skin is jungle-camouflaged, olive-green with darker patches. I saw one, just its skin, stretched out around four walls in the Georgetown museum.

My father told us other stories too. We heard about pork knockers, men in search of gold, who sifted the silt of Guyana's jungle rivers, swirling amber water for its glint, for its glint of diamonds or of gold. My father liked those men. Pork knockers were a bit like him, because he'd panned for gold himself when he was younger, a new engineer and working the mountains of B.C.

Rough pork knockers were not the only ones to search for gold in Guyana's jungle rivers. No. Gold has been a thread that's pulled for years and years, drew ships across the widest seas, dragged them up Guyana's rivers deep into the jungle. Sir Walter Raleigh was one. He went there, went to Guyana seeking gold, hunting high and low. He travelled up the Essequibo River far inland, following rumours of the gold he never found. The Spanish and the Dutch went there for gold as well. El Dorado. Someone said it was out there, in the middle of a lake, an island with a city made of gold. El Dorado was that city's ruler. He was covered all in gold. But it's not there. There was no island and no lake where they all thought there was. That lake, it was a flooding. Flood waters flowed thickly over Rupununi flatlands, covering the flat flat land but only for a while, and then receded, vanished, returned to riverbanks. Gold brought a lot of people to Guyana, but they all left without the gold they sought.

Yet it was there. Look harder and you'll find it. It doesn't gild a man, and it's not shaped into a city's walls. Guyana isn't where you'd find rich veins of gold, but it is lying bit by bit by tiny bit among the muck, beneath the water, in the rivers and the creeks. Ask any pork knocker bent over pans or running gritty water through a sluice. They knew the gold was there. Ask me. I wore it on my finger, a ring of jagged nuggets, red Guyana gold, laced together for my finger. A Christmas gift. I wore it while we were flying over jungles. I felt it on my finger while I looked out and wondered what else was hidden in the green below.

Plenty secrets. Plenty secrets hidden there beneath that canopy.

People asking, "Why yuh daddy fly so much?" and "Where he go to all da time he gone?" I said he flew to every corner of the country, criss-crossing over all that land. He flew to every river and to every waterfall. He camped in places that the Venezuelans said were part of Venezuela but the Guyanese staked claim. He followed rivers that the Dutch thought they still owned, that they claimed were part of Surinam. He flew and flew while looking for the thing that water carried, not for gold or diamonds though, for power. Water carries power and that, for the new Guyana, was as good as gold.

How's that? some wondered. It was explained inside my school textbook where Wilma Williams wrote, on page 38: "At present the Government is finding out how much electric power Guyana can make." Electric power made from water, flowing, falling, tumbling water. Enough electricity to burn Guyana's bauxite down to something valuable, down to aluminum.

*Cum nah, she say, who gwan pay fuh dat? Surely surely big job like dat tek plenty plenty dandra, plenty money.* Who would pay for that? Not Canada, oh no, fuh sure not Canada. Oh Canada, it just lost the ownership of its great bauxite mines deep in Guyana's interior. Ha! Those mines, well Canada had owned those bauxite mines since 1929, then, poof, Comrade Burnham took them away. Took them and other things that then all Guyanese shared equally. Remember, Guyana was a "co-operative," and all things were share and share alike. Yes, I remembered. I remembered Dad explaining why that sort of talk just didn't work. I remembered Farida saying she wouldn't be sharing the new Guyana's future, she wasn't going to be a people's student. I remembered Tiger Bay. The people there were poor, poor, poor. They weren't benefiting from Burnham's taking of the things, like bauxite mines and sugar fields, that others had once owned. But I remembered, too, June saying that it would take time. I remembered that, and I remembered how when working all together like a team, Merici House did better than the other houses at St. Rose's.

The questions were still asked and rumours spread. Was that why there was a quiet listener on the phone?

That land, that jungle that we flew over, that thick thick green down there was not for walking through. It was not for trucks. It had no roads. No trucks with pipes and generators, those could not pass through what I was seeing through the window as we flew overhead. I began to wonder. My father had told us about the man he met who was walking through the jungle, step by step by step he cut his way. He had a sack of Brazil nuts, maybe they were slung over his shoulder like a burlap Santa sack. And there they were, a great big burlap sack of them, one day when I came home from school. The sack was full and leaning up against our kitchen wall. Daphne, our maid, said she don know just what she gwan do wid all dem nuts. They weren't even ripe. We had to wait to taste them, or we'd all get sick from eating unripe nuts. You told us you'd met a man walking in the jungle, just walking there with a Bible and a bag of nuts. He was a missionary. That's why he was out there in the jungle. But, why were you?

They say the look ah duh puddin is not duh taste. I'd heard that before. Farida told me that. She said that when we were talking about Comrade Burnham and his talk talk talk of all a we be one big family. They said only spies and journalists came to Timehri International. They said the place was crawlin thick with CIA and British spymen, Royal Green Jackets too. No innocence was passing through that airport. But, aren't we innocent? Nobody is. True-true, nobody really is.

Green Jackets or Berets I didn't know which, but I did know that while I was at St. Rose's studying with my friends to be The People's Hope, my brother, Stephen, was seeing foreign soldiers shooting guns and marching pretty in a perfect line. He was only sixteen, and things like soldiers and racing cars were what he liked. Tennis too, all day. Riding around Georgetown on his bicycle, he once had to dodge a man, or maybe just a boy, who tried to dump him off his bike, tried to jam a big thick stick into the spokes. One day he and his friend Dennis found a snake. They were out in some cane field just on the edge of Georgetown, and they found a snake living there and catching rats. They caught that snake, put it in a sack so they could take it back to Bel Air Park where Dennis lived. But the gardener at his house chopped the snake's head off. One quick machete chop. He skinned it too, and then he tossed the body in the canal, left it floating in the water there, half-sunk and puffy white. Stephen said he watched a man come walking down the road and saw that man jump and shriek when he saw that skinless snake floating in the canal water like a dead man's leg. Things like that did happen. We read about them almost every day in the newspapers.

Anything could happen. My mother learned that soon enough, the first New Year's Eve that we were there. Stephen, who was then sixteen, went off to party with the American Marines. Midnight came and midnight went. It got late and later, but Stephen was not home. Dad decided he'd go out to find the Marine party and bring my brother home. More time passed and Mom was sitting home alone in the Georgetown velvet dark all night. Anything could happen, maybe it already had, but, she realized, she had no way to know. This was very different from what she'd thought a foreign job would be. This was something else, this fear and waiting in the dark. They did come back, my brother and my father, rumbling home at dawn and full of New Year's commissary beer, but Mom had changed a little bit that night. She knew that she was living in a place where things can happen, anything and anytime.

Stephen had another friend, an expat friend, whose father was a different kind of soldier. He was British, there to train the Guyanese to shoot and march and fight. Stephen and his friend would watch. Green berets and jackets. Inside my head a little voice su-sued. It asked again, "What else is hidden in Guyana's jungle?"

BELOW ME, through the airplane window I saw colours flash. Our plane had startled birds. We skimmed so low the parrots hiding in the trees were shaken out. Macaws burst from greenness humped below the shadows of our wings. I saw long feathers, purple, blue, and yellow, trailing like banners following behind them. "See me. Here I am." George, the pilot, told us that he sometimes picked up cockatoos and macaws in the jungle, caught by Amerindians, and flew them to the coast for export overseas. Guyana's jungle birds perched in pet shop cages all around the world.

We were flying to the southern corner of Guyana, going to the Rupununi for a holiday. The Rupununi was remote. None of my friends had ever seen its wide expanse. Sister Hazel did not want to let me go. My mother had to meet with her to ask if she would let me miss my classes at St. Rose's for two weeks. Sister Hazel said no. She said I couldn't be away that long because I should be studying. Studying for tests, exams I'd never take, but Sister Hazel didn't know that then. My mother told her we would go, that I'd be taken out of school, regardless of the tests that I might have to take—O Levels, that's what they were called—sometime later, next year in Form 3. We were not supposed to let our teachers, or anybody else, know that we were planning to fly home to Canada, that we weren't going to stay forever in Georgetown, in Guyana. We were not supposed to say that we were leaving soon.

Flying inland over jungles, over mountains, over rivers, there was much to learn. That's what my mother said to Sister Hazel. I saw things I never could have seen if I'd stayed home. If I had stayed in Georgetown and studied hard for tests, I wouldn't have seen sheer cliffs, escarpments rising straight up from the red-brown river's edge. Our plane swooped in for a closer look, and sideways then, I saw caves, pockmarks in the cliff, and some spewed water, shot it out as if a giant faucet somewhere hidden in the rocks behind was turned on full blast. I saw jungle pelt made patchy, eaten like a mangy coat. Those were clearings cut by men who were stealing logs, harvesting them illegally. The pilot pointed them out, and in my mind they matched photographs my father took when he was flying there a few weeks back. In those photographs I saw a small open space with tangled vines for walls. The ground was red. Logs were built up into a frame, and on that frame a man was standing with a great long saw embedded in a thick log. Beneath him, underneath the frame and on the ground, another stood and held the other end of that long saw. They looked like old-time loggers from B.C., splitting wood and sawing it to planks by hand. Those photographs my father took were not taken from a plane. He was there, right there, and standing on the wet red ground inside the wall of vines and listening and smelling, watching as they cut that log.

A moment later as we flew, thinly separated from the clearing we'd just circled in our plane, was another open piece of land, this one crissed and crossed by paths, grass worn flat or gone completely by the footfalls of the Amerindians who lived in the round houses made from silvered palm. We saw no people from our plane. Were they there? They must have heard us, if they were. Or were they hiding, were they hunting, were they cutting logs?

Far south we came to where the Rupununi spread its grassy flatness, and we landed, bump bump along the ground. The Rupununi reached far, spread yellow wide between the Takutu River and the Kanuku Mountains. Flat flat flat. Savannah. The air was full of grassy smells and grassy sounds, and the sky was very high. We landed at Manari Ranch, where vaqueros rode their horses to drive cattle on the savannah. That word, *savannah*, sounded unlike a word a Guyanese would say. It is smooth, too smooth for Guyanese. And yet it is a word that came from there, a word invented by the Guyanese, one of the six, the Arawak. The Amerindians gave us that word, passed on through Spanish conquerors and twisted as it went from zabana at its start to savannah at this end. I said it while standing out on the open treeless plain ridged in the distance by a set of mountains, faint wash of grey against the bright blue sky. Guyana. Savannah. Water and grass. So flat that when those waters fell, the place became a lake, and that was where Sir Walter Raleigh's men thought golden cities were. The very place they never could have been.

Manari Ranch was so big it could have been a country of its own. You would have to ride and ride and ride some more before you found its edges. Inside those edges it had lemon trees and lots of grass, men in leather chaps and leather hats, and parrots kept in cages. There was a spider monkey hiding in the rafters of the kitchen house. Long-armed and bushy black, it had small black eyes, a solid colour without irises that I could see, and it stared down at us and yawned. The kitchen house was separated from the building where we slept and where we ate. Between there was a garden and an orchard. In Manari's orchard we found lemons big as grapefruits and as sweet. We ate them plucked straight from the trees, biting into lemons, eating peel and pith and all, and they were sweet, no bitterness.

At Manari we rode out on horses with the vaqueros. My brother, Stephen, Chris, and I. We were not past the paddock gate, not yet out and wandering the plain, when Chris's horse turned sharp and bolted back toward the barn. It ran full speed, stretching out its legs and neck and back, flattened like an ironing board, toward the barn. Its tail was straight and streaming like the feathers of a terrified macaw. Chris, flat out as well, clung, a scared and skinny ten-year-old. A cloud of dust. They were in the barn and Chris had slid, limp, to the ground before we'd got our horses, cantering the distance, to the barn. She stumbled back to Manari's ranch house, wouldn't ride again with us, so it was only Stephen and me who took the horses up a dried creek bed to where we saw a giant termite's nest. It was six feet tall. We rode until we were sunburnt and tired, but the faded mountains on the Rupununi edge never grew closer.

One evening my father said we were going for a drive, going to see Brazil, he said. It was cold, the temperature just twenty-three degrees Celsius, a drop from coastal twenty-six. When we saw that and felt the cold, we knew that we had been in Georgetown long enough to be a little Guyanese. We drove out in a Land Rover along two ruts worn into the earth, red stripes between the dry gold grass. The sky was lapis blue then orange then black. The sun set like a match dropped into water. Fumph, it now is dark.

Our track ended just as suddenly at a river's edge. My father said it was the Takutu River, and there, where we were standing, the dusky sandy bank was called Guyana, and the other bank, across the sluggish water, was Brazil. Dry season made the river crossing easy. Water to our calves. The only thing that I could see to mark that we had crossed a border were the pans of disinfectant. There are no border guards or customs agents, no passport checking and no stamps. Just trays of liquid disinfectant in a shed that was by the river's edge. Our driver from the ranch stepped in the pans then out. So did we, because when in a place that's strange, it's best to copy what the others do. My father said the pans of disinfectant were there to protect the cattle. Those were cattle lands on both sides of the river. Shoes that walked across from one land to another, from Guyana to Brazil, might spread infection. I wondered how many walkers went that way, how many pans of disinfectant were in sheds along the riverbank, and what if cattle, driven by vaqueros, walked across the river?

My father walked in front beside the driver, and we strung out behind like ducks. It was very dark, and in Brazil, right there, there was nothing much to see, no lights, no streets, no town. One narrow width of dirt—a road—three or four bleach-boarded buildings, just like we were on a cowboy movie set. Wood-plank sidewalks and a lot of mud. There were people, mostly men, small and watching us. We were the strangest things walking down that road that night. Strange at any time of day. My father strode along ahead. He didn't act as though there was anything strange about us there in that place on that night. My brother's leather cowboy hat smelled of new tanned leather. It was stiff. Made by Rupununi Amerindians. Even it was strange. The men who watched us all wore cowboy hats, but theirs were mostly made of straw, sweat-stained and dark and tattered.

We went into a shop and found flour, sugar, bullets, alcohol, and oil. I wanted to buy something. Once I'd decided that, then finding anything to buy was all I wanted to do. There wasn't much, but then I found a T-shirt. That would do. It had something written on it in a language I didn't recognize. The script was ornate, the letters curled and curved in gold on bright turquoise blue. I decided that it was from a perfume ad. Maybe cologne or aftershave. Cowboy aftershave. Do vaqueros wear that sort of thing? My brother laughed at me, and that made the men nearby grin white teeth. I looked at Stephen and I thought, "Sure, laugh, but you're the one that's got the leather cowboy hat."

We walked up, then down that strip of road in unilluminated darkness except where a spill of pale and foggy light leaked from a window, maybe from a shop or from a bar. A saloon? Above us, a band of sky, only as wide as the road at our feet, showed so many stars there seemed no space between. We walked back to the river, through the pans of disinfectant, through the shallow river to Guyana on the other side. "Now," my father said, as we bumped back through pitch-black night to Manari Ranch, "you've seen something special. You've been to Brazil, a Brazil that's rarely seen."

"Rarely seen," I thought, was what had brought us there as much, or more, than water had. The Land Rover's headlights revealed the Rupununi in bright discs, fuzzy at the edges, ahead of us. The darkness was so solid beyond those yellow-coloured spots. I remembered arriving in Guyana, standing at the airport listening to my father tell the Guyana customs agent why we'd landed there that night. I still couldn't remember what Dad had told that man, but he could have said that we were there to seek for what was strange. He could have answered that he and Mom had brought their family to Guyana to show us the "rarely seen," the power of a waterfall deep in the jungle, the gift of golden frogs and friends whose lives were carved by things we'd otherwise have never known.

# 11

## LOVE: JUNE

June is standing in her yellow uniform. She's wearing a pastel-yellow, box-pleated skirt, white socks, and shiny shoes, and all is clean and crisp. There are no wrinkles in her cotton tunic. She's standing by the baby grand piano in her family home, there, amid the shadows of the corner of the room. Her legs are so dark, they blend into the background, but white ankle socks mark where her long legs end. All that, contained within a square of plastic, bordered white and small enough to tuck inside a pocket.

Maybe that photograph was taken after school. Maybe June's just finished practising piano. She looks as though she might be just about to bow. Or maybe she was photographed in the morning, before she rushed off to catch the bus that would get her to St. Rose's before the door-guard nuns closed the big doors. Her hands are clasped in front, her back is straight, her feet together, chin up. She is standing just the way a good St. Rose's girl should stand. June is smiling big and bright, and looking straight into the camera lens. Beneath her feet, on the band of white that rims the Polaroid, she wrote, "Love: June."

I was holding June's photograph and standing at a window looking out, and I was alone. I was in a hotel room. I had told my mother and my father that I was sick, and so they'd gone off to sightsee with my sister and my brother and left me there. I was alone in a hotel in a city called Cayenne, in French Guiana. There was another country, Surinam, between where I was then and where my friends, June and all my friends, were. I was in Cayenne because we were going home. I didn't know exactly where home was that day.

We had left Georgetown the week before. Georgetown felt like home, Georgetown and our house on Kaieteur Road where we'd moved to after Almond Street and after moving from the Pegasus Hotel. The house on Kaieteur Road was home for almost all the time we lived in Georgetown. Almost two years is not so long sometimes, but it was long enough for me to think of Georgetown as my home.

Was Daphne in the kitchen making puddings, making peanut punch to drink right then? Or was she sitting on the back steps gossiping with the drinks man who came each week, his bicycle weighed down and tinkling as he pedalled up the street with racks of bottles, fizzy drinks like Ting and Red Spot soda, loaded in his carrier? Where was Victoreen, who chased the floor polisher because she always turned it off by pulling out the plug—just yanked it from the wall— so when it was next plugged in, that polisher would dash across the hardwood floor of purpleheart with bouncy Victoreen full speed behind? That was home. I went home to Kaieteur Road each day after school. I walked through the high wide gate and underneath the passion vine and past the eight-foot walls of thick hibiscus hedge and up the concrete stairs all polished down to aggregate and speckled, and up to where the outside room, a kind of balcony, hung overtop of all, almost close enough to pick the flame tree flowers spreading flat and crimson at the top. Boys climbed that tree right to its top to pick the pods of seeds, foot long, curved, and flat. They called them shack-shacks and shook them to make music. That was home. That was where bananas and papaya grew, and where the guard dog, Duffy, and the guard man, who was also a good gardener, were both afraid of nothing except men, particularly thieves. But that never happened. Nobody ever tried to tief from we, except for once when Stephen was out with his girlfriend, Barbara, and a man ran past them and tore the necklace right off Barbara's neck. That's why they call them "snatch-and-grab tiefman" in all the Georgetown papers. Stephen chased that snatch-grab thief, and when he caught up with him, the thief turned fast and stuck my brother with a little knife. It was a small knife, and the tiefman didn't stab my brother hard, just a little prick, not hard enough to make him bleed. Not hard enough to make him have to tell our parents when he came home that night.

That was home, it became home. That's where my bedroom was and where I had a desk to study at and where there was a ceiling fan that stirred the air, except that after a few months, I hadn't needed that fan because my blood had thinned—that's what they say when you become acclimatized—it had thinned so that the high Guyana heat did not seem hot. Thinned enough that when the rainy season came and temperatures dropped even two degrees, I had to wear a sweater, sometimes a hat, to keep me warm.

I sat at the airplane window when we taxied down the Timehri airport runway. I watched the sugar cane in fields blurred from stalks bending in the wind, blurred into a wash of living green. The green of Guyana, a green I knew. A field of cane, blurred by a speeding plane, blurred by tears.

My mother and my father sat in seats across the aisle, and Stephen was alone in one behind; my sister, Chris, was right beside me. On board were lots of women who were wearing golden earrings, great big hoops that stretched their lobes. Solid gold is heavy. They wore rings on every finger, sometimes three or even four, and necklaces and bracelets. Bangles clanged from wrist to almost elbow when they walked past us to the bathroom, and after that, when they came down the aisle to take their seats once more, they padded silent and without that golden syncopation. All that gold was put away, tucked inside a purse or bag. They carried out their wealth. They were leaving home as well and carrying out what they would need to start again, to start a new home somewhere else.

My mother carried gold as well. Inside her skirt, sewn in the hem, a beaten disc of rough red gold wrapped in tissue paper. And tucked into her bra, a secret pouch of tiny diamonds, rough and uncut, just as the pork knocker had found them when he saw them sparking light in mud. These were things my father brought from trips into the jungle, bought from pork knockers right by the very river where they'd found them in the gravel. Spotted there by sharp sharp eyes. Panned out. My father said these things were not worth much. They were not valuable. Rough diamonds look like chunks of sand, grey and uninspiring, dirty quartz. But gold is gold, though flaky in the packet that my mother stashed. She hid them because my father said it was illegal to take these things out of Guyana. Guyana's wealth must stay inside Guyana, even when the wealth that's stitched into a hem is just a little wealth.

That plane carried secrets, lots and lots of secrets. Hush hush. My father told us all to hold our silence, let him do the talking at the airport, stand behind him quietly. We did. We stood silently while others, not foreigners, not white, were led off to a little room. My mother said that they were being searched. She whispered warningly that those people were being strip-searched in that room, searched for foreign currency, perhaps for hidden diamonds or for gold. I didn't know about my mother's diamonds, didn't know about the disc of gold, but even so I worried. I watched my father hand the customs agent our bundled passports. Déjà vu. His broad back was there again, casting shadows on me where I stood behind. The customs agent smiled. "Where are you and your family going today, Mr. Plunkett?" My father tells him we are flying off to Surinam. That's true. We are. But then he says that we are going for a holiday and that we will be coming back to Georgetown. Back to school, back to Kaieteur Road. I rolled my eyes. How could those airport men not know the truth? Why would they believe this story when our furniture and all our books and all our Christmas decorations, even those, had all been crated, packed, and sent away from Kaieteur Road? Our house was emptied, and those trunks and crates and suitcases and boxes, all were stamped in letters inches high: VANCOUVER. No more phone calls being made for quiet listeners to hear. Even that's gone silent. We weren't coming back. The truth was that we were leaving Georgetown and flying back to Canada and never coming back.

I had a secret too. My secret was that I wasn't able to obey. I didn't hush as I was told to do. I kept my silence at the airport, yes, but just that time. I didn't say a single word when we were there. But, I told others we were leaving and that my parents planned to stay away and never to return to Georgetown. I had talked about it with my friends. And that's why, hidden in my suitcase on that plane, all folded up and tucked away, I'd stashed my pastel-blue school uniform. It's just like the one June's wearing in the photograph I hold, except mine's blue. It was my favourite. And on it, my St. Rose's friends had signed their names in brown and green and orange felt pens. I brought it to my last day at school, and everybody wrote on it, criss-crossed and scribbled over all of it. Some just wrote their names and some wrote messages. "Bon

voyage," and "Adios," and "Sock it to me." June signed
my uniform more times than any other friend. She wrote
her name on it six times with different pens in different
colours. Some places she just signed her name, and in
other places, underneath the collar, on the back, or near
the hem, she wrote a message. She wrote, "Stickle like
pickle!" and in another place, "Lot 4 Friendship, Seafront,
E.C.D., Guyana." That's her address. She wrote it there so
that I'd write to her, so that I'd know where to send my
letters. She was hoping that we'd write, send letters back
and forth, and maybe even see each other someday, once
again, somewhere somewhere, I don't know where.

My father said that we might be moving soon to Kabul,
in Afghanistan. He said we might live there for at least
four years. Kabul's nothing like Georgetown. Afghanistan
is nothing like Guyana. I know that because my father's
been there once, or maybe more, and he came home with
films he'd shot outside Kabul. Those films showed Afghan
horsemen riding in a dry and treeless landscape. Hills with
scrubby bushes. Waterless riverbeds of rocks. No water,
yet we might be moving there, and if we do, and if I write
to June, imagine where that letter will have flown. So far,
so far from somewhere to Georgetown, Lot 4 Friendship
by the sea.

But June was not the only one who wanted me
to write. That was another secret that I had, another
photograph as well. That secret's name was Jimmy Chong.
A boyfriend. Annette said he was. He'd taken me on dates.
Well, one. He took me on a date to see a movie at the

Astor Cinema. My parents knew that's where I was going, but they thought that I was meeting June and Farida or maybe Annette when they dropped me off outside the Astor's doors. But it was Jimmy Chong, wearing his dark glasses, who waited for me, and it was Jimmy Chong who sat beside me on leather-padded seats inside a box, up in front of the balcony and overlooking all the other seats, including, down below, the pit. Only boys were ever in the pit, where they sat on benches, wooden backless benches. I had heard that in the pit the boys would sometimes pee right where they sat, right on the concrete floor, and the one who peed would shout out, "Raise yuh foot!" I never heard that, though I heard fights and other rumblings from the pit seats when the film broke down. If that happened, or if the reels were mixed and they showed the ending of the film before the start, or if the film was playing upside down, then the people in the pit would riot. They would shout and stomp and throw their shave-ice at the screen. They got mad and threw Red Spot soda bottles, shattered glass and eggs and fruit, and I heard once they even threw the benches at the screen. Then the manager would have to turn the lights on high and come out on the stage and shout that no more film would show till everybody settled down. Then even people in the balcony would start to shout down at everybody in the pit. *Sit yuh down!*

When Jimmy took me to the Astor, we sat in a box, separated from the other seats by three high sides, panelled in dark wood and with a swing door like a box-stall gate. It had brass hinges and a shiny latch that clicked.

Inside the smells were leather from the seats that sighed
when we sat down and wood that someone wiped with
lemon-scented oil. The front was open from above our
waist, just high enough to rest our feet, but we would not
do that. We looked across a broad black void to where the
screen glowed through the dust. The air was darkened
for the show, but shafts of leaking light showed lazy dust
throughout and swooping bats. Oh yes, bats lived in the
Astor Cinema, high up in the ceiling, and when the lights
were off, the bats came out and swooped and swirled in
angled silhouette across the giant screen.

Jimmy opened up the box-stall gate for me and, with
a flourish of his arm, ushered me into the box. Inside he
took two oranges from his pocket, gave me one and peeled
the other. Lemon-oil and orange. Cigarettes from down
below us and from the balcony behind. Fried chilies, curry
sauce, and chickpeas cooked in oil. Jimmy leaned out over
the balcony, over the house seats where my friends and I
would often sit, and through the darkening air, he tossed
his orange peel into the pit. He said he did that because
his friends were there, and it's true, somebody turned and
looked up at us, and Jimmy waved and smiled.

Annette said Jimmy Chong was my boyfriend and
that I was lucky that he was. She called him hip and funky.
I thought she was right. He wore platform shoes and
paisley shirts. His hair was halfway to an Afro because
Jimmy's father was black. Jimmy always wore dark glasses,
aviator glasses tinted dark green. He's wearing them in the
photograph he gave me. He gave me it to take away when

we flew off from Timehri. And, just like June, he wrote in the narrow border of that photograph. He wrote "me" beneath his feet and "John" below his best friend John, who is sitting there beside him in that picture, and on the side he wrote "hi" and "me and John" and then, up in the corner at the very top he wrote, "love."

He's staring straight into the camera in that photograph, right at me. He and John are sitting on a set of concrete steps, a big glass door behind them and some potted plants along the side. I think they might be at the Pegasus Hotel, sitting on the steps out front. Who took that photograph?

Jimmy was a secret only Annette knew about. Oh sure, I'd had a boyfriend, once before, and he was not a secret. His name was Patrick and I took him on a date. I invited him to film night at the American consulate. The Americans are organized, my mother says. There are a lot of them and most are army, navy, air force. But all are likely with the CIA. That's what Annette says. The Americans held dances, games nights, and showed films. Once when we were going, I asked my mother if I could bring my friend Patrick along. She said yes and made a joke about the fact that my first boyfriend had my father's name: Patrick. But, she laughed, this one looks very different. Sure, sure he did. My father's skin was pasty white and freckled red, and he had copper-coloured hair. Patrick is black, just black. Hair and skin and eyes. I didn't think of Patrick as a boyfriend though. He was just a boy I took to a movie at the consulate. He was June's brother's friend, and when we went to see that movie at the consulate, I invited June as well. So that was not a date, and he was not a boyfriend.

Not like Jimmy was.

Love: June. Love Jimmy. The driveway I can see from the hotel room I'm standing in snakes and bends, slides down a hill and out of sight. Down that driveway, down that hill, and out of sight, my family is maybe sitting down to lunch. I know they're going to a restaurant my father read about. A place where strange animals are served, things like monkey stew and alligator, even ocelot, he's heard. I don't want to eat strange animals today. I want to be alone, unwatched, so I can run away. I want to run away, to run back home, to Georgetown where my friends are maybe walking arm in arm right now, walking down the Camp Street boulevard, or sitting in a classroom at St. Rose's taking lessons. Right now, I know that's where June is. She'll be in the dark-brown panelled library, up the wooden spiral stairs and overlooking Camp Street, where the market boys splash naked with the lily pads all up and down the Camp Street canal. Sister, Sister Pauline, my eyes hurt me so, we would say. My momma's not got my new prescription glasses yet. I have to stand right here beside the window where the light is best. I need the light to read this book of Plato's. Sister Pauline is the smallest and the whitest of the nuns, with skin like roses soaked in milk. She's from Ireland and so small that she can barely see above the windowsills up in that room. Even if she could, could see high enough to see outside the windows, her pale-blue eyes are so ancient that she can't see what we see when we stare out at Camp Street's boulevards. That's where June will be right now. Right now, a country and a half away from me.

Yesterday I thought I had a plan. I thought that I could sneak away, find a time when I was left alone, just like I am right now, and then I could sneak off on my own and make my way back home, to Georgetown. That's what I thought yesterday. But yesterday we took a taxi tour down to the waterfront outside of Cayenne city where the ruins of a prison crumbled on the shore. Across the water, chopping froth that day, the taxi driver pointed to an island humped and foggy in the distance. Devil's Island. The jungle and the sea, he told us, were the keepers of that jail. And yet one man, one famous man, escaped. He told us all about that man called Papillon. How grand he was, how brave, and how determined. We, all five of us, my entire family, stood on a parapet, a tall stone wall that bound the prison yard and overlooked the tangled jungle. Not even light passed through those vines. There—our guide was pointing down into impenetrable green below our feet— was where our hero Papillon passed by. He crossed the sea from Devil's Island to this shore—perhaps not quite right here, the taxi guide admitted—and dragged himself out of the water and hacked his way to freedom through all that. He pointed down again, "Imagine that!"

Imagination's not required. We saw the movie. Jimmy, Annette, John, and I saw it when it showed at the Starlite Drive-in Cinema out on the East Coast Road. Oh, but this is not a movie. No, this place is real. Its dome-roofed cells are made perfectly to echo, hollow, to reinforce your loneliness. Its thick-walled corridors have tiny cut-out windows showing just enough for you to think that maybe it is a paradise out there, out there beyond the wet stone walls and past the choking vines and through the rising heated mists that surely hold within their water droplets some tropical disease. Out there what you can see is sky and sea of perfect blue, and you smell the sea salt on the air. Out there across the water, even Devil's Island seems a dream.

I dreamt and even thought that I had planned an escape, planned to run away to where I thought of as home. But the jungle is there and I know its sounds and smells. I know that it is darker, thicker, wetter, noisier than I had dreamt. It is much more dangerous. The jungle here is real. The country in between this place and Guyana, that place where June is working right now, sneaking peaks at naked market boys, the distance between us now is real. That's no imagined space that a mind, a thought, or an imagination can float over, can traverse.

I am admitting this right now, right here where I am standing at the window of our hotel room in Cayenne, French Guiana. Looking out and down the curve-away driveway, down the hill, I know there is a distance between me and Jimmy Chong and June that can't be crossed. I won't run away. I am not a Papillon. I am not a hero.

PART TWO

*Indonesia*

# 12

## ABLUTIONS

At the Hotel Borobudur in Jakarta, my sister's hair, blond and baby fine, turned green. It glowed. And on August 1, 1976, at night, I stole a Dunhill lighter, made of gold, and an open pack of Rothmans King Size cigarettes. I found them in the hotel lobby. They were there beside the chair I chose to sit on, underneath the crystal chandelier.

At the Hotel Borobudur pool in downtown Jakarta, Chris and I would float for hours on our backs. Biding time, spending it in water, purified and cleansed. Our long blond hair would trail beneath us waving languidly in that clean, clear water. It trailed like tentacles, like seaweed, like the waving arms of jellyfish. There was a lot of water in that pool. It was Olympic sized, and no one ever seemed to swim in it but us. A third of an acre of clean clear water just for us. We swam, and just as in Georgetown, we lay out on lounge chairs too, hour after hour, in the tropical sun. Satellites of boys, liveried this time, dressed up in fancy uniforms with little pillbox hats, circulated, arms stacked high with white towels, trays, and notepads to take our orders. A room number and a signature would bring us anything: tonic water, peanuts, sandwiches made specially for foreign tastes like ours, and even Bintang beer, though we were still too young for that. Chris was twelve and I was just fifteen, and we were not allowed to order beer. Besides, we didn't want Bintang, we wanted Ting or Red Spot soda, but those we couldn't get.

We missed the steelpan band that always played beside the pool in Georgetown at the Pegasus Hotel. We missed the Mighty Sparrow singing jump-up songs about Miss Mary trying to find a husband, or about his rum-shop days. But Indonesians don't drink Ting, and music here is made for meditation, not for swinging hips. Beside that pool the sounds came from the angklungs, bamboo tubes the players shook while sitting cross-legged on a little platform. They wore sarongs made of batiked cloth, elaborately wrapped and serious. That's not music meant to teach you how to dance. The music was thin and watery, sounding like it came from somewhere people can't inhabit or like wind chimes playing tunes, but tunes a Westerner can't catch. That's okay. We were here. We were no longer in Guyana, so we asked for Coca-Cola. Everybody all around the world drinks Coke. Even Indonesians.

Jakarta. Java. We were waiting, once again, to fly, this time to Timor. Timor is a small island, one of hundreds, my father told us, that make up this country. Indonesia has its water too, but here the water is the in-between, the ocean that surrounds the little bits of land that make this country. It's where my father had been living for some months while my mother and my sister and I packed up again. My brother stayed in Canada. He was to come for visits, to spend his summer holidays with us, time off from university where he'd be studying back in Canada. We waited in Java for permission from the Indonesian army for special stamps inside our passports that would allow us to take a plane to Timor. I wondered why we had to ask the army, why we needed their special stamps, and while I wondered, my sister's skinny arms grew brown, her hair turned green. It was the chlorine in the pool. The chemicals that made that water safe for us to soak in made my sister's hair turn softly subtle green, a green so quiet that it took two looks to see. Two looks, but it was green for sure, and in that Java light, it glowed. She turned brown and greenish-hued, but I stayed pale and my hair kept its wheatish whitish blond. Stretched out on water and on land I tried to darken, but my skin stayed white, as white as if I'd never felt a tropic sun.

Floating like a starfish, my arms and legs stretched and reaching wide, I wore dark sunglasses in the water, and my bathing suit was a bright bikini bought those months ago in Georgetown at the Pegasus Hotel. My mother didn't make me cut my hair short this time, though soon we would be living just as close to the equator as we had been in Georgetown. In Jakarta I thought about the past: Hong Kong, Vancouver, Cayenne in French Guiana, Surinam where we saw people whose skin was bluest black. A tour guide took us to a village where those people lived.

Exhibit A. They were, he said, direct descendants of the slaves the Dutch had kidnapped—he didn't use that word—and brought across the world to work in sugar fields. Look, look, he pointed at a fire where a cooking pot hung from a tripod frame. "See what they eat." Inside the pot was a little hairy hand, curled up with nails that shone. It was a monkey that they were cooking in a stew. We stepped forward, clustered in a group, just close enough to see, bent forward at the waist. "Eww," my sister said. "Yuck." But later, in Cayenne, Dad would take us to a restaurant to eat exotic animals: ocelot and snake and maybe even monkey. I didn't go with them that day to eat exotic animals. I stayed at the hotel and went for a walk, the last walk I took in any of the three Guianas, thinking of my friends a country and a half away. I walked along a path I found when I went out and took the hotel's bending snaking driveway. Followed it down out of sight to the bottom, where I found another brown dirt path as wide as my arms stretched out to the sides. It was edged by eight-foot thorny hedges standing tall, plants with small green leaves all sifted over with fine dust like talcum powder. Fine brown dust that choked the glossy green and coloured everything as I walked past. The colour of a young girl's arms, a young Guyanese girl's arms. I scuffed and dusted up the air. I deliberately scuffed the dust to see it rise behind me. Show where I have been. I stretched my arms and fingers out as far as I could stretch and stroked those dusted-over leaves on each side as I walked slowly slowly down that hidden path. Mimosa. As I brushed them, the leaves folded inward, prayer-like, bowing. A silent ripple all behind me as I walked. I walked, thinking my goodbye while mimosa closed its leaves and dipped.

In water in Jakarta now, I dragged my hands, fingers vibrating, through that clean clear water where I floated. My friends were in Guyana, and letters take a long time to go from far-off places like Georgetown to even farther places like Jakarta. And Timor was even farther away.

VANCOUVER WAS IN-BETWEEN. Nine months in-between. I was a high school student in Vancouver after we moved back from Guyana to a new neighbourhood, not the one where we had lived before Georgetown. At that school I didn't know anyone or anything. There were no nuns. No rush to get to school for 7:15 before the doors were closed. No pastel uniforms or shiny shoes. No Merici House. No song sung every morning, and no Sister Hazel slicing over all a we with her sharp eyes or asking why I slept again through my alarm clock.

But there were other things. There were boys, boys in the classrooms, boys in the hall, and boys at tables in the cafeteria. That was something different. There was also smoking cigarettes and drinking alcohol, a mix of everything, small splashes, found inside my father's liquor cabinet. A splash of whisky, a splash of sherry. Splashes mixed up inside a Mason jar and gulped down. Don't drink it for the taste. There was skiing on the mountain, where we lived halfway up. Skiing drunk at night and in the dark. Then there was smoking pot and smoking cocaine rolled in honey oil, that's hash oil, and it's amber brown and thick and sticky. Drop it on a cigarette and it ignites; puff enchanted smoke, suck that smoke in deep and hard. That will make a white girl, new girl, strange girl from a far-off place, and has-no-friends girl dance and dance and dance all night; or if she's skiing, she'll be the first one down the unmarked trail, the fastest to the bottom.

And in that in-between time, white was what there was and nothing else. There were no brown or black or olive skins at that new school. No Faridas, and the Junes in that white school were not like any June that I had known. In that white school they all were Debbies. I tried to teach those Debbies, all my in-between friends, how to walk the way Guyana girls walked, the way my Georgetown friends had taught me. I tried to teach them how to walk a little bit less white. *Like this*, I showed them, walking down the crowded high school corridor lined with metal lockers and high school students doing nothing in between their classes. Like this, I showed them, lit up sharply by the bright fluorescent tubes above. You roll your hips. You bend your knees. You hold your torso leaning back a little bit. Loosen up your joints. Like this, I said, you make your ass do a figure eight. That's how to walk. That's how I was taught to walk by my Guyana friends, but—and I don't tell the Debbies this—I never got it right, and it would always make Farida laugh so hard she'd be bending over, hanging down her head, and gulping air to catch her breath. But that was fine and we all laughed together.

The Debbies were not interested in how to walk like a

Guyanese or anything about the things I thought I knew. Guyana? What's that? Nobody's heard of that. Nobody's seen black water flowing past a caiman sunning on a log. The Mighty Sparrow? Is that a joke? The Debbies sang to Captain and Tennille. That Christmas my big gift was a white plastic record player that folded up into a case that I could carry with me. I bought the Rolling Stones' *It's Only Rock 'n' Roll* and sang, "Ain't Too Proud to Beg."

St. Rose's taught me how to study. That was something that I learned from Sister Hazel and the other nuns and from my friends like June. I could study. I knew how to figure out what needed to be learned and could learn it fast. During in-between time, I didn't go to class that much but I kept my grades up. My teachers did not like that. Sometimes I would come to class a little drunk, and sometimes I'd do other things that Sister Hazel surely would have caned me for. Things like swearing at the teachers. Telling them to fuck their stupid lessons, who gives a shit about the periodic table or a poem written by a Scot? But I did not get caned. No. Nothing like that happened to me. Instead, my teachers phoned my mother, said my attitude was wrong and that I needed psychotherapy. That stressed her out. She was very mad at me. She had too much to do; she had to find a house to buy for us when we returned from Indonesia. Then Dad decided that they should buy my grandmother an apartment so she'd never have to move again. He told my mother that when she was kissing him goodbye. Right at the airport when he was flying off, again, to someplace else. She was upset. My father was always off in another place. He'd hardly spent a month in Canada, just home for Christmas, just home long enough to fly away again, back to Timor, back to Indonesia, or maybe someplace else. All I knew was that he wasn't there with us, and while he was gone, Mom and I fought "like Kilkenny cats." That's how Gradgy would have put it had she known about those fights. Sure, I passed grade nine—I knew I would even if my mother and my teacher thought I wouldn't. My grades were good. That made me laugh. My mother didn't like that. The principal told her that I wasn't welcome back in that high school.

That also made me laugh. Fuck that stupid school and all its Debbies too. We were leaving anyway. We were leaving Canada again and moving to a place called Timor. Timor? Where's that? Nobody seemed to know, nobody seemed to care. Timor: I tell my new friends that's where I'm moving to as soon as classes end.

Bye-bye, Debbies. Bye, Vancouver. Bye to Stephen too. He's finished his high school and now is starting university. He stays. We go.

WE GO OVER the Pacific Ocean. Below us as we flew were northern icefields. Sun radiated and blinded me when I stared out and craned my neck to see the land below. Was it land or was it ice? Hour after hour after hour of white. I saw no polar bears. I saw no whales. The planet arced, and we arced with it through the sky, chasing sunlight, landing in Hong Kong half a day later than we'd left and yet we landed in the sunlight of day. Catch my breath as that plane dropped down between apartment towers, flying between them straight toward the sea. It was there, just there, right there where tarmac ended. The wing tips seemed to almost scrape the crumbling concrete buildings ringing Hong Kong's airport. Cotton shirts and pants, laundry hung on poles from balconies, fluttered in the jet-stream breeze as we flew down to land. Hong Kong harbour rushed at us. Would we land in water? We might. We almost did, it seemed, but then we stopped on land. Dry land.

Dry land but air as wet as any tropic air I'd breathed. Air as wet as Georgetown, as Guyana. How, I wondered, can that laundry dry in air as wet as this? Standing on the tarmac, thick air pinned our clothes to our bodies. My father said the humidity was almost 100 percent, and as we walked out of the airport terminal, I felt water droplets bursting on my face, but it wasn't raining—the air was just that dense.

My father met us in Hong Kong. There he was, wearing a light-coloured linen suit and tinted aviator glasses. A tailor in Hong Kong makes his shirts and suits and sends them out to him around the world. I thought he looked exotic, crisp and mysterious with his red moustache and thick wavy hair. Not like he did before we lived in Georgetown, but there, in that new place, he looked just right. In Hong Kong, in the tropics, Dad wore light-coloured shirts and pants, but back in Canada his clothes were always dark. Suits of charcoal grey. Flannel shirts in hunter green and burgundy for fishing trips. Navy blue and brown. Suede and corduroy. But there, where the air was wet and dense, his colours were all shades of white and beige and honey-amber yellow. Shirts were finest cotton, suits were silk and linen. He looked just right.

I had missed my dad. I'd missed him, and because of that, I'd made trouble for my mother. I'd missed my father's smoky smell. I'd missed his smell of cigarettes and the scent of smoky whisky that he drank when he came home from work. I'd even missed his teasing and his jokes. He'd say, "Go out and do your poor best" when I was riding Xanthus—that was my horse—in shows. He'd say it and his face would wrinkle up with smiles, crow's feet my grandmother called them. He'd say this to my mother too, to all of us. I missed his sayings. He'd say a thing was "as common as dirt" or that we were going to live "in the back of the beyond." I'd missed that I could talk with him in ways I never could with Mom. With Dad, I'd have a chance of arguing a point without our voices rising to a shout. My mother said that that was just because I was his first-born girl. She said that I had wrapped him 'round my little finger. True-true, and I missed that.

In Hong Kong, the air was wet and dense, but there the similarities between that place, that Asia, and Guyana stopped. Guyana, on the coast and in the Rupununi, but not inside the jungle, felt expansive, open, full of held-back and in-reserve potential. It was bright and young despite the legacy left by the British and the Dutch, the markings of its past. There, even the old things felt somehow young.

In Hong Kong, that was not the case. Every bit of Hong Kong was in use: the air, the sky, the water, and the land. There was no place, no strip, or bit of land to graze a horse or fill with guppy-laden waters. There were no signs of Hong Kong's past, yet everything seemed newly old, old but not historic, old and worn. To me the entire place looked as if about to crumble or break down.

We landed on the Kowloon side and that was where we stayed. Our taxi took us past the Peninsula Hotel that my father said is famous. There were clean young men outside in uniform, standing straight and stiff in their red hats and gloves of pristine white. They stood, and never sweated despite that blanket heat, rigid and unsmiling beside the doors that they swept wide, in unison, for anyone and all who stepped up to enter the hotel. But we didn't. We didn't stay in that hotel, but somewhere else nearby.

On Kowloon side the only thing that you can do, it seems to me, is shop, and that is what we do. We shop and when we shop we walk. We walk up Nathan Road, and my father says this road is famous. Famously congested. On Nathan Road no distance can be gauged. The perspective's tangled up. The space between where you are standing and where you look is tight with flashing neon signs in English and Chinese, packed with people, cars and buses, guy wires, struts and poles, and everything that anyone could ever want to buy. I see fish. Gold fish hang in rows and rows, tiers of little plastic bags of water, one fish per tiny world, hooked on plywood boards outside a shop.

That shop sells turtles too, every size from quarters up to pancakes. The turtles are in plastic bowls, red, blue, yellow. They are piled on top of one another there inside those bowls. They are greenish brown, and I think I'd like to have one but I don't mention this. On Nathan Road I see stores so full of cameras and stereos and shiny silver gadgets, record players, movie cameras, and reel-to-reel recorders that I cannot see how people make their way inside and through all that to buy a stereo or camera. But they do and we do, walking sideways, careful not to bump a shelf, and my father buys himself the latest silver brushed-aluminum amplifier, tuner, and record player. He buys, as well, a Haminex short-wave radio so we can hear the CBC, he says, and BBC and other stations from around the world no matter where we are. We won't be getting any other news, he says, because on Timor there is no television, no radio, no magazines that we can read. The news, he says, is censored there. Yes, we're going to the back of the beyond. But here, on Kowloon side, I cannot imagine what that Timor place will be like. Here, this Asia that we're in, is overwhelming with its shops and people, buses, trams, and cars, and all its noise. I look up and see a sky that's meted out, a narrow street-wide strip. It's hard to find, but I look hard and find it, there, up above a thousand radio antennas and above the laundry poles that poke their flapping shirts into the light.

We have dinner in our fancy hotel dining room. Black marble everywhere and mirrors veined with gold. White tablecloth, stiff linen napkins, servers wearing fresh white gloves. A group of men come by to sing beside our table. They sing, "Home, home on the range, where the deer and the antelope play." My father smiles a polite encouragement, but my mother almost chokes from trying not to laugh. Tears stream down her face, and everywhere I look the mirrors throw her face at me and I laugh too. Chris ducks her head and snickers to her lap. The men are so so serious, but the words come out their mouths all bent. They don't seem to know the meaning of the words they sing. My father is embarrassed by our smirks. He's been staying at the hotel, and the musicians learned that he was waiting for his family to arrive. They've been practising the song for us. Dad glares and pops his eyes at all of us. That makes it even harder not to laugh. But we try. We try hard and start to learn about diplomacy.

The next day we cross the harbour over to the Hong Kong side. We ride the Star Ferry. My father says it's famous. We pay a nickel to ride the top deck, upper first-class tip-top deck where thin-railed seats have backs that flip from one side to the other so that you can ride and face the front or back. Take your pick, the future or the past. You can watch Kowloon dissolve behind you in the foggy mist or you can sit face-front and watch the Hong Kong skyline slowly loom upon you.

On Hong Kong side the harbour there is filled, as crowded as the Nathan Road, but this place bobs and bumps. Junks have oxblood sails, square cut and wide. Sampans, needle-long and black, slink upon the water. Each one has a canopy where men in cone-shaped hats, just like in storybooks, crouch, bent over birds they've trained to catch them fish. Oh my. This is strange and magical, and all familiar too, from stories that my mother read to me when I was a little kid. Five Chinese brothers. One could swallow the whole ocean and catch all the fish. But once I think of this, I shake my head. Silly. Yes, but I can't stop watching the men whose cormorants swim home and cough up living fish.

After that we take the special tram up the mountainside that Hong Kong's built around and on. Funicular. My father teaches us that word as we ride up and on exactly that, on a funicular. He says it's all about the counterweight. The careful balance engineered, the gravitational force. Then he gives us numbers. He gives us: 27 degree angle, a rise from 26 to 396 metres. Seven minutes, that's how long the journey takes. And at the top we see out and out and out, the view seems ended only by the very distant mists that hang over mainland China. Forbidden land. We can only look from far away.

A taxi takes us down from Hong Kong's mountain. It zigs and zags and speeds past giant trees with smooth dust-coloured trunks that angle strangely at the road. We flash past a street sign near the top. Plunkett's Road. What? My sister, hanging out the window with her camera poised, clicks just in time. Later, in the photograph, we see a blurred image of our name enamelled black on white. Who is this Plunkett? Why is our name up there, on that Mountain Peak of Great Peace on the glittery, knife-edged Hong Kong side? This is not a question even Dad can answer. Seeing my own name up there in that strange place somehow it makes me feel more foreign, even less connected to this land. I feel more foreign than I ever have before.

One week of Hong Kong and we're gone. We're gone as far as Jakarta, where I see nothing that reminds me of children's storybooks. There's nothing in my past to reference here.

Jakarta was the strangest place that I had ever seen. The air screamed all the time. High-pitched shrieks of metal, clash of horns, shrill motorbikes by the thousands circling traffic islands. The women sat sideways on the back of every bike, legs crossed and purses held primly on their laps. In front the men were hunched, intent on where they were going. Their wrists were fine boned and sinewy, torsos were concaved with shirts blown inward, tight against their empty stomachs. They wore scarves, triangles wrapped round their faces. They looked like bandits, but they're just filtering air that's pasty with exhaust.

Jakarta's roads are built like football fields, wide and straight, the perfect size for military marches, parades that might include iron tanks on giant treads and men in uniforms, a river of them all in unison. You could imagine them in poster-painted imagery. See them pass in hundreds with their heads all cocked to the left, their right arms raised and bent, every angle perfect. They salute Suharto, who stands, frowning, on a platform high above the road. These are mighty arteries, and just like mighty arteries all should, they end in traffic circles vast enough to house triumphant monuments. Those monuments are all grotesque and comical, but our taxi drivers proudly make sure we pass underneath them all. A boy and girl in bronze wave through smog, salute and welcome all the cars and mopeds. They have disproportioned hands, even bigger than their massive bodies justify. She holds a big bouquet and they both look crazed. Another monument shows Youth. It is a boy towering above our little car as we sweep past. His chest is thrust out far; his legs are ropey, corded up with strain. He holds a tray of flames above his head and stares with open mouth down at the people, buzzing down below. And in another traffic circle, there's another angry man. This one's also monstrous, and he's lumpy, holding giant ugly hands up high above his head. He's breaking chains, his fingers splayed, the iron links are flying. This is Freedom, we are told, but this man looks down and screams, just like the Youth. His mouth is open wide. He seems to seethe, not happy or triumphant.

That seemed to be the way it was in that place. We saw monsters carved from wood and hung with hair. Their eyes bulged, ringed in red, and they had leather tongues with edges gilt and ruffled round the centre black. We saw men at night in long red sashes sitting circled round a fire and chanting. They were frenzied, beating air above their heads with fists. Faces ran with sweat all shiny in the flaring firelight. Now, that angklung music wasn't watery at all, oh no. Its bamboo sound was sharpened shards of ice. We saw puppet shows. Skin puppets, casting lacy shadows, beat each other; murder done in silhouette.

In Jakarta everything was jagged, steeped with rage and furious, and all the stories there were warlike. That city is angry, and I thought that that was fine.

My father told us that Jakarta held about six million people. That was one quarter of the population of all Canada. One city. I think about Georgetown, about Guyana, and I know the Guyanese, all six nations of them, didn't even add up to a million people. But in Jakarta six million people buzzed round and round in a single city. Inside the Hotel Borobudur, right downtown, right in the middle of the land that those six million shared, inside the hotel's walls where almost no one ever seemed to be except for Chris and me and boys who hand us Cokes and towels, inside those walls, there was a garden. I read in a booklet in my hotel room that the garden was vast and green, twenty-three acres walled up and carefully kept for people just like us. It was quiet there inside those garden walls where only parrots screamed sometimes, and in the distance, faintly faintly, you might hear the swish of bamboo brooms on pebble paths. The air was tinged with green and smelled of flowers, of freshly watered dirt. There were lizards too—there always are—and they were lazy there inside that quiet place.

Inside that quiet garden, the water was bluish greenish, clean and fringed with palms, and spread out regally for us to swim in every day, back and forth, floating underneath a sky that was dishrag grey. But there, down where we were breathing, everything was filtered by the green that was growing all around, and within this garden, I am bored. I am bored and tired of waiting. I think Jakarta is ridiculous and I'm bored.

I wandered through the hotel looking for something to do. It was evening. The pool was closed and dinner had all been had. I sat down in the lobby underneath a crystal chandelier. Cool air-conditioned air, polished marble floors, and leather chairs deep and bound in chrome. I stretched out my legs and thought that they looked long because the pale-blue pants I wore flared nicely overtop my platform shoes. My arms were pale, but I was wearing something light and white to make my skin contrast and look a little brown. Beside me on a little table was a Dunhill lighter, gold, a pack of Rothmans King Size cigarettes. A servant came to ask if I would like a drink. No, no thanks. She put an ashtray at my side then polished her way into the distance. It seemed there was no one else inside the lobby on that night. The lighter and the cigarettes could be mine. I was sitting there beside them. Do I want them? Yes. Yes, I do. I will pick them up, nonchalant, because I like that word, and saunter out of here. Most likely up to where I share a room with green-haired Chris. That is what I'll do.

But now a man has come into the lobby, and he is sitting down right here, right beside me on the far side of that table where the lighter and the cigarettes are still unmoved. He's dark and swarthy, and he says he is a trainee manager. He is learning how to run a hotel like this one because his family owns it and many others like it. He's from Kuwait and I don't know where that is. It's far away. Oil and sand and camels. Ali Baba thieves. Magic carpets, magic lamps.

He knew my name. He knew my name without me telling him that I was Shelagh Plunkett. He said he'd watched me swimming in the hotel pool. "You are a good swimmer, a strong swimmer." And, he added, "I don't know how to swim." Oh. I told him I'd been swimming ever since I was a little child. My mother taught me early. I can swim in oceans. I can swim in lakes and I can swim in pools. "I believe you can," he said. "I have watched you. I've been watching, and I've seen you swim from end to end of our great pool, underwater all that way, without a breath from end to end." He knew that we were almost finished waiting, that our documents had finally come through. He knew that we were leaving, flying off to Timor on the very next day. "Perhaps when you return to Java, and you will, perhaps then you will teach me how to swim. I would like that very much." He smiled. His teeth were very white against his skin and I liked that. He smiled and he was very nice. "Let us have a drink," he said. "Come, we'll have a drink and we will talk some more. Come. Come with me." And when I stood to follow him, he told me not to leave my lighter and my cigarettes behind. He smiled again.

He took me to his hotel room. It was a suite high near the hotel roof. He told me that Kuwait, the country's name, meant little castle by the sea. That made me smile. Little castle by the sea, just like a storybook. He told me all about the stories that the princess prisoner told every night so that her captor, the king, would not kill her yet,

not yet, another night. One thousand and one nights of
stories woven, perfumed, all around his head.

I stayed the night. Of course I did. That man was
very pretty, dark black eyes and tinted lids that looked as
though he'd lined them but he hadn't. He knew my name
and he had watched me swim. He was gentle and exotic.

In the morning a fuchsia light woke me early. Fuchsia
smudged the navy-blue sky. Dawn. I was at the window
looking out, and I heard something that I hadn't heard
before: a wailing call. The muezzin, he said. I am Muslim
too. What's that? I didn't know this word. The muezzin
is calling us to pray. He said the muezzin called the adhan
five times a day, called out the faithful to their prayers.
Look down, and you will see them coming out to pray.

I did. I looked out and down, and from that height I
saw beyond the garden's walls. I could see over them and
out beyond that concrete spiked with glass. I saw Jakarta,
different and infused with dawn. I saw a river curving tight
along the garden wall. The river was slick with plastic bags
and fringed by greasy bottles, water thick and sluggish,
foul and garbage-scummed. I saw things, houses maybe,
yes, homes made from broken billboards, some saying
"Coca-Cola," some saying "Sony Stereo," and bright-blue
plastic, rotting planks, and bamboo poles thickened up
with matted paper, string, decomposing vegetables, and
the carcasses of fruit. I saw a platform built ten feet above
the ground. It tilts on skinny bamboo legs; there is a hut
and inside it a birdcage. Inside the birdcage, I can see a
tiny yellow spot of bright canary.

"Watch," he said. "They are coming out for their ablutions. You will see them coming out to pray, to purify themselves with water so that they can pray. This is what we do, what Muslims do each day and many times a day. We must perform ablutions each time the muezzin is heard."

I watched and, yes, I saw them coming out to pray. I saw women wash their hair and splash water on their faces, water from that river. They came out and waded through the shoreline, through bands of floating trash. They bent and dipped their hands in that thick water, ran their hands, flat and wet with river water, over faces, over mouths.

The muezzin calls: "Allahu Akbar." He stretches out the words. Soothing, lovely song. Little castle by the sea. The muezzin says: Come to pray. Come to salvation. Come to success. He says: God is great. Standing at a plate-glass window high above Jakarta, I can hear the muezzin but nothing else. Below, the women wash in silence.

Come, he says, the moment broken. He says that he must also go to pray, and now it's time for me to hurry to my room so that I'm there when parents come to gather up my sister and me for breakfast. But wait, he says he has a wish, an entreaty, he calls it. He says he never wants to lose this morning or last night. He wants to remember me forever. To remember me forever, he says I must leave a mark, and what that means, he says, is I must bite him on the shoulder, near his neck, up high where his skin is milky smooth and cocoa-coloured, where the muscle's thick and strong. Will I bite him? Bite him hard. I must make him bleed, he says, so that a scar can form.

But I cannot do that. I cannot, although I try. I stand on toes and crane my neck and hold his milky skin between my teeth, and I bite down. I bite but I cannot draw blood. This makes me cry. My failure makes me cry, and so I bite a little harder, but all I leave on his fine skin are two curved lines of deepened marks. Wet, yes, but not with blood. I am ashamed. Ah well, he says, if you cannot, then please, please, sign my Koran. And in his book with its cracked pages, paper dry and thin, and where I see the writing sweeps like dragon's whiskers, scimitars, and diamonds, there I sign my name, the one he knew before he even sat beside me in the lobby where I stole a Dunhill lighter and a pack of cigarettes. I sign my name.

# 13

# A SMALL, UNTHOUGHT-OF PLACE

We left Jakarta on Garuda Airlines, named for a Hindu god, the one that carried Vishnu. We left Java where the mosques were growing big and bigger, best and biggest of them all. We left where muezzins call out and people everywhere in that vast city wash before they pray. Ablutions. Ablutions cleanse and purify even if the water used is greasy grey. Where were we going? We were flying on Garuda Airlines to the back of the beyond, to Timor Island. To live in Kupang town where the people are mostly Christian. I thought of this while all the Timorese on board that flight clambered out of seats to kneel down the centre aisle, crossed themselves, folded hands, and then began to pray, and pray and pray until our little plane had reached its altitude. Chris and I just stared at that. What were they praying for? What did they know? My father told me later that Garuda Airlines is unique. Among all airlines in the world, it crashes most. Garuda planes fell out of skies all over Indonesia. Is that why they prayed? Could that be true?

The Hindu god Garuda fed the earth with nectar brought down from the heavens. But, that August our Garuda bird brought only us, my family and me, and some unnamed Timorese who knelt and prayed some more when we were coming in to land. They were on their knees when we touched down, jolting down the lumpy runway. Only then did they stand up and cross themselves and whisper, their voices rustling like leaves. They whispered, "Pujian kepada tuhan." Hallelujah. Hallelujah, we are safe. Hallelujah, we still breathe. Hallelujah, please protect us.

Water cleanses. So does fire. The land we moved to that August was parched and scorched. Timor in August is dry with heat so hungry that it sucks the water from your mouth, your eyes, your skin. There was no watery wall of heat to greet us as we stepped off that plane. Timor land is pocked and pitted. It is a moonscape that you scan when pausing at the airplane door. The air you suck into your lungs feels serrated. You might think that all the dusts of all the world have gathered there to coat your thickened tongue, to sift through your hair and mix with sweat for momentary mud before that little bit of moisture too is eaten by the sun.

Hallelujah. Death and dying. The place is tomb-like in its very nature. It is a coral island, made from the cast-off shells of dead and dying creatures. Coral, an ever-growing lump, once living, tiny creatures spitting out their hardened shells. Over time, those exoskeletons have piled so thick and high that people, cattle, monkeys, markets, roads, and homes, lines of coconut palms leaning, elegantly, over rustic boats drawn up above the tide line all live here. The gritty shore is dotted with exotic shells, curled nautilus all zebra-striped and sometimes glossed and pearled, and a few ancient sandalwood trees are sustained on a bed of coral. Hardened and ungiving, the world is thin-earthed here, and yet, for all the life that it sustains, it seems deserted. A remote unthought-of place.

We landed in full daylight. The light was so so bright it seemed to shout, "There's nothing here to hide," but even I could see that that was untrue. I knew all about the military, Javanese soldiers who issued permits for this place. I learned that while waiting and waiting for the army's special stamps inside our passports. The army held sway. Except for military planes, no others but Garuda flew to this cratered island, and Garuda came but once a week. Oh yes, it seemed abandoned. A moonscape: barren, dry, and pocked with dust-filled craters. Like the moon, except that Timor had no seas of Dreams and of Tranquility, no romantic-sounding names to fill my head.

The place we'd come to live was small. It wasn't even three hundred miles from end to end and barely sixty-five across. A long and narrow bit of land. I saw no shining silver rivers glinting through that barren landscape. No waterfalls to survey or to map, no falls to study for their latent hydro power. No waterways to tap for farmlands needing irrigation. No, not even farmland to be seen, though that, my parents told me, was the reason we had moved. We had moved to Timor because somebody wanted my father and his team to seek out ways to irrigate this land.

First, I saw that barren terrain, and then breathed air that seemed to slice my throat, and next thing were the soldiers. Yes, this was a place where the army had control. The soldiers were everywhere. Suharto's men, though many seemed to be just boys, were all dressed up in olive-coloured camouflage and boots laced high and tight, and some wore special red berets. They all had guns. There were a lot of guns. I'd seen my father's hunting rifles. He had kept them in a rack on the panelled wall of his office at home. I'd seen them, but never guns like these. Machine guns, loaded at the ready. And, in case those weren't enough, they also all wore pistols and knives. Guns and pistols, knives on every belt, and all were glinting in the barren sun at us while we walked down the runway to the little shack, the El Tari airport shack. Every soldier stared at every one of us who walked that path. Each of us was given equal doses of those soldiers' blank yet piercing stares. I was afraid of their hard looks.

Inside the silvered barn-like shed, the airport terminal, it was shady and cool. Suharto's soldiers gave extra-careful study to our passports and our papers. Of course, they knew that we were landing there that day. Of course they did. They were the ones who had given permission for us to be there on that day. But that was not cause for us to pass right through. Oh no. We were stared at and questioned just as much as any others on that plane. My father had been coming and going through that airport for some months and was familiar with the routine. It had become that, a routine, for him. I could see that he was relaxed and used to it, that it was nothing special, nothing to tense up about. He smiled, said hello in Indonesian, and handed over our passports. The soldier was not a customs agent like the sort you see at borders; he didn't smile or answer back. I looked around the shady shed and saw the others who had come off that plane with us. Were they Timorese? Were they businessmen or politicians? Were they coming home to families, back to where they'd always lived? Did everybody have to get permission from these soldiers to return, to come and go? We all were silent while the soldiers flipped through papers, looked in passports, stood and stared. Every one of us stood hushed and silent. It was that sort of place, a place to hold your breath, a place to clench your jaw and hold still as if, as if just anything, a cough or squeak of shoe on concrete floor, a voice heard whispering, might set some thing in motion, something nobody would want. I felt my head tilt downward, eyes to floor. What is this place? I wondered. What is going on?

What was going on was bad, bad, bad. Even I knew that much, though I didn't know it all, not yet. I didn't know how much was going on or how much of it was so so bad. I knew about the Australian journalists who had been shot and killed, and that Australia said Suharto's soldiers had killed them. Five men. Shot by soldiers with machine guns in a place called East Timor. We, however, had landed in the west and that was where we'd stay. We'd live in West Timor, in Kupang, which was the only town

in West Timor. I didn't know that East and West were so
so close, only a few hundred miles apart. The island was
barely three hundred miles from end to end, so just how
far was East from West? Not far.

My father had told us about the journalists. He said
that that was why we'd not be holidaying in Australia,
though that country's coast was close, only five hundred
miles across the Timor Sea. I wondered about that,
because my father often said Australia was a place he'd like
to see. It seemed on Timor we were then the closest we
could ever hope to be to Australia, and so I thought that
we would probably go there one day. But that would never
happen, because if we went to Australia, Suharto's soldiers
would never let us back onto Timor. Not ever.

Dad also said, to explain the soldiers and machine
guns, that there was trouble brewing on the eastern
part of Timor Island. East Timor not West. There were
freedom fighters called the Fretilin. But that's not how
he put it. Dad called them "troublemakers," which made
me think of scruffy, bearded, hungry men hiding in the
mountains. Wearing red bandanas, eating food smuggled
to them by the villagers. Unhappy people, just a few, he
said, who make a lot of noise and trouble for the rest who,
he made it sound, are happy to be Indonesians. Aren't
they practically that now, weren't they always? They're
just a couple hundred miles apart from East to West.
Everybody here in the West is quite content. No fussing,
no troublemaking going on at this end of the island.

That, my father said, was why we had to leave our

fingerprints on special cards filed somewhere in an office on that island. Filed away forever. The soldier looked as puzzled by the process as I was. Sweating, frowning, concentrating hard while he held my adolescent fingers down, each blotted with sticky ink and pressed hard against a creamy yellow card. They were there to stay forever, my own unique, sweeping, swirling whorls. The Indonesians didn't trust us. I felt their hostility as we waited for the army man to let us pass.

A driver in a Land Rover, blue-grey and white like all the rest, was waiting to drive us down the hill and through Kupang to where we'd stay. My father called the driver Andy and even this made everything seem odd. My father was familiar with that place. He seemed comfortable with its odd rules, and even though I knew that he'd been living in Kupang for months, this ease of his was strange and unexpected.

Andy took us to the Wisma Susi. Wisma means "home." Susi's Home is where we stayed until our house, custom-built for us, was ready. Wisma Susi was where they served you sandwiches for lunch, and every day those sandwiches were made of processed cheese and red jam on soft, white, crustless bread. Wisma Susi made these especially for us, for foreigners, and that seemed nice, as if they wanted us to stay. My father said the Timorese didn't ever eat bread. He said that Indonesians, the Javanese and Timorese and even those on Bali, did not eat cheese or jam. He said, "This bread is specially made just for us." And that meant we had to eat those cheese-jam sandwiches if we liked the taste or not. But we didn't eat the rainbow jelly cake. It was special too. Blocks of squishy, rubbery jelly in layered rainbow colours and cut into little blocks. It looked pretty but it tasted bad. We didn't eat it. We flushed it down the toilet so the Wisma Susi cook would never know. That meant they made it for us often. At Wisma Susi, we were special guests.

At Wisma Susi I sat at a desk inside the room that Chris and I slept in, a desk beneath a window slatted over with venetian blinds. The window overlooked a walkway, second storey up, that everybody passed to come or go. I sat at that desk for days. Day in, day out, I sat and played cards. Solitaire. I played and played and tried to beat—I thought of it this way—I tried to beat the Chinaman. My grandmother had told me once that many years ago in Vancouver's Chinatown, the gambling dens, where opium was often smoked, would let you bet on solitaire. She said each card in every deck of fifty-two was bought, one dollar each, and every card that made the stacks up at the top, the stacks I built in suits, each one of those paid out at five. Five to one. So I collected matches, fifty-two were paid before each deck was shuffled and five collected back for every card that made the top. I played this way for hours every day and recorded every game. Weeks and weeks. The Chinaman cannot be beat, I learned. Over time, because I sat and watched out through the window, I also learned who had come to join my father's team. Everybody stayed at Wisma Susi. It was the only place to stay. So all the foreigners went there.

We all spent time waiting at the Wisma Susi because our houses hadn't yet been built. The Timorese were building special houses for us, enclosed and all together. It was called a compound. There were seven little houses, concrete boxes tiled and roofed in tin when they were done. But they weren't getting built too fast. The work was going slowly. They had started building back when Dad flew out ahead of us, and the compound was still not finished. There was history that caused the creeping pace. Oh yes, there's always history, I learned.

Indonesia had once been a colony of Holland. But Timor showed no signs of that. All of Holland's traces had been removed. The Timorese (or maybe it had been the army) had designated land for the compound: It was a cemetery, a graveyard for Dutch soldiers. They had died at war, at war, I guessed, with Indonesians, maybe even Timorese. They were buried there, and there had been a statue standing in the middle where our compound drive was later built, a statue of a soldier standing on a plinth. He would have been a hero to the Dutch. The statue was gone, but the plinth, a high stone platform overlooking where the graves had been, was too big and heavy to be moved. And so it stayed. An empty plinth smack in the middle of our little foreign compound. The graves remained as well, beneath our houses, now unmarked. We learned that a year or two later when some children living in the compound dug up leg bones. They were playing in their garden and stuck the long bones upright, neatly, like a picket fence, outside a fort they'd built.

They called that place the "strangers' village" after we moved in. Kampung Orang Asing was the Indonesian name. That was the compound where our houses were. Full of strangers, some dead and some alive. It was up the hill along the main road into town, into Kupang, where the buildings were jumbled, crumbly cubes painted white and stacked like children's blocks. They were piled up along the shore, and some were even out beyond the shore on pylons in the water. The ocean was underneath, lapping at the pylons deep in darkness like a cave. Kupang was mostly grey, with here and there a slash of colour: a turquoise tarp, a red-streaked rusting roof, a flash of orange and yellow where the Kodak film was sold. Sometimes a bamboo screen of emerald green. That was Kupang. It was small.

Kampung Orang Asing was on the main road, and that same road led out of town and off some three hundred miles to where we'll never go. To Dili in East Timor. That road was busy with armoured trucks and armoured cars and transports moving soldiers here to there. Soldiers marched uphill each day. Each day they ran right past our house in rows that filled the width of that main road. They wore their red berets and stamped their heavy boots, pounding out in unison the shattered coral making up that road. Everyone and all were pushed off to the sides. Nobody held those soldiers back. Not cars or even bemos, little vans all painted with slogans and with images from movies showing in Kupang, not bemos and not ponies, not women carrying their squawking chickens by the legs, not the bent and skinny men with bamboo poles across their shoulders laden down with tins of kerosene or strips of bright red meat. Dog meat, my father said, who added that was why we hadn't brought our dog from Canada. Our house was right in front of that road, but just inside the compound behind two flagpoles. One pole flew the Indonesian flag and one was meant for Canada's, which had to be a little smaller. That caused problem number one, the first one to address. Our flag was huge. The only one we'd brought had been my brother Stephen's and it was as big as a bedsheet. There were no Indonesian flags that large, so Dad had to have one specially made. Those two giant flags made our compound easy to pick out. And from our house right in the front, we saw everything that passed. Each day we heard soldiers coming up the hill from the barracks down the road, and when we heard that sound we learned, like everybody else, to step aside, to go inside and wait for them to pass.

## 14

## KAMPUNG ORANG ASING

When we first moved to Kampung Orang Asing, it was a swath of broken coral. No gravestones standing, just a plinth surrounded by dead coral. The coral was mostly still in chunks, finger-shaped and full of holes, hard and jagged. Walking on it hurt your feet if you were wearing thin-soled sandals. The coral down the centre drive, where Land Rovers passed up and down, was crushed to fine-grained dust. Dust and chunks were white and grey. Our seven houses, two straight rows that lined the drive between, were coloured much the same. Grey and white and made of concrete. Nice and tidy, flagpoled at the front and plinth-marked in the centre. Light-coloured coral radiated intense heat. If you were standing at the flagpoled entrance to our world, you'd see the distant houses at the end through shaking waves of heat. Distortion and mirage.

Timor Island lies near the centre of the earth, within 10 degrees. Almost the same as Georgetown, but this time south of the equator. And, just as it did in Georgetown, here on Timor Island, the sun roared up the sky at dawn. The world was dark one moment, then the next, fierce and fiery, deadly hot and bright. Once up, it travelled slowly, a long and drawn-out day with shadows barely moving once the sun was at its peak. No shade to hide in, just a smudging of the ground around your feet. For twelve full hours, it hung above your head and beat you down, and everything around you too. Then, at 6 P.M. precisely, almost every day throughout the year, the sun dropped like a stone, as if it had been suspended by a rope that was cut suddenly. It plummeted through the last few minutes of the day and vanished, without the glow of dusk to let you grow accustomed to the sudden dark. It fell so fast that photographs of sunsets had to be planned because there was so little time to focus once the daylight's end began.

Our compound, Kampung Orang Asing, was built fronting on the road called Jalan Sumatera, and there the equal parts of light and dark, twelve hours of each, of day and night, were bracketed by noise. Each day began with the sounds of barrel boys and ended with the pigs.

The thunder sound of empty wooden iron-bound barrels rolling over rough, potholed road would wake me every day. The barrel boys with slap-slap running feet rolled barrels past our house and down the little dip to where a sluggish stream emerged to meet the road. They filled their barrels with the water there, then pushed them back, sweating, rumbling, and calling out, "*air bersih, air tawar.*" Clean water, fresh water, 25 rupiah for a pail. Water fresh, fresh from the creek, but sometimes laced with cholera and yellow fever. Ours too came from that stream, but ours was pumped and brought in tanker trucks and stored, then piped into the house to flow through taps for washing clothes, bathing, and watering the garden. But boiled and stored in sterile bottles if we used that air tawar for cooking, coffee, tea, and brushing teeth.

At night, when all the world was blackened for the next twelve hours, the dark was ripped with sounds of pigs, snuffling and screaming. They knew that something bad was up, as villagers who lived behind the compound drove those pigs down paths beside our house. They drove them past our windows, out onto the road and off, away to someplace where their throats were slit, someplace where they were slaughtered. They were consistent. So consistent that my father called them the seven o'clock pigs. You could set your watch by the sound of squealing pigs.

Pigs were not the only things that passed along the path beside our homes. The villagers had paths, old paths that surely they had used long before our compound reclaimed that cemetery land. New paths formed, old ones split and branched and encircled where we lived. The villagers passed by our kampung every day. They passed to gather water in their silver-coloured jugs. They passed to catch a bemo to take them to another village, perhaps to visit friends or maybe relatives. They passed with poles, bent heavy, baskets full of roots to sell at market down in Kupang town. They passed with woven cloth, pink threads mixed in amongst the turquoise blue and chocolate brown, to wash beside the creek. Their feet made new paths, side paths, paths that branched off and led up to our houses, right up to our windows. Then the villagers would stop their passing-by and stop to watch. They would stand, just there beyond a sheet of glass, and watch us in our house. Sometimes their faces seemed expressionless, they stood so still with hands relaxed and clasped behind their backs, fixated, riveted by what was going on inside the box we called our home. Sometimes the villagers would press their faces up against the glass so they could see as much as possible, see around a corner of the room inside, see through a bedroom door and out into the dining room perhaps. Sometimes crowds would gather, groups would form and stare, and they would talk among themselves and point and laugh and wave and smile at us inside our house. Sometimes we'd wave back. And in the rainy season what better way for villagers to shower than to stand and scrub with soap beneath the downspouts at the corners of our house?

Eventually my father had a high stone wall, ten feet of stone and coral crush, built all around the compound. That stopped the villagers from tapping on our windows when whatever we were doing on the other side failed to keep them riveted. But the wall didn't stop everyone. Sometimes we'd see a long stick come blindly over top of the wall, poking, poking, trying to hook our clothes. These were the sock-divining villagers, and sometimes they struck sock-gold and hooked a pair or two. The agile or determined villagers climbed up the wall and sat, legs dangling down our side, or squatted on the top. They perched there, looking down into our yard. They gathered there, jostling for space on nights that we showed films. My father had films sent to us by the embassy on Java. We showed these projected on a sheet pinned to the back wall of our house. We watched documentaries from the NFB. We watched films about the Canadian North. Those films showed tundra, rock, and spiky plants. One showed an Inuit man in furs, thick furs and hooded. He ran and ran across a rocky barren land. Everything was grey and black and white. The villagers leaned forward as throat-singers droned from the speakers of my father's film projector. That was a landscape I had never seen and a sound I'd never heard. It was as alien to me as to the villagers who lined the wall behind us in our Kupang garden. When the action in the film became exciting, we would gasp and lean forward in our chairs, and then the villagers would cheer and clap. We watched the film and they watched us.

Soon, the villagers and other people living in Kupang and all around started coming to our door. They came with things to sell. Two men arrived with a burlap sack, and lifted it with a groan. It was stretched with weight because it was filled with snake. A boa. It was thick, as thick as Chris who then was twelve years old, and it was heavy. They dumped the snake right there, right on our doorstep—poured it from its sack to show us what a lovely snake it was. Others gathered, men just walking past came close and stood with hands behind their backs and watched. They watched us as we stared at the snake on our doorstep. There was a woven rope tied tight behind its head, and that rope ran through a piece of thick bamboo. The man who brought the snake showed how he could yank the rope and force the snake's head up into the bamboo piece just like a hood. Hooded snake. It stretched and slithered on our doorstep, trying to escape. Our living room that day was filled with women because Mom was hosting a bridge party. Some were foreigners and some were Indonesian, but all gasped the same when they saw what was at the door. My mother said a clear "no." *No.* That word's the same in any language in the world, and though my mother hadn't learned much Indonesian yet and still communicated by drawing pictures in the air, she knew that much. The two men waved their arms and hurried words at us. I think they were saying what a beauty the snake was. *No. No.*

The price dropped down and down as they bargained with themselves and not with us, and still the price kept dropping. But, we didn't want that snake. *See how fat and healthy, see how strong and lively. See it shine. It's very fresh.* My mother tried to tell them snake is not a thing we eat. Foreigners eat fish and chicken, never snake. *Oh but this one's different, this one's special. It will taste the best you've ever had.* Our maids Bette and Lin heard the talk. Lin opened the kitchen door. She saw the snake, her eyes widened more than ours, and she said a quiet "no" and faded back into the kitchen, the door clicking softly closed. Then Bette came out. She yelled at those snake-selling men, yelled enough that soon they stuffed the snake back into the sack, and we watched as they went off to dump it on our neighbour's step.

I don't know how Bette, our maid, arrived to work for us. Perhaps she came to the door one day like the others. Waves of black oiled hair around her face. Sometimes she'd paint her skin with paste, pale-pink and thick. It was supposed to bleach her skin. She had skin the colour of creamy chocolate mousse, but she tried to turn it white. Bette was tiny. Standing beside me, she made me look tall. I, who always was the shortest, stood a head or more above her. Bette was fierce and competent. My grandmother would say she took no guff. She worked efficiently and ruled the house. That's what it seems maids do. In Guyana, Daphne had ruled our house and ruled our other maid, Victoreen, who scuttled around the house on Kaieteur Road avoiding Daphne's glinty stares. I was afraid of Daphne too, and I think my mother was as well. But by the time we lived in Kampung Orang Asing, Mom had learned a bit about managing maids. She had learned it was important not to lose the maids' respect while also being friendly.

Bette was not a Mrs., like Daphne was, but that was what she planned to be one day. She had no children and saved her money so that she could marry, marry well because she'd have a dowry by the time we left Timor. She didn't laugh at things we said or did, at least not in the way that Daphne had. My mother had learned. She never got on hands and knees to show Bette the proper way to polish floors. She was never dissatisfied with how Bette got things done. She was our cook and that, we'd learned, was higher in status than a cleaner. So Bette bossed Lin, who was older but who had been hired to sweep and wash the floors, to beat our clothes to cleanliness and iron them too, to scrub the bathrooms, fill the mandi bath, a tiled basin four feet tall and four feet wide, a cube that was always full of water that we scooped and dumped onto our heads to have a shower. All that work was Lin's, and Bette bossed her, to make sure she did those things the way she should. Bette bossed all the maids. Even maids who worked in other houses. My father was the boss and so, Bette thought, the boss's maid should boss the other maids.

Bette found us. My mother didn't seek her out. How could she have when there were no expat wives but her, at first, in Kampung Orang Asing? There were no expat women gossiping or passing round the news of who had moved and left their maid behind and unemployed and looking for another home in which to clean and cook. No women telling Mom which maids were good and which were not and who to hire and how to hire and what to pay.

What to pay was discussed a lot. It was an issue of concern. Pay enough but not too much. Too much pay would throw the economic balance off and leave trouble in our wake. The owner of the Wisma Susi told my mother this. After Bette and Lin were hired, the Wisma Susi owner came to our house complaining. She was very angry because, she said, the maids in Kampung Orang Asing were being paid too much. They were earning

$15 every month. The Wisma Susi owner said this high pay was making her life difficult. Her maids and cooks expected much more money now that we had come to town. How could she afford to hire staff when the foreigners had set that rate of pay? My mother had to scramble for an explanation. She told the Wisma Susi lady, "Maids for foreign households have to learn to cook our foreign food. They have to boil all the water used." Mom thought some more then added in a voice that meant this was the final word, "And they have to wash the floors each day."

The Wisma Susi owner learned my mother liked the woven fabric that symbolized every Indonesian island, and she started bringing fabric in to sell to Mom. Each cloth was different, with different colours and different patterns, and was worn wrapped around by men and women in different ways. They were called sarongs and each had symbols, a secret picture-language woven tight into the fabric. If you knew that language, you could learn a lot about the person wearing the sarong. You could read that person's status, family origins and lines, and where someone was from. Bette brought sarongs too. She was from Sumba and she brought me a special cloth from her island. Blue and white. The threads were dyed, tied off in little bundles that the weaver knew would eventually make a pattern. When woven, those threads of indigo and white would slowly build, weft on weft, into a pattern showing horses in a row. Bette showed me how to wear it. Tucked and wrapped and folded in a way that made a

single piece of cloth into a piece of clothing. She said that
blue and white, two colours, just two colours, made up
the cloth for slaves. Bette said she brought that cloth for
me because my eyes are blue, my hair is white, and on my
desk were photos of the horse I'd had before we moved to
Georgetown.

Bette liked it when my father came home for lunch,
when there was a man about the house. She called my
father "master," called him Tuan. Every day, when Dad was
not away in Jakarta or in the field, Bette baked a cake for
him and he ate it all each day. So, Mom and Chris and I
began to call him Tuan Kue. Master Cake.

Bette told us Kampung Orang Asing was a haunted
place. Some maids, she said, could see the ghosts
wandering around our houses in the night. I imagined
shimmery figures wavery like the heat waves that we
saw at midday. We knew that soldiers had been buried
where we lived, that we weren't the only strangers in the
strangers' village. But the maids seemed fine until the day
those bones were dug up. After that they were terrified,
and Bette was the only one who'd stay in Kampung Orang
Asing through the night. The others abandoned their
maids' quarters despite the privacy and single beds each
had. They'd come into work at dawn and leave each night
at dusk. Only Bette continued living in her maid's room,
identical to the servants' quarters built on every house. I
saw Bette's room only once. It was at the back and down
the side, outside access only, near the kitchen, past the
place where clothes were washed in concrete tubs built

up against the wall. There was a mandi bathroom there as well. Her very own. Bette liked her room and liked, particularly, that my mother had made the curtains for its window. The curtains matched the cover on Bette's bed.

Each house in Kampung Orang Asing had the same arrangement for the maids, but none but ours was used. This was a problem. The other wives didn't like the fact that their maids would not sleep in. They didn't like the fact that theirs were "day maids." Because my father was the project manager, it became my mother's job to solve domestic problems for the other wives. So my mother had to figure out a way to banish ghosts so maids would stay the night. How does one banish ghosts? In Vancouver's Chinatown, my mother used to buy wind chimes. She liked the sound. And she remembered that the Chinese said the sound of chimes scared off bad spirits. She hung a set of chimes she'd brought from Vancouver on a corner of our house and told Bette, who told the other maids, that ghosts were scared away by the hollow jangly sound. Bette smiled. It worked.

Other people came to our door. One day an old man asked to be our gardener. He was a retired policeman and brought his nephew who spoke a little English. He'd seen my mother with a hose, pouring water from our reservoir each day on dusty ground. One scraggly plant, a single stalk, rose out of the coral. Just one branch, a single leaf. My mother watered it each day, and it grew quickly. In weeks, it seemed, that single stalk became a bush that grew to more than twenty feet and arced its branches gracefully, holding green shade where we could hang a hammock and lie rocking, lapped by breeze. It was the only green thing in the compound walls. The old man said he could make a paradise for us. He said he could make a garden lush, luxuriant, a jungle for us in behind our house. My mother hired him and his nephew, Leaf. At least, the old man said that was his name. He made a fence of bamboo stalks that magically stood up and held together, even though he hadn't used a single nail. He and Leaf broke the ground with mattocks, sprayed coral fingers, shook up the dust, dug deep, and mixed in dirt and planted things. They planted bougainvillea and palms that came out of the ground as spears, then unfurled, spread out, and widened like an opera fan. They planted bamboo, green and black and orange, that in the wind sounded like waves breaking on a pebbly beach and grew inches overnight. Before we went to bed, we'd mark the stalks and in the morning grin to see how much they'd grown. Jack and the beanstalk in our own backyard.

And when the monsoon season came and all the dry dusty coral ground became a knee-deep lake around our house in minutes, in moments, suddenly we were standing on an island in the sea, and just beyond our vision, there beyond the curtain wall of falling water—was that a dolphin, a flying fish that leapt from Jalan Sumatera? The flood was fierce and in moments covered all the land. Standing on our doorstep, we would stretch our arms out to the front and see them vanish, hands melting out of sight, disappearing in a fall of water. Then, when the rains made horses stampede on our roof, that was when the orchid lady came and spread her orchids at our door. She always came in rain. She wore a leaf, a giant leaf, three feet long and just as wide, like a cape. Shiny scarab in the rain. Beneath her cape, she had a basket filled with plants, all orchids, that she laid, one by one, in rows across the tiles at our doorstep, underneath the overhang where it was dry. Then she'd step back out into the rain and stand and wait. She never seemed to say a word, just nodded when the little pile of coins my mother placed out on the step was big enough. Then she'd turn and go, leaving behind orchids of sparking colours bright with their spidered roots and leaves like thickened shoe-sole leather. Yellow red-flecked flowers, dragons with their jaws wide open on the world.

And then more people came and called out at our door. Two men came with a monkey, tightly belted and held by string. Macaque. A special kind that lived along the sea, with fur down the centre of his back in yellow-green, with tiny wrinkled thumbs and tiny nails, black and manicured. We named him Quibo, short for "Essequibo," the river in Guyana that turned the blue Atlantic Ocean brownish grey with silt. Maybe it was strange to name a monkey that, but we liked the sound. We liked the memory it brought of where we'd lived before. We took Quibo to the sea, where reddened cliffs that looked like lava rock were jagged and pocked, full of caves, and the sand was made of shell. We swam with snorkels and masks, and Quibo rode our shoulders as we swam, standing, clinging to our snorkels, scanning water with his deep-brown eyes, looking far beneath its surface. Suddenly, he'd dive. He'd dive into the water and we'd follow, watching through our masks while Quibo swam down to the bottom, pawed through shells and sand, stirred it up, and stuffed whatever little crabs he found into his mouth. His cheek pouches bulged and his tobacco-coloured eyes blinked at us underwater; he stared at us while we watched him through our glass masks. He would swim to shore, shake like a dog, and squat, his hair spiked with salty water, to eat the crabs he'd caught.

Next came a baby monkey, Tik-tikki. Her head was bald, her body bristling, thinly, with black hair. Her eyes were large and full of fear. If she wasn't held, she would flatten herself on the ground, spread her arms, and try to grip the tiles on our floor with splayed fingers. She would scream and scream. She was too young to put down or to leave alone. We wondered if she was even old enough to be weaned. The man who brought her to the house had shot and killed her mother. On Timor they ate monkeys, so Tik-tikki's mother was most likely cooked and eaten in a stew. But the baby monkey was too small to bother eating. She was all skin and bone and hair. Besides, this baby had greater value. The man who shot her mother had heard there were foreigners who paid money for these things. Chris and I took turns keeping Tik-tikki tucked inside our T-shirts, T-shirts tucked into our jeans. She slept almost all day, clinging to our bellies in our shirts. We improvised with food, chopped egg in milk and bread, mashed fruit. We invented monkey diapers. For weeks Tik-tikki could not be put down.

Tik-tikki grew stronger and braver. Eventually she didn't have to live inside our shirts. She was free to run around the house, to climb the Christmas tree, and throw ornaments at our cats. We tethered her outside, where Quibo lived as well. They both wore belts around their hips, and we tied long lengths of nylon rope, thin and weightless, to those belts and to the tree where they could climb. Dad tied those knots because he'd been an Eagle Scout, the tip-top highest Boy Scout one can be, and knew how to tie elaborate knots. He'd won badges for his knots. But Tik-tikki had tiny fingers and bright-brown eyes that watched everything, and soon she'd learned to undo buckles and to untie the best of Dad's Eagle Scout knots. She would free herself and then free Quibo. Quibo would climb the wall and scare the villagers walking past. But Tik-tikki would run on all four feet, or hands and feet because that was what they looked like, into the kitchen where Bette and Lin were working. She'd clamber up the shelves, up high where nobody could reach her, and open jars of flour, bags of lentils, packages of raisins, coffee, tea, and biscuits. It all exploded, food was bouncing off the walls around the room. Then she'd throw containers too. Empty tins would clatter in a cascade down on all our heads. Flour dust billowed through the little kitchen. Bette shrieked and Lin ran from the room. Tik-tikki looked like she was grinning, her teeth bared and lips spread wide, but those were signs of fear. The noise she caused had scared her and what had been fun was frightening. I would have to lure her with a biscuit then, quietly; she'd blink at me and climb into my shirt.

Outside, Quibo scrambled through my mother's garden. He'd climb our shady tree trailing his long nylon tether. He kept it clear and untangled, trailing freely behind him as he wandered up the tree. He would climb as high as his rope allowed and then would jump, just like a cartoon circus diver, down into a plastic washing basin full of water. He'd swim in circles round and round the bright red bowl or sit in it, his wet hair flattened and ears sticking out. Seeing laundry drying on the clothesline, sheets beaten bright by Lin, Quibo would squat in the sun, blinking, his tether stretched taut behind him on the ground. He'd sit at the limit of his rope, waiting for a puff of wind. When the wind wafted the clean sheets near enough, he'd grab a handful and hang upside down, swinging and laughing in a monkey manner. He would bounce above the ground, held up and tight between the stretched-out sheets and stretched-out nylon rope.

One day I watched him sit and watch the gardener, Leaf, dig holes to plant a row of trees. Quibo watched him carefully. Later, in the afternoon Leaf left his hand trowel on the ground but took away his shovel. The trowel was within the monkey's reach. Quibo picked it up, tucked the trowel handle up beneath his armpit, just like he'd seen the gardener do all day, and dug a hole.

Quibo was a mischief-making monkey. He played tricks on Bette and Lin. One day Chris and I watched him sitting with his tether stretched out taut again behind. Or so it seemed. It looked that way, but it wasn't really taut. We knew that Quibo's nylon rope was longer than it looked as

he sat nonchalantly chewing on a blade of grass. We could
see that behind his back he'd bunched that skinny nylon
up, made a little pile of it and hid it out of sight. He sat
and blinked and rolled his eyes, slewed them to the corner,
looked at the purple bougainvillea, and looked back at the
sky. He looked everywhere except in front, where Lin,
who was afraid of him, edged round the yard to where the
clothing hung. She was nervous. Bette thought that was
funny. She thought it was very funny that Lin was scared
of the monkeys tethered in our yard. As we watched,
Lin made her way around the edge of the garden to the
clothesline, but by then her back was to Quibo. Then he
burst across the foot or two of space between himself and
Lin, and grabbed Lin's skirt and dangled by two hands,
chattering shrilly while she screamed. She screamed and
we came running. Bette, Chris, and I, my mother, even
Leaf came running when we heard her screams. But then,
once we were there, it was hard to keep from laughing. I
grabbed Quibo and pulled him off. He climbed onto my
head and continued chattering, and bared his teeth but
not as if to bite. He was laughing too. A monkey making
jokes. Even Lin laughed then. Bette slapped her on the
back. They both covered up their mouths and giggled.

In daylight they were playful and active, but darkness
scared the monkeys. When the sun began to set they
grew nervous. Then they'd climb into the bougainvillea,
clinging to its trunk, scanning the sky through its leaves,
and becoming more agitated as the shadows grew. If a
plane flew overhead, they'd panic. My father built a home

for Quibo, another for Tik-tikki. He took a wooden packing crate, large enough for even him, at six feet tall, to stand up straight inside, put wire mesh across the front, and ran planks and boards inside for Quibo to climb up. It was a cave for him to sleep in, a place where he felt safe.

With Leaf and with his uncle, with the water that my mother poured on it each day, the garden stretched wide and reached high. It uncurled and then began to tangle. Thorny boughs of bougainvillea spread, paper-petalled pink-and-yellow flowers, tinted like a sunset on a postcard from Tahiti. The more it grew, the more shade and shadows it contained. Our garden filled with things that people sold us at the door. Orchids. Monkeys. Parrots and a myna bird that mimicked cat fights perfectly. Cats came to live with us and then had kittens. A small and honey-coloured creature called a cuscus, woolly with a pointed nose and curling, half-bare tail that was prehensile. It was shy and silent. Its eyes, as big as quarters, shimmered dark like water in the night. At first I kept it in my bedroom, with the air conditioning turned off. It was nocturnal. All day it huddled on the curtain rod up near the ceiling. I didn't know what it could eat. I gave it fruit, leaves, and water. It lived, first in my bedroom, then outside and in a cage, like Quibo's den, sheltered, tucked into a corner of the yard among the bamboo forest. It lived there for a while, but gradually it slowed and slowed. It lived, but not for long.

## 15

## HELLO, BLUE-EYED WHITE GIRL

In Kampung Orang Asing, in our garden, beautiful and lush, we were sheltered. We were tucked away and hidden out of sight. Chris and I didn't go to school. There was no school for us, and though my father thought of sending us to Java, to a private school, he did not, and we stayed on Timor, earning grades through correspondence school. Tucked away inside our rooms and working by ourselves. I took math and English, social studies, and all the other courses Canada required its grade ten and eleven students to take. I took biology. I had a microscope, and boxes packed with jars were mailed to me. They contained things that I dissected: a frog, a fetal pig, pulled from thick, sweet syrup and spread out on a tray for me to slice apart at home, right in my bedroom, at my desk.

School packages came in the mail from Vancouver, but they weren't censored the way our magazines and letters were. Schoolbooks and papers, forms to fill, exams were left clean and unadorned by the censor's ink, not like the letters that my grandmother and friends sent out. Those arrived with the pages stuck together by the censor's black ink. I would pull apart thin sheets of onionskin, my grandmother's handwriting jiggling on the pages that I had to carefully tug apart because the censor had put her letter back inside its envelope before the ink had dried. I wondered what she wrote that censors felt I should not know about. The sentences were unreadable. The paper was ridged where the ink was laid on thick. What secrets did the Indonesians want me not to know? What secrets were there trapped beneath that ink?

There must have been secrets, more than we'd been told about, more secrets than the killing of those journalists, though that was not a secret anymore. It never really had been. That much we knew. Chris and I heard things. We heard Mom and Dad talking in the evening about the Fretilin. The Fretilin were still out there, still active, still making trouble in the East. I asked about the Fretilin again. Who are they? Why are they making trouble? What is going on out there in the East? My mother waved a hand, fly-swatting, waved the question off. The Fretilin were rowdies, troublemakers, nothing much, not anything to worry about. I wasn't worried, I was just curious. Fretilin made fusses where no fusses need to be. Everybody just wants to get on with their lives, but these Fretilin cause trouble. My mother said the Fretilin were just a handful of people and not a concern to us. And yet, and yet, the soldiers were still there in Kupang, still everywhere and always armed. And we were watched, watched carefully. And yet, and yet, we had to leave the island every six months or so, not just to renew our visas—not just that, no—we also had to leave the island so that we could be scrutinized again by army men who gave (or perhaps withheld) permission to be there on Timor.

And yet, though Fretilin were few and far away, no concern to us or anyone really, at least that seemed to be the message, and yet, my father tells us, "Pack a suitcase. Keep it by your bedroom door." In case we have to leave? In case we have to flee. Run away. Take a powder in the night. Escape. Why would we have to run away if everything was fine and all was safe?

I did not worry about the Fretilin, but the soldiers made me nervous. I didn't like walking past them on the street. I didn't like seeing them in training, running up the hill past our house. I didn't like seeing those machine guns or those bullets hanging off the boys who seemed my age. I knew that most of them were Javanese, or maybe all were Javanese, and Javanese scorned Timorese, they treated them with contempt. I'd seen them snarl and shout at Timorese, push them aside and laugh at them. The Timorese were silent, knotted tight, held in. They were scared and so was I sometimes.

But, my parents said that Kupang was a safe place for us. It was safe, they said, for Chris and me to wander freely, anywhere we wished. They said it was safe, much more than Georgetown ever was. Sure sure, I saw no tiefman there. I saw no snatch-grab thieves. There were no guard dogs at the gates, no men patrolling property, no need for locks or fences, no barbed wire topping anything in sight.

There, on Timor, we didn't have that super-extrasensory alert that let us know when someone, a stranger, stepped within three feet of us. It was true, we didn't feel that. And yet, and yet, even the soldiers seemed nervous, twitchy in their role, and that scared me. They scowled. They never smiled. Why was that? Perhaps they were the ones with extrasensory alerts that let them know when we stepped near. Were they afraid of us?

Bette told us why we heard loud noises in the night sometimes. The soldiers were burying their dead just down the hill. There was an army graveyard down the hill about a half a mile and near the barracks just outside of town. They dug the graves and buried soldiers only in the dark. The Fretilin. The war in East Timor. Except we were told there was no war, and Fretilin were only troublemakers, just a handful. Nothing to be worried of, no concern of ours. But, somebody was killing soldiers sent to Timor, somebody was killing Javanese. Somebody was dead, someone was being buried.

Bette told us other stories too. She said the Javanese are Muslim and Muslims don't drink beer. Timorese are Christian. Beer, for Timorese, is fine. The soldiers, even though they were Muslim Javanese, got drunk sometimes. They were young, they were there on Timor where beer and whisky could be bought in almost every store in town. It was all around them there. Sometimes the soldiers got drunk, and when they drank, their nervousness and their contempt, their twitches and their shoves grew stronger. One morning Bette told us that the night before a dozen girls had been raped and killed inside the Kupang army barracks. Those girls were Timorese and from Roti or Savu or Sumba. They were from the little islands scattered in the Timor Sea. They weren't from Java. Everybody whispered about what had happened in the night; the story went round the Kampung Orang Asing, travelling from house to house amongst the maids and gardeners. The whispers could be heard in Kupang too, the story seen in villagers as they passed by. Their heads were down, their eyes were on the ground and staring at their own bare feet when soldiers were nearby.

That day a man, a foreigner, who was on my father's team, a man who spent a lot of time away, out in the field I think, and didn't live in Kampung Orang Asing, that man invited some soldiers to our house for tea. He liked to drink. He liked to drink Bintang, the Indonesian beer, and show us tricks, like dousing houseflies in a pool of yellow beer, then prodding them to show us they were dead. "Now look at this," he'd say, while sprinkling table salt on the fly. It would twitch, vibrate, roll over. Soon the fly was standing on its feet and soon it flew. He liked his resurrection trick and performed it almost every time we saw him.

That day he came to our door with six or seven soldiers clustered behind him while he knocked. My parents were not home. Bette went to the door, and the resurrection man said he'd got some friends he'd like to introduce to us, to my sister, Chris, and me. He'd brought his friends to tea. He told Chris and me that he'd met the soldiers on the road out front, and that they'd asked if he knew us and could he, please, invite them in for tea and introductions. There they were, all grouped behind him at the door and smiling at us. Some seemed shy, they craned their necks to get a better glimpse of us, the blondes. He said we must invite them in. We must not be rude and turn them away. Bette was angry, even I could see she was and so could he, and probably the soldiers could as well. I doubt they cared. She wasn't Javanese. She was a woman. She was just a maid. Perhaps by scowling at her, they felt better, felt braver. We could not be rude. That wouldn't be the thing to do, the boss's daughters should not be that way, and so we invited him and his soldier friends inside to tea. Each one stepped through our doorway and carefully unslung his gun and left it propped against the wall outside. At first they all sipped tea, but soon tea wasn't good enough. The resurrection man told Bette to get some Bintang beer. He sent her off to the shaggy grass-roofed stall across the road. Then everyone, except Chris and me, was drinking Bintang beer and watching flies brought back to life with salt. The soldiers laughed at that trick. They roared and stamped their feet while Chris and I sat stiffly in our chairs and stiffly smiled.

Safe. Even Bette said we were safe. We were blue-eyed blondes. We were white. It made a difference there. White on Timor was not like being white in Georgetown. No one would ever spit on us when we walked down the Kupang streets. We were safe to wander anywhere we liked, wander into Kupang town, wander out through the

flagpoled entrance to our safe and sheltered home. Chris
and I had no friends on Timor, just each other. There were
no people there our ages, no foreigners, I mean. We were
the only white-skinned blue-eyed blondes on that entire
island. We were the only foreign teenagers. There were no
other strangers quite like us. Somehow, that made us safe.

Safe, but also stranger than the other strangers there.
We were an exhibition. We were a show whenever we went
out. When we ventured beyond the walls of Kampung
Orang Asing, we trailed a crowd of Timorese fifteen feet
behind, an audience that grew larger every step we took
out beyond the walls. Everybody watched and commented
on our clothes, our hair, our height, our walk, our eyes, our
skin, our odd colour.

First, two lanky boys who leaned against the counter
of the hut across the road began to follow us. That was
where I'd send Chris sometimes to buy me cigarettes. Oh
yes, I smoked and smoked in secret. Yes, I bribed my little
sister, sent her off to buy my cigarettes for me. Sometimes
I would go myself, go to the thatch-roofed hut and say I
was buying cigarettes for Dad. Philip Morris, in a jet-black
box. I thought that was sexy and sophisticated. Perhaps, I
sometimes thought, I should smoke Marlboros.

The Indonesians smoked clove-stuffed cigarettes that
popped and sparked, crackly, smelling sweet. At night,
when we were coming home from the cinema where we
saw films that always seemed to feature Charles Bronson,
while we were walking home, the sidewalk was narrowed
by the vendors, old men with hollow cheeks and long thin

moustaches who squatted in the shadows up against a
wall. They'd squat low on their haunches, sarongs bunched
up and tucked between their legs. They'd sit so low their
knees were up around their shoulders. They'd sit like that,
silent, with a cloth spread out to make us step aside, and
on that cloth were tidy pyramids of cigarettes: Marlboros,
Dunhill, Peter Jackson, Rothmans. Those men all seemed
to smoke clove cigarettes, and in the night all roads
through town were bordered in the dark by lines of clove
sparks popping. This was how they smoked: Make your
hand a fist, hold the cigarette between your fingers, push
the filter of your cigarette up tight against the knuckles
near your palm, now with your other hand, clasp your
fist, put your mouth up to the hole where thumbs curl
round. Inhale. That was how they smoked, filling all the
air around with spice and sparks.

The vendor men called out to me to buy their
cigarettes, but usually I didn't. I'd buy them secretly, from
shops, but not from vendors on the street. I thought that
they knew who I was, they surely did know who I was, and
that they'd tell my father that I smoked. They'd come to
the door one day to tell my father that I smoked. So that
was why, sometimes, I bribed my little sister, sent her off to
buy my cigarettes instead of crossing Jalan Sumatera to buy
them myself. I sent her off because I knew that there were
spies, spies who wanted to tell my father secret things.

Oh yes, I was sure that there were spies. Those lanky
boys, the ones that always seemed to hang out at the little
shop across the street, across the street, staring, always

watching us in Kampung Orang Asing, I thought they might be spies. They followed Chris and me. They were the first, the ones who started the train that trailed us, fifteen feet behind.

It was hot and dry. We rarely wandered out in monsoon season when the sky was full of water, when little boys took baths in potholes in the road, and the villagers came to our house and clustered underneath the downspouts, soaping hair and bodies, showering beneath the spouts that tumbled water off our roof. We never walked in rain, so when we walked the air was dry and very hot. There were no trees on Jalan Sumatera, no shade. I wobbled on my platform shoes because the coral was uneven even where it had been crushed to make a road, but that was fine. I sauntered anyway. Why rush when there was not much to do in Kupang or on Timor. Bemos passed, minivans that were the buses there, privately owned, elaborately painted. Each one had a set of horns that blared out tunes, each one distinct. Bony Nancy, that was our favourite, with its fancy lettering above Charles Bronson's giant craggy face that stared at us as it went by. Bony Nancy shrieked an elaborate cacophony. The driver set the horns off as he passed us. Greetings. Dust, fine as talc, rose and then fell. More bemos—there were a lot of them—passed by. Then we were coated in a gritty shroud of fine grey dust. Inside my head, I sang along with Jim Morrison. Together we sang about the beautiful end. I sang "My only friend." Those days Jim Morrison's music was almost the only thing I wanted to hear. I listened to it while I did my school work, singing "Riders on the Storm," waves hissing on a California beach, played again and again while I dissected an unborn pig.

When bemos passed and sang their horn songs at us, the ticket-taker at the back, the one who hung out of the open back to entice riders in, who helped them shove their bags of chickens, always live and squawking, on the bemo roof, that man shouted out and waved his arms above his head and waved at us. He shouted, "*Gadis putih Salam! Salam indah mulus gadis bermata biru!*" He said "Hello, white girls. Hello, beautiful smooth blue-eyed girls." Sometimes when it was very hot and sun glinted harshly and beat the world to paleness, when dust was thick and dry, sometimes when we were bored, we'd take a bemo ride to town. Then the ticket-taker hanging off the back would make us sit right near the bemo opening, the open back. They'd make Chris sit on one side and me across from her, and we were right there with dust and wind catching up our long blond hair and whipping it about. And then the ticket-taker would lean out, a full arm's length off the bumper at the back, and hanging on by one stretched arm, he'd shout out to everyone the bemo passed that white girls, the foreigners, were there, right on that bemo then, come take a ride, you can sit beside one or the other, both are here, come, come. My father said the bemo fare went up when we were on board. The ticket boys crammed people in, made some girls sit on others' laps or even ordered other people off the bemo to make room for more young men, young men willing to pay extra just to ride with us.

Walking into town meant I could smoke. I held my cigarette curled inside my fist, turned my head away from the road and puff-puffed short and sharp, took secret puffs. I smoked only when the bemos were not passing, when there was nobody in sight. I told Chris to watch and warn me if she saw anything that I should be aware of. Any blue-grey Land Rovers, especially the one my father's driver drove, but any Land Rover would be the worst. Once we'd crossed the stone bridge that marked the outside edge of Kupang, I wouldn't smoke. The town streets were narrow, and the shops were cut like caves out of the walls, dark and small and tight. There could be anyone inside where we couldn't see, but they could see us as we passed. Someone was always watching.

We crossed the river, crossed the bridge, and looked down on the water, sluggish, with bobbing plastic bottles, coconuts with rotting husks, Styrofoam that crumbled to confetti, rainbowed oil, mud-coloured froth. My cigarette hit water with an angry hiss. That was when I saw a different man behind us; he'd joined the lanky boys who had trailed us since we left home. That man was behind the lanky boys, a few feet back. When Chris and I were looking down at the water, he stopped too. He waited. He saw me seeing him. He didn't smile or frown or look away. He stood as if he was watching in a way the others trailing us were not. His feet were solid on the ground. His eyes were watching, yes they were, but not the way the lanky boys watched us.

Let's go. Let's go. I tugged at Chris's sleeve. The water stinks. Let's go.

Now that we're in town, a mob is gathering behind. The lanky boys, the man that watches, they've been joined by others, others joining every time we pass a shop. And when we stop, they move in closer. Looking, wondering what we will buy. We pass Toko Liem, the biggest store in town. It's where my mother shops. The only cheese on Timor Island can be bought at Toko Liem. That cheese comes in big round tins with special keys stuck to the top. Break off the key and slot it in the metal band to peel the whole thing open. Inside the tin, the cheese is grey. But grey cheese is cheese, and this is all the cheese that we can get on Timor Island. Toko Liem's the place my father buys his alcohol: rum, whisky, gin. We pause and look inside. Toko Liem sees us and waves. He rushes out from where he stands behind the counter wrapping round the shop on all three sides. We stand at the fourth side that's open to the world. Behind us is the street that's filling up with people watching us and watching Toko Liem rush out. Toko Liem. I don't know his name, but that is what I call him in my head. Toko Liem gestures at us to come inside.

"Come, come. I have something special for your father. Your father, he likes Scotch. I know he does. Yes, yes. His favourite. I know. Special order for your father, just for him. Come, come inside." Toko Liem holds up a bottle, amber fluid sloshes. It does look like the Scotch I know my father drinks on ice, when he comes home from work and listens to the seven o'clock pigs pass by. He buys those bottles sometimes in the duty-free shop when we have gone to Singapore or Malaysia and are flying home. Yes,

it does look pretty much like the same Johnnie Walker
bottles, but not quite. Something's not the same. There's
the bottle, with its label, burgundy and gold. There's the
little man with his top hat and walking cane. But look, I
point it out to Chris: The name on the bottle Toko Liem
holds up is Johnson Walker. Close, but not the same. We
snicker, lightly, holding up our hands to cover mouths, just
like we've seen Bette and Lin do. The crowd behind us
murmurs, mutters things that we don't understand. Thank
you, thank you. Yes, it looks nice. We'll tell our father that
you've special-ordered Scotch for him. We don't buy and
push our way back through the crowd, out into sunshine
on the street again.

Down the street, around a bend, there is a shop we
know that sells bootleg music, homemade copies of
cassette tapes. That's where we are going. It's hot. The
crowd has grown big now: There are men in sarongs and
straw hats that perch high on their heads, wide brimmed
and with a funny spike on the front. Our gardener from
Roti wears a hat like that. They are a Roti version of
the hats that wealthy Portuguese explorers wore three
hundred years ago. There are women following us too, in
sarongs and skirts, some carrying their shopping bags and
others who are vendors from the nearby shops. They've
come to see why a crowd is clogging up the street. The
lanky boys still are there and now they've gathered friends,
arms crossed and leaning up against a wall, and soldiers,
there are soldiers too, and all these people—there are so
many that Chris and I are nervous now. The murmurs

make us nervous. We push through the crowd, single file, my sister behind me as I lead the way and avoid their eyes. I don't look people in the eye, I look down or up above their heads. I look away and stick my chin out. Tough, that's how I act, like Charles Bronson. Shuffle shuffle, people inch aside, but some reach out and stroke our hair, touch our skin with fingers, delicate and small and damp, as we pass by.

The shop we want is so small it's barely big enough for two of us inside. Stacked everywhere, from dusty countertops to shadows hovering against the ceiling out of sight, are bootleg tapes of every kind of music we could ever want. Elton John. The Eagles. Bee Gees. How can you mend a broken heart? The man behind the counter looks like the lanky boys outside, with his high-waisted pants in plaid, his shirt tight and shiny, and the sleeves cuffed tight and belling wide about his narrow wrists. His fingernails are long. He is eager. White girls in his store. Rolling Stones? "You like? We have the best." The shop is rocked by sound. We jump. Sound explodes. Mick Jagger screams. He screams that he likes rock and roll. He likes it. He likes it. He likes it. Now all the other lanky-looking boys are shouting too, in the crowd that's moving in on us, corralling us inside that tiny shop, cutting off the light, blocking off the open door. They sing along with Mick, words about a boy that's strange. I smile, but that's not good. Oh no, a smile turns the music up. A smile brings crowds in closer still. Chris and I are being pushed against the counter, boys shove other boys and dusty cassette cases, scratched and marked, spill down and all around the counter. Yes, yes, I'll buy the Rolling Stones and Bee Gees too. Bee Gee, bee gee, bee gee. They don't murmur now, they shout, "*Beegeebeegeebeegee. Beegeebeegeerollystone.*" Sweat and dust. Hair oil. Spice. Soft damp fingers on my skin again, but this time they don't stroke. A woman reaches over and pinches my white arm to make it red and pink. Another does the same and pulls the fine blond hair along my arm. I pull away, but that just makes the crowd move in. Somebody yanks my hair, my ponytail that's hanging down my back. I hear words. I hear *putih. Putih. Rambut. Kulit.* I hear white. White. Hair. Skin. My skin is reddening, they pinch so much, so hard. My arms will bruise. We have to get out now before the crowd gets any thicker.

We have to push our way past all of them to get back to the street, to air, to light. We close our eyes, I grab my sister's hand, we put down our heads and push like bulls, like bulldozers, like Charles Bronson would. I want to cry but I do not. I want to shout at them, but I must not. I want to be back home. I hear them shouting, voices turn to follow as we push through the crowd. *Gadis! Gadis! Bermata biru gadis.* Blue-eyed girls. Paul McCartney Wings! Rolly Stone!

Light hits my eyelids, and I know we've made it to the doorway of that shop. Light and air. When we are free and past the shoving, shouting boys, I see that different man. He doesn't smile or frown or nod. He watches. Then he follows us, follows the mob that follows us as Chris and I leave town. Back through the narrow streets, back past the floating Styrofoam that bumps against the pylons of the bridge, back over sludgy river water, back out, and up the hill. One by one, and two by two, the crowd thins out— we're not shopping now, we're not standing still, not close enough or still enough to pinch or poke. We're walking fast, as fast as white girls walking here can do and still feel safe. At least, that's how I think of it. Running isn't safe. I sense that it might not be safe. The crowd thins out, but that man stays and follows us, unsmiling, up the hill. Halfway up the hill, the sky changes colour. White to red to navy blue to black as fast as that. Night falls, and just before the light is gone, twisting to look back over my right shoulder, I see him. He's all alone and so are we. Chris grabs my hand and we walk double-fast. No smoking now. Up the hill as quickly as we can without breaking into a run. He's there for the full ten-minute walk up that hill, up Jalan Sumatera to the flagpoled gates, to Kampung Orang Asing where we are safe. Safe safe at home again. Tucked away, secluded, safe.

The next day, at breakfast, Bette tells us, "You are safe." She says that we are safe because there's always someone watching us because we're different. Someone's always watching blue-eyed foreign girls to make sure that they get home unharmed.

# 16

## THE WIVES

The myna bird, glossy black and beautiful, his beak curved just so, polished, pointed too, was in his cage and always learning. He learned to mimic cat fights, bemos blowing horns as they passed; he mimicked barrel boys and squealing pigs and chirping geckos, little lizards clinging to the walls. He mimicked Bette and sounded just like her when she was telling Lin to wash the floors. *Kue kue kue*. He called out, "cake cake cake." He called out, "Sally Sally Sally," my mother's name, sounding out the selfsame voice, its tone exactly right, as if the woman living at the compound's other end was at our door and calling to my mother. Sally. Sally. Sally. "Damn that bird," my mother grumbled when, again, she had to stop whatever she was doing and walk through the house to check if it was the myna bird or not. Damn the bird. Oh, that time it was not the bird. The woman standing there had heard my mother loudly curse the myna bird. She was not smiling, even though some others would have seen it as a joke.

That woman came to our door almost every day; that was how the myna bird had learned to call out my mother's name. She came to gripe. Her husband was working far too long, his holidays were not quite right, he didn't get a car and driver often enough, his status wasn't high enough, the house they lived in wasn't big enough, the maids were lazy, the dust came through the windows and the doors. She wasn't happy. She didn't like the way the project was being run. Her husband wasn't getting his full due. Sally, Sally, Sally.

My father was the head of the project, in charge of the team. My mother was the boss's wife, and so she had to chat, facilitate, negotiate, and manage all the things the other wives needed done, mediate their problems and complaints. The myna bird knew who complained the most.

It was my mother's job to arrange banquets and events, the parties that we, the foreigners who occupied that compound, were expected to hold. On Canada Day, of course, there had to be a party. There had to be a band, and the band members had to learn our anthem. They learned to sing "O Canada," though they didn't know what the words meant. They learned to play it on a gamelan. *Plang plang and clong.* Nobody had ever heard the anthem played that way. A man from the embassy, from Java, from Jakarta, would be there, he was coming to the show. A restaurant was booked and decorated full of red and white. We, Chris and I, were told that we'd be standing with our parents in a receiving line, and we'd shake every

hand of every person coming through the door. So many
hands, limp and clammy, clasped in ours while we stood
and looked as pretty and polite as we were able. I wore a
sari that our neighbour, newly married and just flown in
from Canada, had taught me how to fold and tuck.

Benny, one of the drivers, asked my mother if the girls
from Surabaya—he meant prostitutes—were coming to
help us celebrate our national day. Would the Surabaya
girls be there? No. No, they weren't invited. No, they won't
be there. But there they were, that night, sitting along the
fringes of the banquet room, waiting near the back for
the party to really start. Maybe Benny snuck the Surabaya
girls in. At least whoever snuck them in had waited till the
dinner part was done. Once the eating and the toasts were
finished and the dignitaries had all left, then the party
started for the drivers. The tables were pushed back, the
chairs were stacked, the band went home, and cassette
tapes played the Top 100 singles from the U.S.A. Surabaya
girls were good dancers.

A young man came to ask my father if Chris could
dance with him. He said, "I would like to have intercourse
with Miss Chris." My father barely cracked a smile. Social
intercourse, of course. Dad told him to ask Miss Chris
herself and she, reluctantly, said yes. She understood. It
would be rude to have said no, and that wasn't something
we were allowed to be, especially on nights like that when
Canada and foreigners were on display. We were always
on display. Miss Chris danced with that young man, the
last dance of the night. They looked stiff and awkward as

her golden hair swayed across her downcast eyes. She was embarrassed. I sat back and grinned, grateful I was not the one up on the dance floor. But during the mandatory social intercourse that followed, that brave young man learned I was the older sister. He'd picked the wrong blonde on display and said he was devastated. Devastated because the elder girl should always be the one who dances first, she'll be the one the father is most anxious to marry off. Though my sister's three years younger, she was then my height, and we were often taken to be twins. It was rude of him, he said, to ask Miss Chris to dance and leave her older sister sitting in a chair.

Social intercourse. My mother met the wives of aristocratic Timorese, the ones high in the social pecking order. The raja's wife and cousin and the raja's niece. Mrs. Nesnoni. Essy Tarek. Mrs. Nayfack. Or, perhaps, they were "Your Royal Highnesses" because they were Timor Island's royalty. Mrs. Bambang too. She wasn't royalty, but she was rich. They came each week for English conversation and for tea. For tea, and to look inside our house to see how foreigners live. Our bathroom with its flushing toilet was a feature that they liked; each week they'd flush the toilet, sometimes going to the bathroom grouped in twos. We'd hear them whispering and giggling, maybe making jokes about our toothpaste. They often spoke in Dutch and Indonesian too, thinking that my mother did not understand. But Dutch is close to English, so it wasn't hard to figure out what they said in Dutch, and Indonesian was a language we were learning, taught each week by a tutor who came to our house. *Selamat datang*: welcome. *Pohon*: tree. *Pohon pohon*: trees. *Anjing* is a dog, but hot dogs are not *anjing panas*; my mother tried explaining this to Bette when she planned the menu for a beachside bonfire picnic. My father had brought Oscar Mayer wieners from Jakarta. That was a treat. Mom was telling Bette what sort of bread we'd need to make the hot dog buns, but not buns to stuff with dog meat. "Yes," she'd said when Bette had asked, "that's what they're called. Hot dogs. But they are not that sort of dog." She told Bette that eating dog went against our religion. Canadians don't eat monkeys, snakes, or dogs, but we love to cook hot dogs on open fires at the beach. Sometimes we were invited to the governor's house to dine. Those were always banquets, lots of people wearing traditional Indonesian clothes while we looked oddly casual no matter what we wore. There were formal rules, as well, we learned when, right off, my mother, Chris, and I were made to understand that food was always eaten first by men while we, the women, sat in straight-backed chairs around the borders of the room.

The same eating rules applied when we were asked to dinner at the raja's house. But in other ways, aristocratic Timorese and foreign women shared a lot. Essy Tarek and Mrs. Nayfack talked together, and my mother understood a lot of what they said. What did they chat about that they thought she couldn't understand? I asked my mother what the Royal Highnesses discussed. Wives, my mother said, talk the same wherever they are in the world. It always was the same; they talked of sex. *Seks*: sex. The Timor raja's wives and daughters, princesses and queens, they talked about their husbands and the sex they had with them, how often and how good or bad.

The raja was quite old, his wife as well, and they'd lost their crowns long ago. When the Javanese took over all the little island kingdoms, they took Timor too, and took the crowns and thrones that all Nesnonis had. But crowns and thrones are not the only things that mark a family royal. The Timorese of Kupang knew the names Nesnoni, Tarek, Nayfack, knew they were royal family names, and so the people with those names were treated royally. To me, the raja's wife looked the same as any other Timorese—elderly and wrinkled as a nut, dressed in plain worn clothes, not wearing jewellery—but she had a regal way of walking, her back held straight, and she never bowed her head to Java's soldiers. When Mrs. Nesnoni took a bemo anywhere, she never paid, and all the passengers on board when she waved down that bemo would get off. They weren't even asked to leave, they just got off. One day when she and Mom were riding back together from somewhere and chatting, the bemo passed our house without my mother noticing. But the raja's wife thought it was not okay for Mom to walk the distance back up the hill. She told the bemo driver he must back his bemo up the hill, back it up on Jalan Sumatera, against the traffic zooming into town, against the flow of bemos and of villagers who walked, back it up so that my mother didn't have to walk that little way.

Mrs. Bambang wasn't Timor royalty but she was rich, much richer than the others all combined, but even so, I doubt she could have made a bemo driver run his bemo backward up a hill. She was richer than the rest and made sure that we all knew she was. Mr. Bambang's factories were here and there and everywhere and not just on Timor, not just in Indonesia. On Timor he had factories that processed sandalwood. Sweet-smelling oil that was rare and getting rarer. Sandalwood would soon be gone, the slow-growing forests all chopped down. Soon there wouldn't be any more of those trees to grind and process into oil. Mrs. Bambang was very rich, but she was Chinese too. And that was why she could never get a bemo driver to go backward up a hill. And that was why, Mrs. Bambang said, the Timorese and Indonesians hated her.

It was true. The Chinese were hated in Indonesia. Not because they were rich or grinding up rare trees, making money from the last of Timor's sandalwood forests. They were hated just because they were Chinese. The Indonesians called the Chinese foreigners. They weren't foreigners like us, of course, but they weren't Indonesian either. Mrs. Bambang's family had lived there for a long time. They had history that went back all the way to Dutch colonial times. No matter. That was irrelevant. Indonesia was for Indonesians, even though the country's motto means "many, yet one." Many, yes, but not that one, not Chinese. There was no talk of six nations, no talk of everybody's history and the part they played in the making of that place. No, no, no. Indonesia was for Indonesians. But Indonesia is a group of islands stretched out from west to east, miles and miles across the sea, as wide as Canada, and every island is different from the rest. Different cultures, different religions, different skin tones, different face shapes. True, but Balinese and Timorese and people living on the islands they call Flores, Roti, Sulawesi, Lombok, Surabaya—pick a name, there are almost 20,000 of them—none of those were Chinese. Were they? Chinese people there created what the Indonesians called *masalah cina*. Chinese problem. They were a problem, not one of all those "many" in the country's motto.

Mrs. Bambang said that it was her problem. She wasn't truly Indonesian because the Indonesians said she wasn't. That meant she could not travel, couldn't leave the place where she wasn't wanted. She couldn't travel with her husband when he flew on business trips to Singapore or Kuala Lumpur. It didn't matter how much money her husband's factories produced. She couldn't leave the borders of the country, the place that called her foreigner, because she couldn't get a passport. Indonesian passports are for Indonesians, not for Chinese foreigners. And so she stayed behind and decorated her house. She decorated it with things her husband brought back from his trips. Souvenirs, the kind you see in airports, like toys, stuffed animals, cotton-candy pink, some set up into scenes she made, like dioramas in a museum, behind sheets of glass. We visited her. She showed us all her dioramas. The biggest and most elaborate one had teddy bears and dolls and plastic plants and coloured sand spread out, and was set up beneath the stairs, filling up that triangle of space.

Chris and I made faces at each other when nobody else was watching. We rolled our eyes and barely held back laughter. We whispered at each other, "creepy." Mrs. Bambang showed us all the things her husband's money bought, and all those things—the lamps and brocade furniture and carved wood chests of drawers, the cushions and the chairs—were wrapped or covered, coated and protected in thick plastic sheets. Things squeaked when we sat down to sip the iced tea that her maid served us. Our skin stuck to plastic covers. When we left, she handed Chris and me small batik toys, stuffed toys, stuffed up with sandalwood, fine dust. A smell that's getting rarer.

Mrs. Bambang had no children, but all the other ladies did. Essy Tarek had six but only five of those are hers. Only five lived with her at home. She gave away the sixth, the youngest, a boy then just a few months old. She gave him to her brother's wife, who had no children of her own. Essy said, "She's barren." Barren is a wasteland. Barren is a dust-dry place, a coral field, a place where even weeds won't grow. Barren isn't good. So if a woman was barren, she was given a child as a gift, a boy, particularly, if boys were plentiful elsewhere. Children were important. We thought this was strange, the gifting part, and strange, as well, that Essy had the honour, she and not the one she gave the baby to, to name the child. She named him Leonid Brezhnev Tarek. And that seemed strange. We didn't know that Russian politicians were so famous on Timor.

It was shameful to be barren. It was a secret that must be kept, tight inside a family, hidden from the world, but we were foreigners and strangers. We were people that the Timorese felt free to tell these shameful secrets to. Mrs. Nayfack showed my mother something shameful too. She took my mother to a place that was secret, hidden away. It was an orphanage and where some older people lived, a sort of seniors' home, a place for those who had no family. It was secret too, because this was a shameful thing for Timorese. The Timorese were full of shame about these abandoned people with no homes, these children without families, old people without families, and tucked them all out of sight. That was why that place was hidden out of town, along a riverbank, a row of little houses. My mother said she found the place quite nice, tidy little houses strung out beside the water just like cottages, like summer cottages that we might rent for holidays. Mrs. Nayfack took my mother there because my mother had a plastic Christmas tree to give away. Soon we would be leaving Timor, flying back to Canada, and my mother was finding people who might like the things we didn't want to take back home.

Toko Liem would like it all. He liked anything we had to give away. One night when nobody but Chris and I were home, not even Bette because it was her night off, the front door suddenly banged open. Nobody had knocked, they just opened up our door and marched into our house, a crowd of ten or twelve, all relatives of Toko Liem. He was leading them. He led his family and friends into our house, and they spread out and opened cupboards, bedroom doors, and drawers, and looked inside our closets. They found the cutlery we'd brought from Canada. It had shiny plastic handles and was unlike anything that could be bought in Kupang. The woman that opened up that drawer said something loud and shrill that brought four others to her from across the room. Toko Liem was squatting down in front of Dad's stereo, fiddling with the dials and waving his free hand at somebody, pointing at our kitchen door. Go check that out. There might be good stuff there, more stuff the foreigners have brought. One woman started pulling tablecloths out of the linen chest. Chris and I were shouting at them. We yelled whatever Indonesian words we knew. *"Tidak. Pergi. Sama sekali tidak."* No. No way. Go away. They ignored our shouts. We waved our arms and were about to try to push them out the door when, bang, the back door opened suddenly, and Bette was in the house. She roared and stomped her foot, and that made them all stop talking and stop rifling through our house. They muttered and glared at Bette because she was just a maid. They glared but they left. I slammed the door behind them, and Chris and I fell on the floor, laughing but indignant. Toko Liem got nothing from our house, but Bette had anything she wanted. What she wanted most was my mother's mixer, an electric mixer we'd brought from Canada. She told us that she'd put it on display in her new home, it would be an ornament because, she said, she'd likely never have electricity.

Toko Liem did not get what my mother had to give away the day she saw the shameful orphanage. It was our plastic Christmas tree, fake fir, a thing the Timorese had never seen, brought all the way from Canada, complete with lights and tinsel. It looked so real, or maybe not, and perhaps it was just a thing they'd never seen so didn't register as fake or real, but they seemed to think it was real because the people at the orphanage asked how to keep it fresh, how to keep it living through the year.

Mrs. Nayfack and my mother walked along the riverbank, looking into houses, each one cute my mother said, and, she thought, not at all a shameful place. Mrs. Nayfack seemed to know everybody there, and chatted with them all. She asked the man in charge, the caretaker who managed the place, about his child. His wife had had a baby recently. He smiled with pride and said, "My baby, he is very white." My mother later learned from Mrs. Nayfack that the man's wife was Chinese. Chinese, yes, and that meant her skin was pale, paler than the Timorese. That was a cause for pride, a thing to be desired. Skin tone, even there, was all-important. Didn't I see Bette put on bleaching cream each night? She said while she was saving money working for the foreigners, she was also whitening her face. Both things would mean that when we left, she'd marry well. White skin and money meant she'd marry very well.

## 17

# THE LADY WITH A VIPER ON HER HEAD

My mother and my father had a deal. They made a bargain. In exchange for answering the Sally-Sally-Sallyings that came to our door each day, for buffering my father from his team of expats and their demanding wives, and for making sure the angklung orchestras played Canadian tunes, my mother got two trips away from Timor every year. Dad promised that he'd take her off the island so she could have a break from her diplomatic duties, so she could "blow off steam."

Her steam would build, and Dad was often nervous that she'd blurt out irritation or choke on laughter when murmuring politely was required. He said Mom was like a cowboy, prone to shooting from the hip. But so was he. Dad's eyes would bulge with suppressed rage that made his face bright red. He'd mutter, "A degree in Engineering and my job is scheduling drivers for these people." That was when Mom smiled and did her job.

Most of the time she seemed to like her job. But there were times when it was hard. Once when Dad, as usual, was away, a child was killed. There was a deep-green village, the only one like that we ever saw on Timor. It had a mossy-sided pool, deep and carved from stone, a place that we were told was sacred. It was alive with watery smells and watery sounds, and it was very old. The driver of the Land Rover, a member of Dad's team, didn't see the child run out onto the road. The child was killed, and Mom was left to find a way, somehow, to make that right. We had no phone, no way for her to contact Dad. She had to solve it all alone. In times like that, when it was hard to do her job and when Dad was somewhere else, Mom cried. Chris's bedroom looked out into the garden in the back behind our house, and sometimes she'd see Mom out there, in the velvet Kupang darkness after 6 P.M., alone and sitting on a rock, crying. Then Chris would come and knock on my bedroom door and we'd whisper, wondering what we should do. We never knew just what to do, so we'd wait for Mom to come back into the house, and we'd pretend we hadn't heard her cry.

But, those times were mostly rare, and when Dad kept his promise and they flew off to someplace new, that's when Mom was happiest. We were too, because Chris and I were usually brought along. Those were times when Mom and I got along better than we often did, and those trips away were also times when Stephen travelled with us. He'd fly out when his university classes were on summer break. Then we'd travel as a family of five. A Mom who sought adventure. A Dad who found the opportunity to learn in all we saw. Because of them, our times away from Timor were not often spent on beaches.

Mom would take us places that were full of people, full of noise, and full of smells we'd never smelled. She liked streets where food was sold on charcoal braziers in amongst parked cars, where Bangkok's "ladies of the night" patrolled and Mom could see that they were really men before the rest of us suspected. Her favourite places were the markets. Strange and glittery things piled and pyramided there, and fruits and vegetables oddly coloured, weirdly shaped. Some stank and others smelled of perfume. She liked to wander into where the bamboo cages, overhead in hundreds, sang and swayed with tiny, brightly feathered birds or where the woven pens ranged out along the ground held snakes, fattened up like calves, so big they looked as though they'd have no trouble swallowing my sister, Chris. I could imagine just her running shoes sticking out those serpents' mouths. Mom liked the places where artisans squatted on the ground surrounded by silver shavings that they'd carved off ornaments, bracelets, rings, and pendants, or by chips of rock and dust of stone shed to reveal a dancing Hindu princess or a spotted deer. She liked batik. We spent an afternoon in a batik school on Bali where a man told us everything about the history of Indonesian batik. He talked about the wax, the dye, the cloth, the special tools for tracing thread-fine lines in dye-resistant wax. Those were tjanting tools, and they are needle-fine for patterns drawn by hand; for inferior cloth, he said, the design is stamped by tools made from blocks of wood with patterns raised in wire. He told us everything about those patterns, what they meant, their history and geographic origins. He said, "This one is pisau rusak, that means 'broken knife.' Only kings could wear the pisau rusak pattern." He told us what the colours meant and in what order they were dyed, layer upon layer, light to dark, on cloth.

Dad chose the guided tours of palaces, temples, and museums. Every display card must be read, every bit of written information had to be absorbed. That was the point. It seemed rude to stare aimlessly at gilded furniture or wander past a glass-boxed display without pause. We'd stand, heads bent, gazing down through dusty cases on little crumbling figures made of clay and set up to show each stage of every battle fought by the Javanese. My neck would ache from staring down at printed information cards. My feet would ache from inching slowly sideways through museums. The golden Buddha once encased in plaster and found by happenstance when needed most. Caves where sadhus, with their skewered cheeks and tongues, waited silently for money dropped by worshippers or tourists. To reach them we climbed almost three hundred steps rising steeply from the giant golden Hindu god that guards the base. In the hills outside Jakarta, a botanic garden stretched for miles, and every plant was labelled with its Latin name. In a corner, trees were filled with fruit bats hanging upside down asleep. They were three feet long, with wrinkled, leathery wings enfolding fuzzy bodies. There was no information label for the bats, but Dad said don't be scared. They just eat fruit.

We drove the length of Java from Denpasar to Surabaya, Surakarta, Yogyakarta, Bandung, and Jakarta, learning the history of Indonesia from its ancient sites. We saw Borobudur, a mountain clad in blocks of stone, made into a giant temple, Buddhas in their bells—stupas was the proper word—ringed round the upper tiers. If your arm is long enough and you can touch the Buddha statue sitting stony in its stupa, you'll have luck. We were the only people at Borobudur that day, just us and some Indonesian archaeologists working on a complicated restoration of the site. Huge blocks of stone were numbered, numbers painted on in white, and grouped and jumbled all around the site. Some had carvings on their surfaces, parts of stories, and some were cut and smoothed and shaped themselves into an arm, two feet, a hand in prayer. They were lying all about the mountain's base. We clambered on them, sending lizards darting when our shadows fell across their sunny basking spots.

Next it was Prambanan. Borobudur was Buddha's place but Prambanan was for Brahma-Vishnu-Shiva. Three in one—creator and sustainer and destroyer—together in a single body, in one place. Borobudur and Prambanan, first Buddhist and then Hindu. That's the order they were built in. The second one, Prambanan, in answer to the glory of the first. One-upmanship, my father said. Prambanan did its one-up well. Not a mountain clad in man-cut stone, but a compound that seemed miles across and filled with temples, hundreds of them. At Prambanan we were, again, the only people wandering all day long among the steep and pointed temples and the life-sized animals of stone that guarded dancing goddesses and men with many arms. The story of the *Ramayana* was all there in detail, every moment of that saga carved in bas-relief. There was Ravana kidnapping lovely Sita. There was Hanuman flying with a mountaintop carried on his palm, flying south to heal Ram's army with that mountain's herbs. There was the elephant god Ganesha; Hindu, yes, but sitting just like Buddha in the lotus pose. My mother in her cotton sleeveless summer dress, its batik border dark on creamy beige, sat on a bench beneath an ancient sacred tree, sunlight flecking the ground around her sandalled feet.

In Malaysia we drove for miles along a narrow country road through rubber tree plantations. They tap them just like maple trees are tapped in Canada. Tin buckets hung off every tree and slowly filled with milky sap that wept from where the tree was scarred. The bark was slashed away, peeled deeply from the tree in twists that spiralled round the trunk. As each scar healed, another cut was made but only halfway round the trunk each time. You don't want the tree to die. I brushed my thumb along the ridge of scar, milky white and sticky.

In Thailand we saw temples and elephants trained to do the work of bulldozers on construction sites. There was a man who went with us, in the shuttle bus of tourists departing from the hotel where we stayed.

Chris stayed back. She said she wasn't feeling well, but I was there with Mom and Dad. That man was from the Middle East and said he liked the look of me, blond-haired, blue-eyed. My mother joked she had another just the same, and he could buy the pair of us if he wanted a matched set. They both laughed at that while I watched the elephants heft tree trunks overhead and roll boulders into water with a splash.

We saw Buddhist temples, Hindu temples, water temples, temples built for sacred monkeys and another built for snakes. Incense choked the air inside that one. Thick and warm and sleepy-making smoke. Vipers, snakes with piercing poisoning fangs, lay draped in a drug-like stupor over baskets made of sticks above a bed of coals. The keepers of the temple tossed herbs and incense on those coals to make the sacred smoke. That was the Temple of the Azure Cloud, with vipers black and spotted white and brightly banded yellow. The keepers said the snakes had come to the temple on their own. They weren't caught and brought there to display. They came slithering through the jungle, creeping over ground, and along the road out front because they liked the place. They weren't angry. They were happy-spirit snakes, but real and warm and dry when held. The keepers said the vipers were not milked, not drained of the poison in their fangs. It wasn't necessary because the vipers were content. For a donation we posed for photographs with vipers in our hands. The keepers tucked a snake inside my father's collar. It dangled down his front like a tie that slowly moved and looked him in the eye. They coiled one on my mother's head. A snake tiara twisting, flicking its tongue, and tasting air above her grinning face, and we all grinned as well.

We were shown Indonesian palaces by Indonesian guides who told us stories of the Indonesian past. My father liked to speak their language with them and encouraged us to do the same. In Yogyakarta, at the palace of an ancient Java king, we stood together underneath a ceiling carved in teak but made to look like a canopy of silk. Heavy wood, painted red and gilded gold, rippled like a cloth above our heads. The guide was serious and young. He wore a black fez and thick-rimmed glasses, and Dad, his hands behind his back, listened carefully to everything he said. Dad's eyes lit up. "Ah," he said. "I see you wear the king's own batik pattern on your sarong." "Yes," the guide responded with a smile. "Yes," Dad said and looked at us. "Remember from our trip to Bali? It's the pisang rusak pattern. Broken knife for kings." The guide coughed, and Dad's smile broke off because we were all smirking. "Pisang rusak? That means 'broken banana,' Dad. You meant pisau rusak." From then on we'd poke our Tuan Kue with a "pisang rusak" comment when we could.

Click. Stephen took a photograph of us. Chris and me, hair spun out as we turned our heads to look at him, our embarrassed guide with downcast eyes, and Dad, tall and awkward looking. A red velvet rope separated us from the furniture that courtiers and Indonesian kings sat on, carved with animals and flowers. Chris and I looked

like twins. People told us that. It was true. We had been
growing more and more alike. Her hair wasn't tomboy
short anymore but shoulder length, like mine, and banged.
She'd outgrown her checked overalls and ankle socks. We
both wore smooth blue pants and brown shirts, and her
head was at the height of mine. But, we weren't twins. I
was seventeen and, sometimes, resented that my fourteen-
year-old sister was mistaken for my age. So, to make a
point, I flirted when I could. I wore men's dress shirts tied
up tight around my waist, sleeves rolled up to flash the
silver bangle that my parents bought me in Yogyakarta.

While Chris and I grew closer, looking more and
more like twins and becoming more and more like
friends, our brother, Stephen, seemed to go the other
way. His life was taking place in Canada while ours
was spent in Asia. Every time he visited, those summer
holidays, it seemed we knew him less, until he became
more like a cousin than a brother in our minds. One
year, it might have been the first, when he arrived at
the airport, we stood and watched him being pushed
into the terminal in a wheelchair with a crutch across
his lap. Mom's face went pasty white, but later, when we
learned he'd broken his leg while racing on a motorcycle,
she looked a funny mix of sad and angry. That was the
year we drove the length of Java in a car hired by my
parents. Stephen sat in the front where he could stretch
his broken leg and where, as well, he had a full-face view
of the way that Indonesian drivers drove. Sometimes he
flinched involuntarily at things we didn't notice. He said

that we were crazy to ride in a car that was driven in that way. His hair that year was long and wavy, and he'd grown a blond moustache. In a Java market he bought a cane of reddish-orangish wood with an ornate brass handle. For the weeks he spent with us, he limped languidly through palaces and temples. I thought that he looked distinguished despite his cut-off shorts.

In Yogyakarta that year, Mom and I bought batik pictures, cloth stretched and framed to hang. Hers showed three women, stylized in dots and swirls, swaying on their way to market, baskets on their heads. Mine was abstract, whirls of Prussian blue and emerald green and crimson red. It reminded me of photographs my brother bought of nebulae—night skies far, far away from earth. For childhood birthdays I had always asked to see a show at the planetarium. Sitting in the purest dark and breathing purest air, we'd watch the giant projector pick out all the constellations while a voice told stories of the stars. Later that day in Yogyakarta, when we were done with markets and museums, we raced cycle-rickshaws back to the hotel. The cyclists on the bike seats up behind the benches we sat on pumped their legs and laughed with us, careening around corners. Chris and I rode in one, Mom and Stephen were in another, and Dad was on his own. Chris and I passed Mom and Stephen with his cane across his knees. He was leaning back and being nonchalant, but you could see he wanted to win. Dad bumped along behind with his camera at his eye, photographing all of us. Chris and I were dressed like twins and we won the race. That day Mom and I didn't fight about anything. Dad was close by all the time and Stephen too, and all three rickshaws billowed golden clouds of Yogyakarta street dust as we chased each other through that town.

## 18

## MONKEY ISLAND

Timor was a dry and dusty place except when monsoon rains were falling hard. Timor had two seasons: wet and dry. Wet was "winter" weather, cold for us once we had been there for some months. Wet was from December to about May, and then the place dried up again. Rivers flowed but not year-round, flowed with water in the rainy season, flowed with sand the other months. Wide curving swaths of sandy gravel. Silt there was not a blessing of fertility; it choked rivers and blocked streams. Timor was not a watery place at all. Long ago, the Dawan people lived there, and they called the island *Pah Meto*. Dry Land. A frank and candid name, with no poetry in it. It was very dry. And yet my father and his team were there to study water. To study irrigation possibilities. To study what and why and how these systems might, perhaps one day, be built. We were told that we were there on Timor Island to help the Timorese, help them grow stronger, have more food, build a future that was better than their past, better and safer than their present.

Timor Island Water Resources Development Study—
that was the name of the project, the reason we were there.
I was sitting at the table in our dining room in Kupang,
my mother across from me. We had stacks of paper in
front of us as we proofread the project report. Dad's
Timor secretary had learned to type on a keyboard made
of cardboard, not a real typewriter, so there were a lot of
mistakes for us to catch. I'd been reading that report, and
this is what I'd learned: The project team was big. The
report summed up the work of twenty-nine expatriates
and seventy-five Indonesian counterparts, another
one hundred technical and administrative staff. Years
had passed from start to finish, and although we were
proofreading the report, the project was not done quite
yet. We were still in Kupang, though we were heading
home quite soon; Mom and Chris and I were heading
back to Canada, but Dad would stay on there for at least a
few more months.

My mother read aloud while I, inside my head, read
too. She said, "New sentence capital F field operations
required about numeral three years comma with over
numeral two hundred and fifty expatriate man hyphen
months having been expended in numeral twelve
disciplines full stop." Each word was bitten off and spoken
with an equal pause between. Dah. Dah. Dah. I yawned,
tried hard to concentrate. The air was absolutely still and
absolutely hot. We had to read all nineteen volumes of
that report before it could be sent off to a printer, bound
in black cardboard, and signed. My mother said, "New

sentence capital *I* it is not surprising comma therefore comma that the result is a rather large and complex capital *R* report."

But, there *were* surprises. We puzzled over things, Chris and I, we wondered. For every expat engineer, soil specialist, geologist, hydrologist, or sociologist, there was a Javanese counterpart, an Indonesian specialist who shadowed every foreigner as he—they all were men—travelled, studied, measured, counted, asked, or sampled. Why were they Javanese, all Javanese? There were no Timorese who shadowed foreigners. Why were there sociologists among the team? We heard one man say he spent many days in villages inland where he recorded flies. He said he counted flies. We thought that could not be true. Why irrigation? Why study irrigation where no crops are grown? We saw no agriculture on that island, no paddy tiers of rice or fields of wheat. No crops of any kind were grown on that ever-growing island, that expanding lump of coral in the middle of the sea. None that we could see.

We puzzled over why a boat arrived one day, a speedboat made of fibreglass and with a high-powered engine. It was brought to us on a trailer, all high and dry and shiny looking, brand new and parked in the dusty compound. It was orange and white. Coloured like the Coast Guard boats we used to see when we lived in Vancouver. Why was there a boat like that for us to use? The team did all its work inland, away from coastlines. Inland and away from that place that we were told we'd never go. Dili. Dili was not far, just 182 miles away, and that was where Fretilin were making trouble. That's where the Indonesian military said we must not go. And yet, and yet, my father did get very close to Dili. But not by boat. He travelled by land right to the border, close to Dili. Close enough, Chris and I heard him telling Mom one night when they sat in the garden, to hear the sound of gunshots in the distance. If you hear them, can they kill you? Are you close enough? Dili, Chris and I were thinking then, is just a few miles down the road.

We didn't know why that boat was there, but we had fun with it. We went places in that boat. It took us off to Monkey Island. Pulau Kera means "Ape Island," but we called it Monkey Island, where no monkeys lived or walked or swam. No monkeys and no soldiers, no villagers, no Timorese, no trees, no creeks or rivers, and no bemos. Quiet Monkey Island, just a sandbar off the coast of Kupang town. The only sounds were reeds hissing, crabs clacking as they moved from hole to hole along the beach, seawater foaming on the shore. The shiny boat could get us there in minutes, and we'd stay a day, sometimes a weekend, sleeping on the sand, seeking out the Southern Cross. It was hard to find in that night sky, so dense with stars that there was almost no black space between the bright sparks of light up there. They seemed so close, those stars, that we faked fear, pretended to be scared that they might scratch the hands we lifted up, pretending to grab handfuls of that shattered light. All four of us were lying out on still-warm sand. Dad pointed to the Southern Cross. There is where you see it. You can't see the Dipper there, not there where we were lying in the southern hemisphere. My father pointed out other constellations, but they were quickly lost to me in that sky so full of stars. The moon smiled horizontal, crack-grinned and unlike other moons we'd seen.

Best of all on Monkey Island were the tidal pools of phosphorescence. At night in pitch-black dark, we'd walk the shoreline, circling that island in an hour or less, wading into tidal pools to kick up water full of tiny creatures startled into glittering green. Dad said that's what the phosphorescence was. He called it bioluminescent plankton. Our arms and legs, phosphor-coated, patina-ed in stars, would shimmer with them. Later, in the daytime, we would dive off that boat and swim above the coral reef. Fishing, catching barracuda, silver-sided, bony-headed, mouths full of needled teeth. Fish flew, leapt in the frothing wake of the orange-and-white boat. They flew with fins like wings, like wings of dragonflies spread wide. Dolphins too would come, some were spotted, their backs above the waves beside our boat as speckled as the sky at night. Once when diving off the boat, overtop the reef, I saw a shark, long and lurking in the distance. The water was so clear I couldn't tell how close it was. Too close and much too big.

When we were going out to fish or dive or picnic out on Monkey Island, my father towed the boat to a beach far from town. A miles-long crescent bay of sand, a sloping waterline, a place to back the trailer over hard-packed sand and into water. See palm trees lean. See nautili with tiger stripes in orange and white, and see conch shells washed up with tides despite their heaviness. You can blow through them if you cut the tip off cleanly, blow it the way you would a trumpet. It's not easy, but when you learn, the sound the conch shell makes will rattle windows all around. See an empty bay, nobody's there but us.

That's where my father liked to put the boat in water and take it out. That's where he left the trailer when we went to Monkey Island. But once when we were coming back from Monkey Island, the sky above and right down to the water's edge turned greenish yellow-grey. The water all around the boat turned suddenly from tropic blue to solid black. Wind caught the water, tossed it high into the air. We were on crests and then deep in troughs with walls of ocean, dense and solid-looking all around. The flying fish stopped flying in our wake. The wind blew hard, so hard that if the flying fish had leapt above the water's top, the wind would have carried them onto our laps, into the boat, up to the sky. Storms like that can come on suddenly and that one did. We were not far from land, not far from where the beach was waiting emptily. Not far from where my father left the trailer. Not far, but also not quite close enough. We would have to take the boat to Kupang town, to where the river joins the sea, to where the stone bridge into town carved out a sheltered inlet, stagnating there and full of trash.

Oh, but even there the wind had come and made the sludgy water turbulent and rough. The boat could not be landed. The beach was very narrow, squeezed between two walls of buildings, hemmed by Kupang's buildings built right to the shore and out on pylons in the water there. The water bulged in that small space. The surface humped and heaped as if a whale-like creature lurked beneath. The boat surged up, dropped down.

My father said that Chris and I should hop out of the boat and wade to shore and walk up Jalan Sumatera to the house. It wasn't far. The water wasn't deep. But the boat was heaving from the water as it bulged in that small space, tight and narrow space of water churned to thick grey froth, slick with garbage, full of things that Kupang's people dumped into the sea; those things were banging up against the boat. And while the water slopped and while we hesitated, watching for a space, perhaps between the bottles and the boards and palm-tree branches grinding on the boat, while we stood bent over, clinging to the gunwales of the boat, a crowd was gathering along the shore and on the bridge nearby. They'd never seen this boat, at least not in the water, not in Kupang harbour here. They'd only ever seen that boat on land and parked in our compound. They gathered, more and more of them, and watched. We knew the water there was shallow, not much deeper than our waists, but we were scared. Waves spewed. I turned my head but not in time. I was wet with greasy water, stinking as it dripped down my face, ran off my head. Sewage. Kupang's sewage sloshing in that sheltered bay.

"It's safe." My father had to shout above the wind, above the crashing water, above the shouts of all the people gathered on the shore and on the bridge. "It's safe. Jump. Jump now."

"*Melompat!*" The people shout at Chris and me. *Melompat sekarang*. I saw a man on the bridge, his hands cupped around his mouth, stretched and straining and shouting at us. "*Melompat ke dalam air.*" He waved his arms above his head.

That man, the one I focused on, ran off the bridge, jumped down the banked-up shore, and the crowd of people followed. They crashed down onto the gritty narrow shoreline, all were shouting at the *orang asing*, at the two blond girls in the fancy boat, that it is safe. Safe. Safe. Safe. I chanted silently, leaned over, looked into the pewter-coloured water, held my breath, leaned out, but I didn't jump. There were people in the water by then. The crowd was wading out toward us. Plowing through the water, through the garbage, waving arms above their heads, and shouting. My father struggled, cut the engine, tried to make the boat drift parallel but not into the shore. Hands grabbed the gunwales of the boat, wet and slippery hands, hundreds of them, all the people living in Kupang, all the people of Timor it seemed were clinging to the boat. Maybe it was their grabbing hands that rocked the boat from side to side or maybe it was the storm, the waves, the swell that made it jerk about. I slipped and almost fell. *Jump jump jump, it's safe.* Faces stared up at us, mouths were open. I could see their teeth and tongues and almost down their throats. Their eyes seemed to bulge. I saw their fingers growing longer, thinner, sharper as they reached for us. Hands grabbed for our hands, for Chris and me. And then, suddenly, we were also in the water, and the people all around were grabbing at us, and I felt bodies crushing me against the boat; the boat was riding up and down on waves, and everyone was shouting still. I can't see Chris. Where is she? I saw only frenzied Timorese. Where is Chris? Where is she! Then I saw her, tucked up and carried by my father's special driver. Andy, big and tall. He'd scooped my sister up. She was safe, and he was reaching for my hand. Andy plowed like a draft horse through the sea of garbage, sea of people, stormy sea. We made the shore and clambered up the hill, onto the bridge, into the Land Rover parked there. Safe safe, we were safe, and through the window looking down, I saw my father turn the boat and slowly take it further out, away from shore, away from where the people, some still in the water, waved, and then I heard them cheering, saw them smiling, some were laughing. Everybody's safe. I saw soldiers too, standing on the bridge, drawn there by all the noise. But they weren't looking at us, they weren't interested in us it seemed. They were standing looking down at all those people crowded in the water, crowded on the shore. Looking down at them not smiling. They weren't cheering, they weren't waving arms, just standing very still and watching everybody being happy we were safe.

## 19

## A BROKEN MONKEY

From the water, out at sea and sitting in a boat that falls and rises with the waves, Kupang town looked as though it had been slapped, slapped hard enough to send the buildings toppling and off-kilter. Strung out along the shore, one end of town was higher, braced against the weight of leaning structures tumbling at it from the other end. In choppy water, that shoreline was seen in momentary flashes, glimpsed as the water rose and fell.

Life was like that too. Vivid moments hidden in the lull of boring everyday. Some, like flotsam, disconnected from their past and others like the warning spark of what's to come. Standing on a scruffy shore and being told that's where the cast-offs from the *Bounty* came ashore. A crew member was buried there. We had thought that would be a thrill to see, but it was not. Just a piece of ground like any other. Stephen holding up a fish he'd caught. His legs are burnt, scarlet skin and scarlet scales still wet with salty sea.

Chris trudging home, soaked in sweat, and it was barely dawn. Her tennis lesson with the region's tennis star done for that day. A monkey hiding beneath my mother's batik dress, her sandalled shoe, his beady eyes all that we could see. On another day we watched and laughed while Quibo took his frustration out on an egg we'd tricked him with. It wasn't raw that day, not one that he could gently crack to sip the contents from its shell, holding it like a goblet. That morning we gave him a boiled egg that puzzled him to fury. And Dad. My father stretched out on his back, asleep on sand, his hands folded on his chest, sunglasses on his eyes. That's one. Another has him striding, always purposeful, away through an airport terminal. Dad's yellow safari shirt.

Chris and I were salt-encrusted from a day on Monkey Island, stiffened hair and tightened skin sparkly with a dusting of the dried-up sea. Our lips were chapped, our shoulders bound to peel. The Land Rover pulled up beside our house so we could jump out before Dad drove with the boat trailer to the compound's other end. He would hose off the boat and get it ready for another day. We wanted out, to dump our swimming gear and run to the back garden to see our pets, our monkeys, to feel their sticky fingertips on our sunburnt skin.

The house was empty. We ran in from the dazzling outside to the cool and shadowed interior of our home. A rippling silhouette of the Land Rover drifted past the windows, blinds drawn against the sun. We heard the coral crunching under its tires. It took only a moment to drop our sandy towels and flippers and then to bound outside, out into the back, into our private garden paradise, into that quiet place where Tik-tikki huddled in a tree and Quibo hung immobile.

Quibo, arms and legs sprawled, starfished and stiff, hung upside down, entangled in a screen of macramé my mother had been making. It was to be a lacy thing for vines to climb, a screen blocking off the view into our yard from our neighbour's house. She was making it of rough twine, knotted elaborately. Like a net stretched across an open space of air. It had caught Quibo, and now his fingertips were dry and he was dead. His greenish-yellow hair ruffled in a little breeze. Why couldn't he just lift his head and look me in the eye? Why not?

There was a moment of thickened artificial silence. The world wasn't really silent, all the Kupang sounds were still being made, but I had stopped hearing them. Even Chris, close behind me somewhere saying something, asking something, wasn't making sounds that I could hear. Even my own sounds went out unheard by my own ears. Just for a moment. Then I heard myself screaming and screaming, and that seemed ridiculous, but I couldn't stop. My mother appeared suddenly and tried to enfold me in a hug, but I pushed her away. And then I was running and not feeling the jagged coral on my bare feet. I ran the length of the compound to where I knew my father, in his yellow safari shirt, was hosing off the boat. I was still screaming.

My father turned with the hose still in his hand, water changing dust to milky mud around his feet. He looked puzzled. He looked bewildered at this howling interruption. Inside my head, I shouted at him to fix it, fix it for me. Fix Quibo. Fix this thing for me. Fix the *patah monyet*, fix the broken monkey. I did not want to be hugged or made quiet. I grabbed his arm and made him run with me back to the house where Chris and Mom and someone else stood in a semicircle with Quibo on the ground surrounded by their feet.

Mom had cut him down. The centre of the macramé screen was gone, and its strings dangled, ragged and loose. She'd cut the grey-brown twine that had tangled in Quibo's tail and unwound it from where it left a deep furrow in his neck. He was free but lay on the ground splayed out exactly as he'd been when caught and tangled in that screen. His tobacco-coloured eyes were open but just narrowly, a thin slit.

Dad tried to hug me again, but I shouted at him, "Make him breathe," and I saw his bewildered look once more. He seemed to hesitate, which made me shout again and push him. Dad picked up Quibo and held him stretched out along one arm. Quibo's head was cradled in the bend of Dad's elbow. Dad blew air into his mouth. I watched, bent forward, silent now, and hard and tight and absolutely still, and I held my breath and didn't blink. Dad blew air into the dead monkey's mouth more than once, but Quibo did not come back to life. His mouth was stiff with rigor, and his chest would not inflate with air. My father had no magic trick for me, no way to fix the monkey. When he put Quibo down, I backed away from

Dad. All that stillness I had gathered could explode with just a touch.

I BURIED QUIBO quickly in the furthest corner of the overgrown garden, underneath the bamboo's rattling stalks and deep beneath the crushed and broken coral. It was important to me that I bury him before the ants could gather at his eyes and nose and mouth. I sat for a while where it was cool and dark, where it was quiet, where the overturned coral showed Quibo's grave. I sat and thought about my father's eyes when he'd tried to hug me. His eyes were sad, and I saw that they were coloured just like mine, and then I remembered everything I hated about living there in that dead and dusty place.

## 20

## FLY AWAY HOME

We were on our way to see Komodo dragons, two in a pit, kept there and on display outside the governor's house in Kupang town. We usually took new people there, and that time in the car with us was someone new. He was the youngest and newest expat on the team. He'd just arrived, a few days back, and he has asked to see the dragons. Everybody wants to see Komodo dragons. They are the thing that everybody knows of, if they know of anything about this place.

Along the way, we saw other things he'd never seen, like strips of bright-red dog meat dangling in the sun from poles that men are carrying to market. The Timorese eat dogs. You would rarely see a feral dog roaming round the streets of Kupang town. My father said that I had eaten dog meat too, but I just didn't know it at the time. We saw a market, watermelons stacked on dirt. We saw a pig, I didn't know if it was living or dead; its feet were bound and it was slung, hanging upside down, and carried on a pole that bent and bowed as two men walked. I saw

Kupang passing by and realized it was like a western town, a town shown in a cowboy movie. It was booming. I saw it rising from the muck, brand new but also looking as if it was about to crumble back to dust. We saw little ponies, sturdy-legged, thick, and short, with men who hiked their sarongs up to straddle saddles made of woven hemp and straw. We saw barrel boys and palm trees. It was just like a postcard on some streets. We saw brightly painted bemos flashing Bronson's face again and tooting as they passed. We saw a group of people squatting in the road. They were wrapped in dirty rags, their faces and hands bound up and covered. The Land Rover had stopped because they blocked the way. They were squatting and were chipping coral, breaking up lumps of it, hitting it with pipes to make a surface for the road. The Land Rover was creeping past, and I was leaning out the window to look down at grubby rag-sheathed heads.

"What's this?" the new arrival asked.

This, I said, is how the roads are made, by hand, by chip-chipping bit by bit. Six or seven people squatted as we slowly drove past, and each one had a pail of coral lumps, each one a pipe. All heads were bowed and four soldiers stood nearby, their rifles ready in their hands, watching all the chippers chip. What's this? Were they prisoners? No, not prisoners, not prisoners exactly, but they must be watched. All heads were bowed, then one looked up at us in our Land Rover. We were leaning out the windows, catching sights and catching air. One face looked up, a face without a nose. That face had eyes above disintegrating lips and scabby leprous patches on its cheeks. That's why, I said, as I looked up at him. He was the whitest member of the team, perhaps because he'd just arrived, but then his face was even whiter than it had been when he got into the Land Rover. See, I said, and waved my hand above the faces on the street below, they're lepers. The soldiers guard the lepers. They're not prisoners, just lepers working on the road. I smiled. The driver gunned the engine and we were gone.

Chip chip. The houses in our compound are slowly emptying. People had left. The foreigners were flying home, leaving Kampung Orang Asing houses empty one by one. The project was winding down, but my father, the first to come to this dry place, would be the last to go.

The Shortreeds had left. Jim and Esther, who said we all must call her "Easter." He was an engineer, and they lived in the house two doors down from us. Easter Shortreed made a special celebration for me on my sixteenth birthday. I had apple pie for breakfast at their house, rare and special because apples didn't grow there. She had the apples bought and flown in just for me from Java. Easter made that pie, not her maid. Easter also made a tinfoil crown for me, a crown for sweet sixteen, she said, and made me pose in it while holding my new guitar in my lap, a gift from my parents. I'm smiling, sitting in a wicker chair. But see how thin I am, my wrists more delicate and bony than they've ever been. For months I'd been taking lunch and breakfast to my room. I told my mother I was studying, working on my school assignments, making sure my grades stayed high. Sometimes I used the same excuse, hard work, to take my dinner to my room as well. But I was not. I was not working hard. I sat hour after hour in the dark, my curtains closed to block the sun, listening to music, Bob Dylan and The Doors and the Rolling Stones, and wrapping all my food in paper, throwing it away. See me bury breakfast and lunch, and lunch and breakfast in the bin beneath my desk. Sometimes I dumped food out my bedroom window, in hope some creature would come to eat it up before the gardener discovered it and asked my mother questions. I sat in my room and listened to The Doors telling me this is the end, calling me their beautiful friend. I listened. I drank coffee. I smoked cigarettes, nervously puffing beside my open bedroom window. I grew very thin.

Later, when I was seventeen, the Shortreeds flew home to Edmonton. His portion of the project was over. They flew home but left disruption in Kampung Orang Asing. They'd left a maid and now she was unemployed. The Timorese are poor, my father said. In some places on that island, $20 a year was as much as people earned. A year? Yes, he said, a year. Not there in Kampung Orang Asing. I remembered the Wisma Susi lady coming to our door, complaining that at $15 every month we paid our maids too much. Who would hire the Shortreeds' maid once they were gone? Who would pay so much to have a person cook, wash floors, make sure the laundered sheets were fresh and crisp and white? The Shortreed maid came to our house each day with cake. She baked a daily cake to rival Bette's. Cake for Tuan Kue, hoping Master Cake-a-day—our newest name for Dad—would like hers best. Maybe we would hire her? Did we need another maid? No, no, we don't. She left a cake sitting on the kitchen counter on a clean white plate.

I saw it there and remembered at the start, when we first moved to Kampung Orang Asing, how my father and my mother talked about the wages people made when working for the foreigners. They said on other islands foreigners had made a mess, created havoc in the whole economy because they'd tried to outdo one another, this one paying more than that, and on and on and wages climbed and climbed. The maids in other places, on those other projects, were paid much more than any other workers on those islands made, more and more each time a family arrived. Things got out of hand, my father said. Things were not controlled. Lives were thrown off balance. The economy was altered on those islands just because of what the *orang asing* paid their maids. Paid while they were there, but then they left. Not here, I heard my father say. That won't happen here, not on this job. Later, when I saw the cake the Shortreeds' maid had left for Tuan Kue, I wondered: How much money did those others pay their maids? As much as $30 or $75 every month? How much money did it take to mess things up?

I won't eat that cake. It will sit and sit until my sister or my mother or my father, likely Dad, eats it all. I don't eat much anymore. I drink coffee and smoke cigarettes and watch. I watch people come and go and come and go.

A man, his wife, and two small kids arrived. They were passing through, going home from somewhere else, from another island, stopping off to meet my dad, consult, and maybe do a bit of work, here on Timor Island. They came to dinner, and my father said that Chris and I must be polite, amuse the kids, show them our pets, our "menagerie" he called it. We had an orange cat. Her tail was kinked and mangled, knotted in a lump she held above her back. She'd had kittens. Each one's tail was bent in one way or another, twisted into lumps. "They were born that way," we tell the kids. "It was not an accident that hurt their tails." We had another cat, a black one who was always fighting and yowling, always making trouble. "That cat is Timorese," one of the Javanese engineers once said, pointing to the black cat in the garden. My father's driver, Andy, scowled at that, while the Javanese man smirked a little smirky smile. I understood by then what his black-cat-Timorese comment meant. He meant the cat was Timorese because its coat was black. The Javanese think Timorese are black, and black, they think, is bad. But Andy was from Timor, and I didn't think his skin was any darker than the Java man he stood beside. I scowled along with Andy.

We showed those kids our cats, the black one and the orange and the kittens, showed them the myna bird that imitated the cats. My sister had taught the myna bird to say in singsong voice, "Hello, sailor," but that night he called out my mother's name: Sally Sally Sally. We showed them Tik-tikki, who climbed the branches of the bougainvillea bush. She bared her tiny teeth, but seemed embarrassed that she had, then chattered at us while she huddled up against the thorny boughs. She didn't like the strangers. But that man's wife wanted most to hold her, and reached up and circled Tik-tikki with her hand. Her hand was beautiful, manicured and smooth and fine, with red-painted nails. Poor Tik-tikki. She shrieked, and then the woman did as well. She shrieked because Tik-tikki pooped all down her dress. I was smirking then. I wanted to say I told you so, but, of course, I didn't.

Chris and I were glad when they all left. We didn't like those kids. But then they were back. At least, the man and kids were back, and then those kids were at our house each day. I knew that I should think that it was sad, but I did not. I thought it was weird. I thought it was strange, but I didn't think that it was sad. I thought that it was strange their mother died one night when they were on holiday on Bali. Suddenly, she died. That was how the kids told us. Just like that, she died when they were sleeping. Do you know, they ask in little voices, do you know how dead people smell? They start to smell bad right away. They start to stink before sun's up. I looked at Chris. She looked at me. We both made faces, raised our eyebrows, grimaced with our mouths.

Oh, but then another person died, and that time we were sad. That man had lived on Timor just as long as we, and we liked him very much. He was funny, made jokes, and clowned all the time. A great big man who used to wedge a beach chair to his bum, stand up, and waggle

waggle it to make us laugh. Then he was sick, and all of us were told we must give blood. The doctors in the Kupang hospital said the foreign man needs foreign blood. An *orang asing* cannot have the blood of Timorese.

I knew that hospital. When Chris and I needed shots, injections for protection from some tropical disease like cholera or yellow fever, we were taken there. We sat waiting underneath a covered portico and watched gurneys pushed around the walkway in the central courtyard there. We saw feral dogs, the only ones we ever saw in Kupang, slinking round as well, dogs with yellow hair, patched and thin, and ribs and hip bones sharp. They had brittle eyes. They slunk round doorways, skittered in and out of rooms where patients lay on gurneys. We watched a nurse mix liquid in a teacup. She filled two syringes and called us in to get our shots. And then, much later, we were at that hospital again and giving foreign blood to save a foreign man. Then he was sent home, back to Canada where hospitals are dogless and where all the blood is foreign just like his, and yet he died.

And when our time came to go, when Mom and Chris and I were leaving, we all cried. We said goodbye to Bette and Lin, our old-man gardener and Leaf, and they all cried too, as they stood lined up on our front porch. They waved and we waved back until a bend in Jalan Sumatera took us out of sight. Then, unexpectedly, there they were again, lined up and crying still, outside the airport gates when we arrived to catch our flight away. They'd raced us in a bemo and they'd beat us there.

Fly away, fly away, fly away home. The newest, whitest, freshest member of my father's team had to go as well. He had not been there on Timor very long, but then he had to go. I'd been watching him since he arrived. He flew in to help my father with the project as it ended, to help him with the final report, all nineteen volumes of it. I didn't know how old he was, maybe thirty, maybe thirty-five. I knew he was from Vancouver, from the office where my father worked when we lived there. Downtown, black and white and glass. That was what I thought of when I watched that newest member of the team. There was a courtyard in Vancouver at the office, with a waterfall out front and all the plate-glass windows were filled from edge to edge with views of Stanley Park and of the ocean.

We took him with us when we went to Monkey Island. We took him swimming there in clear blue water, saw the reef below, saw yellow, red, and turquoise fish, and sometimes saw a shark. The water was fine, warm and clean. We took him to our other favourite beaches. One that was curved and empty, curved like a fingernail, with whitest sand and sunsets, momentary flashes, hurry hurry now the sun is gone. We took him to the other beach, where caves were carved from coral cliffs, caves we hid inside. We hid inside and listened to the drip drip drip of water, condensation falling into tidal pools caught there when the tide was out, far out. Tucked inside that cave, I smoked a cigarette, leaning up against a jagged coral cliff. I smoked and watched that guy, that guy who'd come to help my father. I knew what was going to happen next, and sure enough it did. And later, a day or two later, when both my parents had gone out, it was nighttime then and he was there, right there, lying on the floor and so was I, and we were kissing, "making out" I called it. That's what we were doing when my father and my mother suddenly returned home. Just like that I'm caught, lying on the floor and making out with him. My father was so mad that he could barely speak. His eyes were shards of blue. His face was red, enraged, and that made me hold mine in flatness, blank and pale. I didn't even blink. Next day, I heard, from Mom, that Dad had sent his new assistant home, sent him packing, that was how I heard it said, back to Vancouver. "You've ruined that man's career." He was never seen again, not in Kampung Orang Asing, not on Timor, not in Indonesia. It was as if he'd been evaporated by my father's rage. Dad didn't speak to me for days.

But before that happened, before my father sent him back, he saw the most exciting thing in Kupang town before he left. He saw Komodo dragons. When you go to Timor, when you visit Kupang, you must see them too, because they are rare and special lizards, the biggest in the world. They are sometimes eight feet long, from scaly pointed tail to shiny blunted jaw. You will stand above the concrete pit that's dug below, and you will see them lying lazily in the bottom, in the depth among the rocks. You should hope the pit is deep enough, because though they are lazy, they are also very big. See them flicking tongues to taste the air, they know you're there above them, they can smell you, they can taste you on the air. They know what you have brought. They weigh at least one hundred pounds, with skin that's amber, umber, grey-green, yellow, scales of many colours make a creature that seems brown to most. Their skin sags around their bellies, even though they weigh one hundred pounds or more. Full bellies. Bellies full of what you've brought, what everybody brings when they go to see Komodo dragons there in Kupang town. The dragons seem uninterested. They seem lazy, anchored down to earth, unmoving, slow, and clumsy. But that's deceiving. The lizards smell what you have brought, and they are gathering their energy. They are waiting. They are poised. Watch this. White chickens, snowy white and pure—they're always pure and spotless white—are tossed, alive and clacking as they flap and fall into the dragon pit. You might hear claws, Komodo claws, on rocks, but you'll hear nothing more. Dragons move too fast to hear or see. Brown flash. White feathers in the dust. Gone. Gone.

# *Epilogue*

## HOTEL DREAMLAND

My mother, my sister, and I left Timor and were back in Canada by mid-October 1978. My father travelled out with us as far as Hong Kong and then returned to the island where he would stay for a few more months to finish the project. The house we moved back to was one my parents had bought during the time between Guyana and Timor, but we hadn't lived in it during those nine months. It was high on the mountainside with the city of Vancouver spread out below, a night-carpet woven in lights. On clear days the view went so far we could see smoke rising from pulp mills on Vancouver Island, fifty miles away across the Salish Sea. Sometimes I would stand at the windows watching red tail lights cross Lions Gate Bridge, watch them vanish into the dark blankness of Stanley Park. That house was a long way from where we'd lived in the years before moving to Guyana. There were no farmers' fields nearby and no cow to chew the grass behind our house. This was a house and an address that clearly marked the rise in my father's status. It had been a rapid career rise. Fewer than five years separated the time between when we'd boarded a plane for Guyana, my father's first overseas posting, and when we'd returned from Timor. Yet, there was little or no obvious connection between where we'd been when we left Canada and where we set up home when we returned.

Fewer than five years, and much more than our address had changed. I returned to high school, but not to the school I'd attended during our pause between Guyana and Timor. This one was larger, there were more students, and it was more structured. There were a few people I recognized from 1976 when we'd last been in Canada, but I started classes more than a month into the school year and had trouble making friends. It was harder this time, harder than the time between. I did things that in this new environment were mistakes. At a high school dance, I wore a sari, yards and yards of flowing mauve silk. I thought I looked beautiful. People stared. People stared and, sometimes, people asked questions. "Why are you dressed like that?" "Where have you been?" "Guyana? Timor?" They asked once, then turned away. Nobody had heard of the places where I had been living for most of my adolescence. Those places I had lived, that shaped my thoughts about the world and about people, that directed my decisions and judgments, meant nothing to my new friends. Those places didn't really exist in this new place, this newest home.

And then that changed too. My mother, my sister, and I were pulling apart crates of furniture one evening. We were in the big family room of the new house, and our shipment had just arrived. It was cold outside. Cold for people who had been living more than two years in the hot, dry climate of Timor. The crates contained bamboo furniture, a dining table and chairs, a sofa, side chairs, side tables that my parents had ordered from Jakarta. The television was on. That was something we'd not seen for years. TV was a novelty. The evening news started and I heard my mother gasp. She stood staring at the screen with her hand over her mouth. Her face drained, shocked, white. Jonestown. It was November 19 and the massacre at Jonestown was being reported. Suddenly the whole world knew what and where Guyana was.

Guyana, Guyana. In Guyana a dried stick driven into the ground will sprout leaves and grow roots. In Guyana the rivers flow clear and cool over gravel bottoms, and the water is the shade of strong tea. In Georgetown, the capital, where the ground is three feet below sea level and canals line every road and are ten feet deep and six feet wide, the ditches are full of guppies, males with electric-green and neon-orange-coloured tails fanning as they hunt for mud-brown females. In Georgetown the deep, wide canals are criss-crossed with pipes that twelve-pound rats use as passageways to and from the city.

That was Guyana. My Guyana. The one I knew, but that Guyana wasn't known by many more. Nobody had heard of it. And now, now everyone spoke the word *Guyana*, and when they did, they had a different picture in their minds beside that country's name. Now Guyana is a field of bloated bodies. Guyana is a photograph of 909 people, the dead lying out in the tropical sun, the followers of a charismatic, paranoid, drug-addled evangelical who ordered them to drink a cyanide-laced grape-flavoured drink. The mixture was there, dark and shining in steel drums, when the dead were found and photographed for *Time* magazine. All the dead were Americans, and the Guyanese would come to say of Jonestown, *"Don vex me wid dat story. Jonestown not we problem, dat not us and we got nutten nutten to do wid dat bad place."* But they were wrong. Sure, the dead were foreigners who obeyed their foreign leader when he said to drink, but Jonestown, it was Guyanese for sure. It had a lot to do with Guyana. Jim Jones chose the country carefully. He picked Guyana because it was unknown and isolated, because it was socialist, and because its leaders, Comrade Burnham's men, were malleable and hungry for the U.S. money that Jones waved in fat white envelopes. But Comrade Burnham's men were sniffing more than money. Later, years later, the world would learn Jim Jones enticed those Guyanese with "public relations officials," blond and blue-eyed women, young women eager to do whatever Jones told them to do. Oh yes, Guyana and Jonestown were bound, and not by random chance. Guyana and Jonestown. Speak the one and always comes the other.

We never met Jim Jones or any of his followers, but they were there. Oh yes, Jim Jones had been to Guyana and to Georgetown as early as 1974, and by the time we left, he had signed leases for the land where Jonestown later would be built. His girls were working hard already in those years to lure, entice, and put big smiles on Burnham's men. I wonder, did those marching students, those National Service girls and boys whose faces smiled on *Stabroek News* pages, I wonder if they helped to clear the land that Jim Jones later filled with death? I'll never know, but I did see the Port Kaituma airstrip close to Jonestown borders. I was there and walked along the red dirt strip hacked from the jungle where three years later, Congressman Leo Ryan and four others would be killed by Jim Jones's henchmen. Paranoid and heavily drugged, Jim Jones ranted at his followers that Ryan was a harbinger of doom, that he would destroy their paradise on earth, that they must all die now rather than suffer that loss.

And Timor, that small unthought-of place, that dry dry island where the monkeys swam in the sea and where lepers worked to build the roads from chunks of broken coral. Timor too is now known for death. While we were living there, the Indonesian soldiers, those same boys we watched run up the hill outside our house, the ones who left their guns politely on the porch when invited into our house for tea, those soldiers killed fifty thousand to eighty thousand people a few hundred miles away, just down the road from where we lived in Kupang. I was right to be afraid. A blood-soaked island, that's what Timor is today. That's what it is known for now.

Known and unknown things. Secrets, whispers, rumours. After my father died, I began thinking, again, about the unknown things hidden behind the memories of the places where I'd lived, where my father had taken his family to live. My father died suddenly, unexpectedly, and I hadn't taken the time to ask him the sorts of questions I would have liked to have asked him.

A few years after he died, I took a contract to research and write about women who were being trafficked out of Bangladesh. I was hired by a group of women lawyers there and paid by UNICEF and Red Barnet, a Dutch NGO. The report was to be used by the Bangladeshi government to modify their human-trafficking laws. It was a very low-paying contract, but I jumped at it because it would take me to a place in the world I had never been. Just like Dad. I missed him even more then. He wouldn't have been impressed by the pay, but I think he would have liked the thought of me following, a little, in his footsteps. I stayed at a guesthouse in Dhaka that catered to foreigners on development contracts. Every morning and every night I ate with a group of German men conducting a feasibility study for the improvement of Dhaka's waste disposal system. They told me wonderful stories of Dhaka's sewage system (warning me not to eat fresh fish served at dinner because it was caught in the sewage treatment fields) and of other jobs they'd had in other countries. They reminded me so much of my father. I recognized in them the addiction to expatriate life that had compelled Dad.

Once my report was written, it seemed a good idea to have my partner and our ten-year-old daughter fly over, so that together we could explore the Indian subcontinent. We spent three months there.

And India was where I always thought of my father dying, despite the fact that my brother and mother were able to get him back to Canada while he still breathed. It was in Shimla that he'd taken his last steps, so I went to Shimla and thought about my father's secrets, and the whispers and rumours, while I walked the thin-aired streets of that Indian town. The last place my father and I had walked together had been, bizarrely, Disneyland. Bizarrely, because Disneyland was not my father's sort of place. The man who had taken his family to remote corners of the world, who had shepherded us through ragged colonial museums and empty palaces, to the temple of the Golden Buddha, the Emerald Buddha, the Reclining Buddha, the obscure and the celebrated and the hidden and the ancient and the new and just about every damn Buddha in the guidebooks of all the countries we'd travelled in Asia, and who had made us read, along the way, every information card in every display case, spent his last days with me in Disneyland.

I wanted to walk the same ground he'd last walked in the place he'd chosen to be when he died. So, four years after his death, my partner and I and our daughter travelled in winter to that small town in India. Shimla was where the British Raj had escaped the summer heat of the Gangetic Plain, a heat that hammers and flattens and kills. Who would seek a place like that when winter sweeps the plains below, when the monkeys of Delhi's Connaught Circle shiver on the rooftops? Who would come to that place when the coldest and most bitter air of India swaggers down its streets? But, that was the last place my father ever walked. Those views were his last. That was where he had expected to die, and that was why I was there.

Secrets and rumours. Why did my father choose to die in that far-off foreign place? Why did he suddenly suggest he take my mother, my daughter, and me to Disneyland just before he flew off to begin his contract in India? Did he know that he would die in that thin-aired land so far from home? The questions drew me up and up the mountain, all the way to Shimla. All the way up from Kalka in the valley, riding the toy train, huddled in the ladies' carriage built for summer heat. Its windows would not close, and snow blew in and onto us for hours. All that way I thought of him. Slowly, slowly we rose six thousand feet over sixty miles, taking six hours to finish the journey, switching back and forth and passing through 107 tunnels. I remembered riding the funicular in Hong Kong, my father's voice rattling facts about the train, the grade, the distance all the way up the Peak Tram.

And at the top, when that train journey ended, there was Shimla, crouched in clouds. High misted air, high frigid air. We stayed two nights at Hotel Dreamland, a place not built for winter use. Our room was marble clad. Our sheets stayed wet all night. The small heater lent us by the manager had no effect unless we huddled in front of it tented by a blanket. In the morning we came down to the lobby and were beckoned to a glass-walled room off to the side. Thick smoke pushed up against the glass like fur. Inside that room, the hotel staff was burning furniture in a steel barrel. They fed lacquered chair legs, smashed tabletops, and wooden shelves into the fire. Flames sparked and flared. The floor was thick with soot and ash, the marble blackened and charred, heat cracks radiating jaggedly from where the waiters and the maids gestured at us to join them by the fire. Come, stand close and warm yourselves before venturing outside. Our clothes, still damp from the day before, trailed smoke all day.

That day we walked into the forest. We took a path I know my father had taken. He had described it in the postcard that he sent to me from Shimla, a postcard I carried in my pocket. He wrote that while in Shimla he had acquired the habit of walking each day before breakfast. One morning, just before his daily walk, a large part of his spine finally gave way, dissolved, and he collapsed. He was paralyzed from then until his death eleven weeks later. Before that morning, though, he'd walked Shimla's zigzag streets and climbed its cobbled stairs. He'd had sweet coffee at the Indian Coffee House where, in coal-smoke darkness, men puffed cigarettes and read the *Hindustan Times*. He'd walked the Mall and passed Christ Church, both still the same as how Kipling said they were. And he'd walked up Jakhoo Hill to see the temple in the clearing at the top. And so, despite not knowing if it's true, I like to think the walk I took that day, through the forest and up to Jakhoo summit, was the walk he'd planned to take the day that he began, instead, his life's final stage.

Jakhoo Hill is the highest point on Shimla Ridge, and at its summit is a clearing, an open space surrounded by the forest, where a little wooden building stands. This is the temple where Hanuman the monkey god is worshipped, and in the forest all around are monkeys too, sacred, bold, and watching.

To get there you must take the path from Hotel Dreamland. It's there, just to the side. When you find the path, turn away from the smoky, three-tiered town and look up into the clouded forest hanging in the air above. Behind you is a view so clear, so high, so far, that if you let it, it might pull you out and off the mountain terrace, pull you out into thin air. But you're not Hanuman, and you don't have the gift of flight and you must keep your feet on solid ground. Turn your back on that and start to climb, and soon you're in the forest. Sharp scent of deodar cedar. Monkeys watch you pass from where they huddle underneath the rhododendrons. Hear the snow melt, drip drip dripping, on their heads. Feel it drip on yours. Now you're in the shrouded forest, mists swirl and views are shadowy and dim. This is a good place to contemplate my father.

When I ask my mother if she ever thought there was a hidden reason, something other than my father's engineering work, that took us to Timor, or to Georgetown just when Burnham's government was nationalizing bauxite mines and sugar plantations, she shrugs and says, "Your father never said there was." Then she adds, "But then again, he wouldn't have told me." And, "There were rumours."

Rumours then and rumours now. It's no secret that Canada was keen to keep an eye on Timor. Allan MacEachen, Canada's secretary of state for external affairs, said at the time, "a hell of a lot of money [can be made] in Asia now if you're in business and you're hungry." While we lived on Timor, Canada signed deals with Indonesia lending that country more than $200 million. In 1976, the year that Indonesia officially annexed East Timor, MacEachen visited Jakarta and signed agreements for grants and loans totalling another $20.8 million. And, in 1978, just before we moved back to Canada, Glen Shortliffe, our ambassador to Indonesia, travelled to East Timor, having been told to do so "in good company" by External Affairs. Shortliffe reported back that he saw no signs of the "alleged heavy fighting that took place in 1975–76." Yet the Indonesian government had admitted killing about 60,000 East Timorese during that time. During the first five years of Indonesia's occupation, two and a half of which took place while we were living on the island, some 200,000 people died, through fighting, bombing, napalming, or forced starvation.* I do not know how much of this, if any, my parents were aware of.

Secrets and silence. My father was no less a complicated man than any other person, and after his

---

* Sharon Scharfe, *Complicity: Human Rights and Canadian Foreign Policy: The Case of East Timor*, (Montreal, New York, London: Black Rose Books, 1996), 134–42.

death we learned a few of the secrets he'd harboured. One was a story that came out at his funeral. Before writing his eulogy, Russ Fraser contacted as many people from my father's past as he could. One of those was a woman who had been Dad's secretary for many years. She was a single mother whose son was at high school with me. The story we heard began with the fact that she'd always wanted to travel but couldn't afford to. She was surrounded at work by engineers who were flying off or returning from exotic locations. Eventually, that company was bought by a larger engineering firm, but just before the handover, my father called his secretary into his office. "I have a package I need to send to Hong Kong," he told her. This was in the days when live couriers were used to transport important packages. "Get yourself a passport, bring it to me, and I'll make the arrangements for you to carry this parcel to Hong Kong." She did that, and when the time came to depart, she learned that my father had made arrangements for her to carry the parcel from Vancouver to Hong Kong via New York, London, Africa, the Middle East, and India. He flew her around the world. At each stop, she was met at the airport, driven to her hotel, taken on a tour of the city, escorted to dinner, and brought back to the airport when it was time to board the next leg of her flight.

Why did nobody among my father's friends or family know about this gift, this wonderful gesture? Dad didn't boast, so maybe he didn't think it was necessary to let anyone else in on the story. But he was also scrupulously honest. Maybe he didn't want it known that he'd spent company funds in such an extravagant manner, or perhaps there were other lies to avoid. Silence was how he did that. Dad never gave away much, and rather than lie, he'd just not talk about something.

Perhaps it was his adherence to honesty that also made my father so very remote emotionally. My mother called him "crippled." Maybe that was because, to avoid lying about his emotions, he controlled any situation that might bring them up. On Jakhoo Hill I thought of this as well.

In the Hindu epic *Ramayana*, Hanuman saves Ram's army from defeat when he flies north to the Himalayas and uproots a small mountain covered in medicinal plants that can cure any wound. Hanuman returns to Ram with the mountain balanced on the palm of his left hand, and just smelling the scent given off by the plants revives Ram's exhausted warriors. Though my father lay so near the Himalayas, Hanuman's healing mountain peak did not cure him. From the moment his spine gave way to when he died, my father's life was first confusing then frustrating and finally very painful. The only scent associated with this progress was decay. I believe my father anticipated this and tried to die alone in Shimla so he could avoid his family's messy deathbed emotions. I don't know this, but I do believe it.

Up Jakhoo Hill on Shimla Ridge where the path from Hotel Dreamland ends, the clearing opens up before you. Across the way and barely visible through swirling snow and swirling mist is the little temple, red and gold, pointed roofed and belled. Though it is solid, made of brick and stone, it appears and vanishes from view. The longer that you contemplate it from this distance, the more it seems to fade into the trees behind. Even when you leave the monkeys that have dogged you up the hill, leave them hiding in the forest underneath the rhododendrons and the deodar, and step across the clearing, into the temple, slipping on the icy steps, even then, the truth of what you seek is thickly cloaked in smoke. A man inside will come out from behind a curtain, offer you a cup of tea he's brewed on smouldering charcoal, say that you can stay until your hands and feet are warmed, but he won't tell you more than that. Whatever else you want to know, you'll have to find yourself, somewhere. Perhaps it's out there, maybe not.

# *Acknowledgments*

You wouldn't be holding this book were it not for a great many people, particularly the following. Each is owed an enormous debt of gratitude, my most heartfelt thanks, and a whole lot of love.

The all and all and ever-patient Kari Szakacs
The lovely, inspiring, and encouraging Linda Kay
The true-true friend and generous Chris Plunkett
The big-hearted Kate Johnston
The constant and tenacious Sally Keefe-Cohen
The masterful and heartening Diane Turbide
The spranksious and artful Niamh Malcolm
The elaborately meticulous Eleanor Gasparik
The diligent and buoyant Jacqueline Mo, Amy Smith, Charidy Johnston, and Ashley Audrain
The master of gyaff Stephen Plunkett
The graciously enthusiastic Helen Reeves
The Mighty Sparrow himself, who was not so big-time that he couldn't meet me

To everyone at Penguin Canada, the Canada Council for the Arts, the Conseil des arts et des lettres du Québec, and the Quebec Writers' Federation, many many thanks.

Mon 18 March 1974

Kabul

I haven't seen very
many horses, but
there are many
donkeys here. They
usually have big
bags slung on either
side which are filled
with goods for sale
— usually vegetables
such as carrots,
cabbage etc. or
sometimes orange
I may see some be
before I leave.

Love
Dа.

P.S. I did. 22 Mar

POSTES
2 AFS

24 Yaks in Pamir

۲ افغانی